COLUMBIA UNIVERSITY STUDIES
IN ENGLISH AND COMPARATIVE LITERATURE
Number 130

Ballad Opera

Ballad Opera

BY

EDMOND McADOO GAGEY

Benjamin Blom

Printed in U.S.A. by
NOBLE OFFSET PRINTERS, INC.
NEW YORK 3, N. Y.

To S. M. G.

Preface

FOR ONE reason or another the story of ballad opera has remained practically an unwritten chapter in the history of English drama. Of Gay's *Beggar's Opera,* thanks to numerous scholarly editions and studies, a great deal is known. The same is not true, however, of the scores of plays interspersed with ballad songs which followed, in and after 1728. The present book is an attempt to supply this missing chapter. Several valuable earlier studies have provided much of the necessary groundwork. Allardyce Nicoll, in his *Early Eighteenth Century Drama,* has given a brief review of ballad opera, as well as important information in his appended hand list of plays. In an article, "Early Irish Ballad Opera and Comic Opera," W. J. Lawrence has thoroughly covered one phase of the subject. For identification of ballad operas and for lists of tunes I am indebted to works by George Tufts, William Barclay Squire, O. G. T. Sonneck, and William Eben Schultz. For the necessary English and Continental background I have consulted numerous scholarly works and read widely in the literature of the seventeenth and eighteenth centuries. Most of my research, however, has been devoted to the ballad operas themselves, which I have been fortunate enough to find—for the most part—at Harvard and Yale and in the Longe collection of plays in the Library of Congress.

If sometimes I have dealt rather fully with operas that are relatively unimportant, my excuse is, first, that they are little known and, second, that they are interesting in their own way, for they offer us a realistic and often a topical portrayal of the life of the time that we are not so likely to find in the more ambitious and more serious drama. For the same reasons I have chosen a somewhat informal presentation and have often yielded to the temptation to quote passages and songs. In an effort not to include too much, however, I have omitted mention of the actors unless—like Charles Macklin or Kitty Clive—they are of considerable importance. The operas have been treated throughout from the standpoint of drama rather than of music. In ballad opera this limitation is easily justifiable because the music is often incidental and never all-important; strictly speaking, we are dealing with plays that include songs, not with mere opera librettos. There remains, however, an opportunity for some interested and better-equipped scholar than I am to write on the complicated subject of ballad-opera tunes. While it has some disadvantages, my organization of the chapters according to types seemed in the writing the most natural and the most convenient. The active period of ballad opera lasted no more than nine or ten years (one might almost say five) and a strictly chronological arrangement of the material would make any division into chapters meaningless and artificial, to say the least.

What, if anything, may prove of most interest to the reader it is impossible to predict. To me several phases of the research seemed particularly enjoyable. I found special delight, for example, in the malicious Latin wit of the Comédie-Italienne and the Théâtre de la Foire, and became absorbed in the task—worthy of a Sherlock Holmes—of tracking down the topical references in the political and satirical ballad operas. The pages of the *Grub-street Journal,* yellow and illegible though they might be, brought ample compensation in their revelations of the life and spirit of the century.

For their courtesy and assistance I wish to thank the staffs of the libraries of Columbia University, Harvard University, and Yale University and of the Library of Congress. I am indebted to Dr. Edward A. Richards for his kindness in looking up material for me at the British Museum and to Miss Edythe N. Backus for a similar favor at the Huntington Library. I am also grateful to Mr. Walter N. H. Harding of Chicago for his patient and helpful correspondence concerning items in his private collection of ballad operas and eighteenth-century music. To numerous scholars at Columbia University, including Professor George Sherburn, Professor Paul H. Lang, and Dr. Henry Willis Wells (to mention only three), I wish to extend thanks for valuable suggestions. For inspiration, guidance, and helpful criticism I cannot fully express my debt of gratitude to Professor Ernest Hunter Wright, to Professor Oscar James Campbell, and particularly to Professor George Clinton Densmore Odell, who suggested the subject of ballad opera to me and whose love of the theatre aroused my own profound interest when I was an undergraduate in his classes, many years ago.

Columbia University
June, 1937

EDMOND M. GAGEY

Contents

Ballad Opera

CHAPTER ONE

Introduction

BALLAD opera, engaging but impudent newcomer in eighteenth-century drama, took London by storm during several years when the fashion demanded that old plays be revamped and new ones adorned with popular or "Gothick" tunes. Then, after one or two decades of undistinguished survival, it lost its identity in the new comic opera that became popular in the second half of the century. Not meant for permanence but for passing entertainment, ballad opera—except for the initial example—rarely survived beyond 1750, but during its span of life it received wide applause in the London playhouses, either as main attraction or as afterpiece; it amused the more democratic audiences of Southwark or Bart'lmy Fairs; it took to the road in strolling companies, such as the ones described so vividly in Charlotte Charke's *Narrative*; and it established itself in the repertory of the provincial theatres. Its tunes, now sad, now gay, but always simple and melodic, found equal favor in the kitchen and in the ladies' drawing-room. On the boards, many an engaging Polly, or Betty, or Clarinda ogled and sang in her sprightliest vein, hoping no doubt to secure theatrical renown —like Kitty Clive—or to be taken into keeping and perhaps eventually to marry a lord—like Lavinia Fenton. Despite the lamentations of the "tragick Authors"—the devotees of Rowe, Otway, and Shakespeare—the Grub-Street fraternity, including more than one of Pope's victims, ransacked the plays and themes of the past as well as the song collections in order to satisfy the prevailing taste. Even a few Gentlemen of the Universities, with a gesture toward popular frivolity, condescended to dash off ballad operas in their less scholarly moments. Among the many amateurs who entered the operatic lists were an auctioneer, an army officer, an apprentice to a clothier, a law clerk, a former footman, and one or two misguided female authors. The supply of adequate popular airs, unfortunately, was limited, and their repeated use became a factor

in the degeneration of the form. Outside of the theatre proper, a
number of "operas"—taking the hint from Gay—entered the fields
of political polemics or court scandal and undoubtedly contributed
to the eventual downfall of Walpole, "Bob the Poet's Foe." Although overlooked by scholars, these political ballad operas are
extremely interesting.

Eighteenth-century opinion in England, as represented by the
newspapers and such standard works as Colley Cibber's *Apology*
and Samuel Johnson's *Life of Gay*, recognized in *The Beggar's
Opera* a new dramatic form or species of poetry. To contemporary
audiences the novelty consisted primarily in the liberal use within
a comedy of familiar and popular tunes—*native* as opposed to the
"effeminate sing-song" or operatic Italian music. In a measure this
English, hence patriotic and presumably masculine, music was designed to counteract and ridicule the popularity of Italian opera,
which since *Arsinoe* in 1705 and *Camilla* in 1706 had captivated the
aristocratic audiences of the town. The employment of popular airs
necessarily required that the songs themselves should belong to the
simple and unpretentious type that might be heard in the repertory
of the street-singer—hence the name ballad opera, the ballad being defined in 1728 as a "Song, commonly sung up and down the
Streets."[1] Songs, of course, had figured extensively in Elizabethan
and Restoration comedy and the airs were occasionally traditional
rather than specially composed, but never had ballad ditties appeared so consciously or so profusely as in *The Beggar's Opera*.
Later writers, especially in the shorter ballad farces, began to use
songs more sparingly, but nevertheless ballad opera (no matter
what it happened to be called)[2] depended for its effects upon music
familiar to the audience, much as though a modern review should
set its songs to "My Old Kentucky Home" or "Yankee Doodle," or
even to a recent musical comedy tune.[3] In the words of Allardyce
Nicoll, "Part of the worth of a ballad-opera, therefore, comes from
the subtle juxtaposition in the mind of the auditor of the *original*
tune and words and of the new words written to the music."[4] This
important association or relation between the new words and the
original ones might afford pleasure or surprise to the listener; as in

the French *vaudeville* it might also allow opportunity for parody. In this connection we should be inaccurate if we believed that all, or even many, of the original songs and airs were of great antiquity. Most of them came from the seventeenth century. Tunes were frequently appropriated from the songs of D'Urfey or of Dryden, and even from such recent favorites as Gay's "'Twas When the Seas Were Roaring" or Carey's "Sally." These were essentially in the ballad vein, but the writers were not at all averse to invading the Italian enemy's camp and stealing his thunder, particularly in the way of marches and dance music—sometimes for purposes of parody.⁵ Or along with the ballad tunes might be included a few specially composed pieces—by Mr. Seedo, or Mr. Charke, or Mr. Carey.⁶ These few exceptions, however, do not alter the essential fact that ballad opera depended almost entirely on airs already known to the audiences.

In their quest for familiar tunes the authors must have shown considerable diligence, about a thousand airs appearing in the acted operas alone. Most of these, however, were used only once or twice. Among the fifty or sixty favorites we find the "Black Joke," "Moggy Lowther," "Polwart on the Green," "Lillibullero," and—most popular of all—"Tweedside." A few airs resurrected from Restoration comedy and opera are interesting because the composers may be identified. "We've Cheated the Parson," from *King Arthur,* for example, was set by Henry Purcell. Ballad opera took special delight in dialect songs, for which numerous Scotch, Welsh, and Irish airs were utilized. Some fifteen or twenty tunes came from the French and at least twice that number from the Italian, including marches and dances from the serious operas. That the English airs, in turn, often made their way on the Continent is apparent from Horace Walpole's letter to Richard West: *"Then I have danced, good gods! how I have danced!* The Italians are fond to a degree of our country dances: *Cold and raw* they only know by the tune; *Blowzybella* is almost Italian, and *Buttered peas* is *Pizelli al buro."*⁷

Our brief consideration of the songs may help us in arriving at a definition of ballad opera, for the use of simple ballad airs and the recollection of original words by the auditor serve to distinguish the form from the dozens of earlier and contemporary musical types— from the masque and native English opera, from the French *ballet de cour* and *comédie-ballet,* from Italian opera with its formal recitative and aria. Only two earlier genres show similarity to ballad opera. One, the Elizabethan jig, employed popular ballad airs but was nothing more than a brief dance in dramatic form with singing but rarely with spoken dialogue.[8] The possibility that Gay had any acquaintance with the long-obsolete dramatic jig appears exceedingly remote.[9] On the other hand, he may very well have had knowledge of another form, the French *comédie en vaudevilles,* which anticipated *The Beggar's Opera* in the use of familiar airs. The entire question of French influence will be considered more fully in the next chapter. Adequate definitions of ballad opera have been offered by Allardyce Nicoll, William Eben Schultz, and the 1927 edition of Grove's *Dictionary of Music and Musicians.* Perhaps the most thorough critical study of the term appears in an article by W. J. Lawrence in *The Musical Quarterly.* He writes:

Broadly speaking, "ballad opera," together with its variant, "ballad farce" (the term usually employed when the entertainment was in single-act form), signified a play of humorous, satirical or pastoral order intermixed with simple song, the music for which was for the most part derived from popular ditties of the street-ballad type. But, as no rigid formula had sway, both original music of a light order and pre-existent music of more scientific quality were occasionally pressed into service.[10]

It remained for the comic opera of the second half of the century to abandon ballad airs for more elaborate and specially composed music. Mr. Lawrence traces the beginning of comic opera to Bickerstaffe's *Love in a Village* in 1762. The distinction between the two genres, he finds, was not so much one of form as one of method. He adds aptly, "Ballad opera was designed for the player who could sing, comic opera for the singer who could make some attempt at acting."[11]

Accepting the conclusions of Mr. Lawrence, we may consider ballad opera, for purposes of this book, as designating a play of three acts or fewer,[12] usually but not necessarily in prose, interspersed with a variable quantity of songs, all or part of which are set to familiar or popular airs normally specified and numbered in the printed play. While the songs may have proved the main attraction for a contemporary audience, they are not usually the prime concern of the dramatist, and their omission would not incurably ruin the play. Overtures are frequent, particularly in the full-length operas, but recitative is never employed. Dances appear frequently and spectacular scenes occasionally, but in comparison with those of Italian opera, the stage and musical effects are modest. In treatment and content, the great body of ballad operas remain realistic and satiric, though concessions are made to pastoral, romantic, and sentimental themes. Unable or unwilling to preserve strict purity of form, moreover, ballad opera welcomed other dramatic types of the time, such as pantomime, burlesque, or "rehearsal." As a result, a number of plays will be found on the border line; their classification as ballad operas will depend on the irreducible minimum of our definition—they must not be downright tragedies, and they should include at least a few songs set to old or familiar airs.

Chronologically, ballad opera's life-span was short—from 1728 to about 1750. This period will provide our main concern, but some mention will be made also of the earlier musical drama and of the later survivals of the form. In accordance with eighteenth-century opinion, *The Beggar's Opera* will be considered the first of its line, at least in England. Grove's *Dictionary* and various histories of the drama assert mistakenly that Allan Ramsay's *Gentle Shepherd* (1725) was an important precursor or even the original ballad opera. Burns Martin, among others, has dispelled this fallacy in his book *Allan Ramsay* (1931)[13] by showing that in its original form *The Gentle Shepherd* had but four songs, and a glance at the early editions of Ramsay's pastoral will quickly bring confirmation. The fact of the matter is that Ramsay, who was a great admirer of Gay, ballad-operatized the poem himself late in 1728, no doubt under the influence of *The Beggar's Opera,* in order to adapt it for theatrical performance in Scotland by the boys of the Haddington Grammar School;[14] and this revised and somewhat inferior form has appeared in subsequent editions.

From its very beginning the story of ballad opera is one of degeneration. In his first attempt Gay had brought the form to such
high perfection that it could not be improved upon, although a
number of capable authors, like Fielding, adopted it and were successful in their own way. After 1750 ballad opera simply died out,
to be replaced by comic opera of the Bickerstaffe-Dibdin-Sheridan
type, even as in France the *comédie en vaudevilles* had given place,
by the time of Favart, to the new *comédie à ariettes,* set to specially
composed music. Even after ballad opera had become outmoded,
however, *The Beggar's Opera* and several other pieces continued to
win acclaim upon the stage. Some critics have seen a direct relationship between Gay and Gilbert and Sullivan. While it is true
that they belong to the same operatic tradition, it would be a mistake to overstress the resemblance or attempt to discover too specific an influence. Little similarity may be discerned in their works,
either in form or in music. The content is essentially different. The
airy and delicate fantasy of the Savoy operas, the bubbling and
irrepressible gaiety of versification, the high moral tone are all alien
to the age of George II. A century and a half separates Gay from
Gilbert and Sullivan, and their work reflects their different ages.

A few words may be devoted to the influence of ballad opera
on the Continental stage. *The Beggar's Opera,* in spite of its immense popularity in England, Ireland, Wales, and the American
colonies,[15] did not take kindly to translation. In its own century it
proved a dismal failure in French and scarcely received a hearing
in German.[16] Another opera, however, Coffey's *Devil to Pay,* played
a singular part in Continental drama. Translated into German in
1743 and adapted numerous times thereafter,[17] this all-but-forgot-
ten ballad farce initiated in Germany a vogue for musical plays
which led to the creation and development of the *Singspiel,* a form
which attracted such diverse composers as Hiller, Wolf, Schweitzer,
André, Neefe, Benda, Dittersdorf, and even Mozart. By the second
half of the century, however, the influence of French comic opera
had likewise reached Germany, and the *Singspiel,* in its dependence
upon specially composed music, comes nearer to the form of Favart
and Sedaine than to that of Coffey.[18] *The Devil to Pay* appeared

also in French, and later in Italian, while its sequel, *The Merry Cobler,* enjoyed several adaptations in the German *Singspiel.* A few other ballad pieces may perhaps have made their way across the Channel, but none of them, certainly, rivaled the influence and success of the Coffey operas.

In *The Beggar's Opera* Gay initiated a tradition not only of ballad music but of realism and satire as well. It is therefore an entertaining but not altogether pleasant world that ballad opera presents to us—a world of intriguing chambermaids and rebellious daughters, of "oyster-meeters" and hypocritical Quakers, of highwaymen, bawds, and stallions, of stupid rustics and drunken squires, of coxcombs and unscrupulous rakes—male and female. The country village, the cobbler's stall, the poet's garret, Billingsgate, Bridewell, St. James's, Mother Pierce's—they give us a picture of the century which has justly been called Hogarthian. But comedy was never averse to the depiction of knaves and rogues, and as frequently as not the rascals were exposed to defeat and ridicule. To complement the picture, a few sentimental operas give us scenes of sweet reconciliation and noble sentiment, and in Fielding's ballad farces we are generally offered at least one example of true and sincere love. As for the language—both in the songs and the dialogue—it is for the most part the idiom of the time, racy as well as realistic, and the many dialects attempted should bring joy to the heart of a philologist.

The uneven quality of the plays renders them no better—and no worse—than the average comedies and farces of the century. Like the non-musical dramatic works, the ballad operas are at their best in dialogue and characterization and at their weakest in plot. On the whole, they preserve the comic spirit of English drama far better than do the genteel and sentimental comedies then coming into favor. At least a dozen make excellent reading, surpassing in quality some of the better-known plays. While, as a matter of course, *The Beggar's Opera* heads the list, Johnson's *Village Opera,* the anonymous *The Footman, The Jovial Crew, The Jew Decoy'd,* and several of the political operas have considerable dramatic force and effectiveness. Fielding's farces and burlesques are "mixed pieces," difficult to classify but always interesting. Some of the more popular afterpieces—like Coffey's *Devil to Pay* and Hippisley's *Flora*—were undoubtedly quite satisfying on the stage. On the other hand, some of the other ballad operas (usually maiden efforts) are unspeakably bad. In the succeeding chapters, after a review of the facts concerning *The Beggar's Opera*, the various easily defined types will be considered in turn—the "low life" operas, the village operas, the operas of intrigue, the classical and mythological operas, the "rehearsals,"[19] and so on down to the end.

If the critical estimates appear distorted or inaccurate, it must be remembered that this type of antiquarian research is not unlike the reconstruction of a prehistoric fossil on the basis of a recently excavated toe or femur. The dim candle-lit stage of the eighteenth century is missing, the rich leisurely life of Drury Lane and Covent Garden has yielded to a faster and more nervous tempo, the songs have lost their vitality and the Kitty Clives their voices, and the footmen no longer interrupt the play from the gallery. The printed lines tell us only one small side of a story buried in the theatrical past. Colley Cibber's skill in the impersonation of fops may have given life to some apparently stupid parts, and the Spillers and Hippisleys may have brought down the house in an endless succession of clowns and rustics. Two centuries from now, imagine judging the Broadway revue of today on the basis solely of the printed dialogue! And what a task for the brow-beaten scholar of the twenty-second century to clarify for his breathless reader the countless topical or political allusions! One may hope perhaps to reconstruct ballad opera—this genial and rather innocuous monster—but only to the merest shadowy semblance of its original self.

CHAPTER TWO

Low Life and the Musical Background

WHILE critics may disagree in their determination of the first novel or the first short story, there is little question about selecting the first ballad opera. At least, the contemporaries of Gay appear to be unanimous in their assumption that the author of *The Beggar's Opera* initiated the form. Writing in his usual authoritative style, Dr. Johnson points out the novelty of this new mode of comedy and declares that whether it "was the product of judgement or of luck, the praise of it must be given to the inventor," a pronouncement to which he adds that "there are many writers read with more reverence to whom such merit of originality cannot be attributed."[1] The modern suggestion that Ramsay anticipated the type in *The Gentle Shepherd* has been proved, as we have noted, inaccurate. A model in the matter of mere form may be discovered in the French *comédies en vaudevilles,* some of which Gay may possibly have seen either at the little theatre in the Haymarket or on his visits with the Pulteneys to Paris, but there exists at present no direct evidence of such a relationship. The apparent absence of any earlier ballad opera in England does not, however, indicate that Gay created the form out of thin air. There were obviously some sources of inspiration or influence in English life and literature which were utilized by the author. A brief review of these—and of the possible French influence—may prove helpful in tracing the genesis of ballad opera.

In 1727 (and possibly earlier), Gay sat down to write his opera—under the same roof, according to Spence,[2] with Pope and Swift, two other members of the Twickenham Hotch-Potch. The play was substantially finished by October 22, 1727, if we accept the evidence of Gay's letter to Swift, who had by then returned to Dublin.[3] At the end of 1727, Gay was no novice in the art of writing. He had experimented in a variety of fields. The *Fables* had recently come out with a hopeful dedication to the young Duke of Cumberland. In the *Pastorals* and in *Trivia* he had shown his ability to treat realistic and "low life" material with such grace and elegance of diction as to lift it far above the merely commonplace or vulgar. In *The What D'ye Call It* and in *Three Hours after Marriage*[4] he had attempted novelty of form and personal and literary satire.

The traditional story is that the initial hint of *The Beggar's Opera* came as early as 1716[5] in a letter from Swift to Pope with regard to verses written by an ingenious Quaker in Dublin to his mistress.

It gave me a hint that a set of Quaker pastorals might succeed if our friend Gay would fancy it.[6] . . . I believe farther, the pastoral ridicule is not exhausted, and that a porter, footman, or chairman's pastoral might do well; or what think you of a Newgate pastoral, among the whores and thieves there?

Swift's suggestion appears also in Spence's *Anecdotes*, where we may find the Dean's well-known remark that a Newgate pastoral would make an "odd, pretty sort of thing."[7]

Here was Gay, then, in 1727, engaged in the composition of a "Newgate pastoral," which he chose to develop as a play rather than as a poem. What were some of the sources and traditions from which he may have drawn in arriving at the form that, in the words of Dr. Johnson, he invented? There seem to be four main ones, which will be considered in turn: the earlier plays of low life, serious and comic opera, ballad song, and the French *comédies en vaudevilles*.

Beggars, whores, and thieves had long found a place in the English drama—in Fletcher's *Beggar's Bush,* for example, and in Ben Jonson's *Masque of Gipsies*—and Gay was undoubtedly familiar with many of the plays in which they appear. Without attempting a complete catalogue of the realistic drama, we must examine briefly a few specific plays which have been frequently suggested as having possible influence on *The Beggar's Opera*. First in time, and one of the most important, is Richard Brome's boisterous *A Jovial Crew, or The Merry Beggars* (1684). It anticipates Gay's opera in tone and subject, particularly in the mendicant background and in the lines of some of the characters. One of the beg-

gars says, "His Father, Sir, was a Courtier; a great Court-Beggar,
I assure you";[8] at another point, Rachel, with some spirit, exclaims,
"Does he think us Whores too, because sometimes we talk as lightly
as great Ladies?'"[9] In addition, the play has six songs, at least one
of which—with the chorus "And a begging we will go"—seems to
have been a popular street ballad. Interest attaches to several songs
in beggars' cant as foreshadowing the numerous dialect songs, not
of Gay's play, but of later ballad opera. Consider, for example, this
amazing specimen, sung by the aged beggar woman, Autumn Mort:

> *This is* Bien Bowse, *this is* Bien Bowse,
>   *Too little is my* Skew.
> *I* bowse *no* Lage, *but a whole* Gage
>   *Of this I'll* bowse *to you.*
>
> *This* Bowse *is better than* Rom-bowse,
>   *It sets the* Gan *a* giggling;
> *The* Autumn-Mort *finds better Sport*
>   *In* bowsing *than in* nigling.
>   *This is* Bien-bowse, *etc.*[10]

After which, the old lady, being properly drunk, "tosses off her
Bowle, falls back, and is carried out." The disporting and dancing,
in addition to the singing, bring *A Jovial Crew* fairly close to the
ballad opera form, and it is not surprising to find it operatized in
1731 as *The Jovial Crew: a Comic Opera.* But that it had any very
direct influence on *The Beggar's Opera* remains extremely doubtful.

Several later plays dealt with thieves and highwaymen, either in
or out of Newgate. In 1715 appeared Christopher Bullock's *A
Woman's Revenge, or A Match in Newgate,* an adaptation via
Betterton of John Marston's *Dutch Courtezan* (1605). Bullock's
play was in turn ballad-operatized in 1729 as *Love and Revenge,
or The Vintner Outwitted.*

A Woman's Revenge presents a parcel of consummate rogues,
including Vizard, Vixum, Mother Griffin the Bawd, and the passionate courtezan Corinna. The play ends in Newgate, introducing
several felons under condemnation, whose leader is the bumptious
Peter Padwell of Paddington, played by Spiller (the original Mat
o' the Mint), to whom Bullock's play is dedicated. Here we find

none of the satirical elegance of Gay, but we do find numerous cynical thrusts at society and the professions, such as Vixum's speech, "You might as well find Truth in a Gamester, Sincerity in a Lawyer, or Honour in a Poet ..."[11]—a type of comparison frequently employed in ballad opera. In another passage, Vizard exclaims, "That's owing to the Corruption of the Age. For as you seem to intimate, few Men, indeed, suffer for Dishonesty, but for Poverty many: The greatest Part of Mankind being Rogues within, or without the Law, so that little Thieves are hang'd for the Security of great ones. Take my Word, Sir, there are greater Rogues ride in their own Coaches, than any that walk on Foot ..."[12] This is not unlike the vein of *The Beggar's Opera,* and some of Gay's contemporaries were quick to discern the resemblance, one anonymous writer making the accusation that Gay "stole from *Mr. Bullock,* who only Borrowed it of *Mr. Marston*; and the Law says, The Receiver is as bad as the Thief."[13]

Not mentioned previously in this connection, it seems, is a play by "Monsieur le Grand" from the repertoire of one of the French companies at the Haymarket. The piece was printed in 1727 in English as *Cartouche, or The Robbers.* In this comedy concerning the celebrated French robber we find emphasis upon the idea of the gang and loyalty to it. The day's booty is catalogued by Cartouche in a way reminiscent of the Peachum scenes and is turned over to Madam Tricksy, a receiver of stolen goods, to be disposed of to a certain Mrs. Frippery. There is incidental satire on lawyers as well as bribery of one of the officers of the guards, who is called "one of our Pensioners." The play has no *vaudevilles* and resembles the subsequent Sheppard pieces far more than it does *The Beggar's Opera.* As in *The Prison-Breaker* the central characters are eventually arrested and given over to poetic and criminal justice.

Harlequin Sheppard (1724) by J. Thurmond, author of *Harlequin Dr. Faustus,* was one of the first pieces to deal with the exploits of the famous English highwayman. It was followed, in 1725, by an anonymous and unacted play, *The Prison-Breaker, or The Adventures of John Sheppard,* which capitalizes on the same material but has much greater importance in connection with *The Beggar's*

Opera. Here the unknown author brings on the stage not only Sheppard but the equally notorious Jonathan Wile (Wild) as well, informer and receiver of stolen goods, and apparently the prototype
of Peachum. Pearce believes that Gay was in some degree indebted
to *The Prison-Breaker*,[14] a perfectly reasonable supposition which
is not denied by Schultz, although the latter believes the authors
may have drawn their material from the same general sources.[15]
Different as are the two plays, they have many points of resemblance in content, situation, wording, and characterization. To list
only a few parallel items, we find in *The Prison-Breaker* the escape
of Sheppard from Newgate and his recapture, the gang of thieves
and their self-characterization as "Rogues of Honour," the disposal
of stolen goods by Coaxthief and Mrs. Coaxthief, the abuse of
lawyers, the close relations between the criminals and the officers of
Newgate as personified by Rust, Jonathan Wile, and Coaxthief.
The names of the thieves bear some likeness to the register of
Peachum's gang. The end of the prologue, intended to have been
spoken by Hulett, may even have suggested to Gay the mock-
heroic reprieve in *The Beggar's Opera*. The last lines run as follows,
with reference to the author's Muse:

> Here, in her Magic Empire, she Reprieves,
> Stabs, Poysons, Marries—Crowns or Halters gives.
> The Heroe whom this Night her Colours paint,
> Is but Low Life, and all her Drawings faint.
> Let him be therefore in your Censures spar'd;
> To Execute him twice will be too hard.
> On the World's Stage he has his Doom receiv'd,
> Shew Mercy here, and let him be Repriev'd.

While Gay may perhaps have read *The Prison-Breaker* and derived
some suggestions therefrom, his total indebtedness must be considered, in that event, relatively small. His treatment, his style, and
his characterization are immeasurably superior. His general thesis
is different. The 1725 piece, furthermore, has no female characters
other than Mrs. Coaxthief, nor does it offer any suggestion of musical treatment.[16]

While these various plays of low life may have been known to

Gay, in no case can a direct and unmistakable influence be detected. Ample Newgate and Tyburn material could be gathered just as well from reading the daily papers or from the confessions of condemned criminals in Newgate. In a more adventurous mood, Gay could easily have witnessed the frequent hangings at Tyburn or ventured upon Hounslow Heath at night. With regard to the Peachums of real life he needed only to glance at the numerous newspaper advertisements in the early Seventeen-twenties, such as the following from the *Daily Post* of March 26, 1724:

Lost on Saturday Night a Pocket, being torn from a Woman in Cornhill, in the narrow Passage going into the Jamaica Coffee-house, in which was a Diamond Ring in a Shagreen Case, in a green and white Purse, a laced Handkerchief, and a Silver Snuff Box with a Cypher on it, a Pair of Silver Buckels, some Money, and a Key. If any Person will bring the aforesaid Things to Mr. Jonathan Wild in the Old Baily, shall receive 4 Guineas Reward; or whosoever will discover the Person or Persons concern'd in the said Robbery, shall have 5 Guineas Reward for such Discovery paid by the said Jonathan Wild.

A complete exposé of Wild's ingenious criminal practices occurred, naturally, with his apprehension and execution in 1725, so that regardless of the exact sources which Gay may have had or followed there was an abundance of prison and low life material available either in print or in contemporary life, all of it properly illustrative for the development of a Newgate pastoral. There remains, next, to consider what particular influences may have induced Gay to write an "opera" rather than a pastoral or comedy and, more particularly, to evolve in the process the ballad opera form.

Opera owed its origin to the desire of Italian scholars and musicians of the Renaissance to recreate the musical drama of the ancients. From its very beginning in Florence in the late sixteenth century it attracted eminent poets and composers in various parts of Italy. Before long it enjoyed an enthusiastic reception in other countries, although it also provoked the criticism of St. Evremond and the ridicule of numerous later writers. Davenant, who had witnessed performances of Italian opera in Paris, was responsible for the introduction of the form in England. His operatic *Siege of Rhodes* (1656), which appeared during the last years of the Commonwealth, was soon followed by a second part and by several other operas. For the next half century the musical influences in England were French rather than Italian. Musicians from France were often patronized at the court of Charles II and several French operas secured production in England, including a version of Molière's *Psyché*. Purcell's master, Pelham Humphrey, it may be mentioned in passing, studied music in Paris under Lully. Whatever its foreign relations may have been, native English opera continued the traditions of the masque and the romantic drama, moving serenely in its own exotic world of absolute unreality, if not always of absolute nonsense. Its primary concerns were war and heroic love, with contests of generosity added for good measure. Its denizens, according to Dryden, were ordinarily "Gods and Goddesses, and Heroes, which at least are descended from them, and are in due time to be adopted in their Number."[17] When not utterly heroic, seventeenth-century opera became spectacular and fanciful, as in the Davenant operatic *Macbeth* (1672) or the Shadwell *Tempest* (1673). The costumes, the settings, and the extraordinary use of machines are described at some length in George C. D. Odell's *Shakespeare from Betterton to Irving*.[18] Two of the crowning achievements of the musical Shakespeare, certainly, were the flying witches in *Macbeth* and the male counterpart of Miranda in the *Tempest*, but these were mere details in the orgies of elaboration. Once, in *Albion and Albanius* (1685), Dryden fluttered near enough to the real world to satirize Shaftesbury and the Whigs, but only through the medium of allegory. Of the dramatic operas—as many were called—*King Arthur, or The British Worthy* (1691) achieved some artistic success, largely through the music of Purcell, and was occasionally revived in later centuries.[19] The native opera continued into the early eighteenth century in the works of Settle, Motteux, Theobald, Carey, and others—a little more restrained in its effects, perhaps, and often imitative of Italian opera, but still heroic and artificial. Neither in content nor in form was there likely to be much influence on ballad opera with its realistic themes and ballad airs. The dramatic opera—whether it used recitative or not, and it scarcely ever did—was normally a romantic play in verse, five acts

in length, with specially written music and songs by known composers, the most famous of these being Purcell. The songs were not
usually assigned to ordinary human characters, but to spirits, fairies,
and other supernatural beings, or to shepherds and shepherdesses.
While similar features might occasionally be discoverable in ballad
opera, they were in no way typical.

Native serious opera may have invited in part the satire of Gay,
but his main victim in this respect was undoubtedly Italian opera.
The latter also was heroic in content but differed from the English
type in the use of recitative and aria and in the rigid conventions
governing the kinds of roles and the distribution of the airs. At first
in Anglicized versions, then in the hybrid bilingual performances
so delightfully satirized by Addison, and finally all in Italian, Continental opera had gained a wide and fashionable following at the
Haymarket, soon eclipsing the native variety. The first opera sung
entirely in Italian was *Almahide* in 1710. The following year was
noteworthy for the performance of *Rinaldo,* the first of Handel's
thirty-five operas. As a result of the increasing popularity of Italian
opera the Royal Academy of Music was formed in 1720 under the
direction of Handel. Lavish funds from noble and aristocratic subscribers, and the acquisition of Senesino, Faustina, Cuzzoni, and
Anastasia Robinson, however, could not prevent the Royal Academy from falling gradually into financial decay until it remained
for the popularity of *The Beggar's Opera* in 1728 to give it the *coup
de grace.* But even Gay's piece was not able to subdue Italian opera
for any length of time. In the fall of 1728, Handel set out for Italy,
where he engaged a new, if inferior, group of singers. In a few years
a rival company was started at Lincoln's Inn Fields with considerably abler singers, including Senesino, Cuzzoni, and Farinelli. This
new opera was patronized by the Prince of Wales, whereas George II
and particularly Princess Caroline adhered faithfully to Handel.
The political implications of this division of the royal family are
amusingly and interestingly presented in Hervey's *Memoirs,* where
the rival factions are compared to the Greens and the Blues of
Rome.[20] The successes and quarrels of Italian opera, along with its
grandiose pretensions, made it a favorite butt for the ridicule of the

native writers. In title, in content, and in music *The Beggar's Opera* may be considered as one of the many attacks upon it. Some writers and musicians, however, including Pearce, Burney, and George Hogarth, have striven laboriously to prove that Gay was not really satirizing Italian opera but merely offering a rival form. Their arguments, which do not appear particularly convincing, rest primarily upon their interpretation of satire as detailed parody. While the entire matter seems of relatively small importance, it will be discussed more fully in the next chapter.

Nearer in method to *The Beggar's Opera* were various burlesque and comic operas, written during and after the Restoration, which may possibly have offered a few hints to Gay. They differ from ballad opera proper in their spectacular effects and primarily in the absence of popular ballad tunes. Early among the burlesque operas we find Thomas Duffet's *The Mock Tempest, or The Enchanted Castle* (Drury Lane, 1674) and *Psyche Debauch'd* (Drury Lane, 1675), in which the author attempts a systematic degradation of serious operas which had been performed at Dorset Garden. In lieu of the characters of Shakespeare, for example, *The Mock Tempest* presents a motley assemblage of wenches, whores, Bridewell keepers, spirits, devils, and masques. The songs are treated in the same spirit of burlesque. In the last act Ariel appears in mid-air and sings:

> Where good Ale is, there suck I,
> In a Cobler's Stall I lye,
> While the Watch are passing by;
> Then about the Streets I fly,
> After Cullies merrily.
> And I merrily, merrily take up my clo'se,
> Under the Watch, and the Constables nose.[21]

This is in the ballad opera manner, but there is no indication that it was set to an old air; in all probability it merely parodied the music as well as the words of the operatic *Tempest*.

Another early comic opera, Elkanah Settle's *World in the Moon* (1697), does not stoop to burlesque or travesty. It combines, interestingly enough, a realistic Restoration comedy of deception with fanciful and spectacular operatic scenes, the latter in the form of a "rehearsal." The two parts are kept fairly distinct and separate throughout—the musical and terpsichorean features being usually reserved for the end of the act, as in the *comédie-ballet* of Molière. The straight comedy part, in any event, could easily be played without benefit of opera. But at regular intervals the flat-scene draws, revealing the World in the Moon and Cynthia's train—or some related spectacle—and we have, for example, "A Dance of Four Swans. To them enter Five green Men, upon which the Swans take Wing and fly up into the Heavens. The green Men dance; which concludes the Act."[22] The music of the prologue is ascribed to Jeremy Clark and one of the entertainments to Daniel Purcell; there seem to be no ballad tunes, although some of the songs have the ballad-opera flavor.

Considerably more fantastic, though it also has strokes of low humour, is D'Urfey's *Wonders in the Sun, or The Kingdom of the Birds* (1706) "with great Variety of Songs in all kinds, set to Musick by several of the most Eminent Masters of the Age" and a dedication to "The Celebrated Society of the Kit-Cat-Club." Tom D'Urfey had the misfortune of having been born thirty years too soon—or, as Whincop perhaps more aptly puts it, "Poor *Durfey* died before his Time, for had he lived till the Ballad-Operas came in Vogue, what a Figure he must have made?"[23] His connection with ballad opera, interestingly enough, is extremely close through his collection *Wit and Mirth, or Pills to Purge Melancholy,* which the ballad-opera writers found an almost inexhaustible source of supply for old songs. Many airs and verses were his own, and he was also much admired for the singing of them. Burney says that the songs of *Wonders in the Sun* were ballad tunes of a true English growth[24] and as a result this play has sometimes been considered the first ballad opera,[25] but neither statement seems altogether accurate. Although none are specified, apparently some ballad measures were used, if we may judge by some of the refrains—"Dub dub a dub, dub a dub dub dub," and "Tantarra rara Tantararra."[26] On the other hand, one tune is ascribed to Mr. Eccles and another "to a Famous Sebel, of Seignour Baptist Lully." The main objection to calling the play a ballad opera, regardless of the songs, is that it does not look or sound like one. There are four acts (really five including the long musical prologue) and no end of machines and spectacular entertainments, proceeding through an involved and rather confused dramatic plan. The characters—except for Gonzales and the Sancho-like Diego—are not even human, but Bramins, Daemons, satyrs, gods, allegorical qualities, or birds, in an endless succession. If Gay was in any way indebted to *Wonders in the Sun*, it could have been only through the songs and some of the underlying satire. There are satirical thrusts at courtiers and ministers, at wits and women, even at the Tories and Whigs, who appear as the High-Flyers and the Low-Flyers, expressing the "Humours of Two Parties in a certain Northern Kingdom." But the satire itself is rather of the type we find in *Gulliver's Travels* or in *Erewhon*, and Swift, as a matter of fact, is probably indebted to D'Urfey's play for suggestions concerning Laputa and the Houyhnhnms.[27]

Of less importance is a short burlesque by Richard Estcourt, *Prunella* (1707?), which was introduced into Buckingham's *Rehearsal*. In this piece, according to Whincop, Estcourt acted Bays for his own benefit before a "prodigiously crouded audience."[28] The usual degradation of operatic high life is found—this time in satire of the Italian opera—with such characters as Racino, "a Grocer in the Piazzo in *Coventino Hortensi*"; Prunella, "young and handsome, something given to Love, and for it turn'd out of Doors"; Bella, who "dangles with *Prunella* every where"; and Sattinisco, "a Mercer's young Man within a Month of being made free." The play, on present reading, appears utterly incoherent, but the scenes were no doubt parodies of operatic passages and hence more intelligible to a contemporary audience. The songs—some fifteen in all —were apparently set to well-known airs from *Camilla* and *Arsinoe*. Gay followed the same device in appropriating the March from Handel's *Rinaldo* for his song of the road, and later ballad opera writers, as we have noted, indulged in similar parody of opera airs.

Still another burlesque was written in 1716 by the celebrated bass singer, Richard Leveridge, with the title of *The Comick Masque of Pyramus and Thisbe*. Leveridge names Shakespeare as his source: "From that Immortal Author's Original, I have made bold to Dress

out the same in Recitative, and Airs, and after the present *Italian*
Mode, hoping I have given it the same Comical Face, though in a
Musical Dress."[29] The songs, like those of ballad opera later, were
designed to be "the quite Reverse" of the "*high* Recitative *and*
Buskin *Airs*" of serious opera. The play itself is slight but not un-
interesting.

A few years later, in 1719, was performed at Lincoln's Inn Fields
Harlequin-Hydaspes, or The Greshamite, ascribed to Mrs. Aubert
and satirizing through the usual method of realistic degradation
the Italian opera *Hydaspes*—the one in which, by the way, occurred the famous scene between Nicolini and the lion already
burlesqued so effectively by Addison in the *Spectator*.[30] The songs
definitely parody the operatic originals, the Italian being usually
printed at the foot of the respective pages in the text. The *commedia dell'arte* tradition enters here in the fact that the characters
are performed by Harlequin, Scaramouch, Pierrot, Columbine, the
Doctor, and the rest.

A few resemblances between this burlesque opera and Gay's play
may be indicated. One song not only belongs to a type used frequently by Gay in *The Beggar's Opera* but also employs the same
general image as in Air X (Act I) and Air XLVII (Act III). It is
sung by Harlequin in Act III, Scene I:

> Have you beheld a Vessel strive
>   By adverse Waves withstood;
> While fierce impetuous Tempests drive,
>   And lash the swelling Flood?
>
> So fares my Soul amidst the Train
>   Of Ills, that hang around;
> For gentle Succour looks in vain,
>   Where none is to be found.[31]

In the same act, Columbine and Harlequin have a romantic parting scene ending in a sung duet and somewhat suggestive of the
pathetic separation of Polly and Macheath in Act I. At the end of
the play, finally, after killing the lion, Harlequin—in burlesque of
Hydaspes—falls down in the arena, presumably dead. But he is not
really dead; the actors cry for pardon, the Doctor relents, and Col-

umbine is his. Is there not a suggestion here of the sudden reprieve of Macheath in *The Beggar's Opera?* Or perhaps Gay may have had the ending of the original *Hydaspes* in mind.

Another opera by D'Urfey, *The Two Queens of Brentford, or Bayes No Poetaster,* was published in 1721, though never presented on the stage. Here we find even more buffoonery and confusion—partly resulting from the favorite seventeenth- and eighteenth-century form of the "rehearsal." A long prologue, satirizing among other things the Mississippi and South-Sea Bubbles, is followed by five dull acts, with the operatic entertainments usually relegated to the end of each act. Of greater importance seems to be the underlying political satire, most of which is at present virtually unintelligible. While the date is rather early for political ridicule of Robert Walpole, the several songs and innuendos about Robin the Sutler strongly remind us of the Robin of Bagshot references in Gay and the Robin passages in Fielding. It is not impossible that *The Beggar's Opera* may have derived some of its impulse toward political satire from D'Urfey, although here again absolute proof is lacking. While D'Urfey, then, foreshadows in some respects the ballad opera, it is indeed regrettable that he did not live to profit by the simpler form introduced by Gay; considering this possibility, we can only re-echo Whincop's exclamation, "What a figure he must have made!"

Gay's familiarity with D'Urfey's work and his appreciation of it are evident from the invocation near the beginning of "Wednesday; or the Dumps" in *The Shepherd's Week,* which, by the way, appeared in 1714, long before *The Beggar's Opera.*

> A while, O *D'Urfey,* lend an ear or twain,
> Nor, though in homely guise, my verse disdain;
> Whether thou seek'st new kingdoms in the sun,
> Whether thy muse does at *New-market* run,
> Or does with gossips at a feast regale,
> And heighten her conceits with sack and ale,
> Or else at wakes with *Joan* and *Hodge* rejoice,
> Where *D'Urfey's* lyricks swell in every voice;
> Yet suffer me, thou bard of wond'rous meed,
> Amid thy bays to weave this rural weed.[32]

This and other poems by Gay show also an interest in the ballad-singers, of which more will be said in due time.

So much for opera, serious and comic, but on the other end of the dramatic scale it must be remembered that music not only had been the handmaid of English drama during the Elizabethan period but had been since the Restoration steadily encroaching upon comedy and tragedy both, so that scarcely a play was acted without songs and dances, either in the text or during the entr'actes. This type of "variety" Nicoll considers as an element in the disintegration of the drama.[33] In any event, we encounter numerous comedies interspersed with songs—an expression which, incidentally, has sometimes been offered as a definition of ballad opera. The difference between these and the ballad pieces lies mainly in the lesser number of songs and in the fact that the old ballad music was not ordinarily used. Dryden and Congreve, as well as Tom D'Urfey, showed partiality for song. Part III of *The Comical History of Don Quixote* (1696) has some eight songs, one to the tune of a minuet, another a ballad measure sung by Mary the Buxome. The latter, a breezy and bawdy song with the refrain (with variations) of "Hoy Was Ever a Maiden So Lerricom Poop'd" appears in Volume II of the same author's *Pills to Purge Melancholy* under the title of "The Jolly Miller"[34] and made its appearance in the ballad opera repertoire. Especially interesting is another play by D'Urfey called *The Fool Turn'd Critick* (1678), a hard-boiled comedy of wit and intrigue. It includes only three songs in the five acts, but these are notable in having the printed music in the text, prefixed to the songs, as was the case in many of the ballad operas later. Obviously the materials for the form initiated in *The Beggar's Opera* were easily available—even disregarding entirely the native and the Italian opera—and Gay may simply have had the inspiration to extend for his own particular purposes the common features of contemporary comedy.

Without ballad tunes, *The Beggar's Opera* would have been a straight comedy or a comic opera. We now turn, therefore, from the tradition of low life in the theatre and from the early opera to a consideration of the ballad songs of the time, which may have

offered additional hints to Gay. For a large body of new songs set
to specified old airs, Gay did not have to search very far around
the corner—no farther than the nearest street-corner, in fact, if he
were lucky enough to find there a ballad singer in the midst of his
"auditory."

This noteworthy character was a regular feature of English life,
though perhaps less popular than in preceding centuries. He appeared on the stage in such characters as "Nightingale" in Ben Jonson's *Bartholomew Fair*. A print of the street singer with his cor-
pulent wife and two children is reproduced opposite page 214 of
John Gay's London by Irving. With a wooden leg, patches in his
breeches, and a nondescript costume, he is to all appearance a beggar. Since professional beggars of the period were often itinerant
songsters, incidentally, Gay's title seems almost synonymous with
"the ballad singer's opera" and helps perhaps to explain the presence of ballad songs.

That the itinerant singer performed indoors as well as out can
be observed readily in the tavern scene of Hogarth's *Rake's Progress* (Plate III), where the rake and his fellow-revellers are being
entertained by a woman singing the "Black Joke." This song, to
which there was apparently a definite dance, was a great favorite
of the time. It reappears constantly in ballad opera and has even
earned scornful mention in Pope's *Imitations of Horace*.[35]

Gay's interest in ballads and their singers as literary material is
evident from his humorous description of the drunken representative of the order in "Saturday" of *The Shepherd's Week*:[36]

> He sung of *Taffey Welch*, and *Sawney Scot*,
> *Lilly-bullero* and the *Irish Trot*.
> Why should I tell of *Bateman* or of *Shore*,
> Or *Wantley's Dragon* slain by valiant *Moore*,
> The bow'r of *Rosamond*, or *Robin Hood*,
> And how the *grass now grows where* Troy town *stood*?

Pearce believes that Gay became himself rather closely identified
with popular ballads through his song " 'Twas When the Seas Were
Roaring" in *The What D'ye Call It* (1715) and his equally popular "Sweet William's Farewell to Black-ey'd Susan," both of which

were set to music and appeared frequently in ballad operas.[37] Even more significant, of course, in connection with *The Beggar's Opera*, is Gay's ballad "Newgate's Garland," written in 1725. Quoted by Pearce are passages from an article, presumably[38] from the *New Monthly Magazine* of 1836, on Gay's relations to the singers of St. Giles's:

We are to look upon the ballad singers from this time forth in the light of a corporation. Custom had established yearly festivals for them in the classic regions of St. Giles's, which were much frequented by some of the wits of the day—Swift, Gay, Bolingbroke, Steele, etc. From these high followers of the Muses yearly contingents of ballads were expected. . . . Gay and Swift had naturally a relish for low society, and were hailed by the fraternity and sisterhood as the most precious sources of profit.[39]

Delightful as the story is, it is unsupported by any other testimony. If credence is given to it, one might find support for the statement of the beggar in the Introduction to Gay's opera—"This piece I own was originally writ for the celebrating the marriage of *James Chanter* and *Moll Lay,* two excellent ballad-singers!"

If one may believe the gossip of Horace Walpole, John Gay in 1714 or thereabouts enjoyed a connection of a different kind with a supposed member of the mendicant tribe. One night in the gallery of the playhouse he struck up an acquaintance with a handsome woman seated next to him. For two years thereafter he had numerous if irregular assignations with her. One day he saw her cross a street in Pall Mall dressed in rags like a beggar, but she refused to recognize him. During their acquaintance she never explained who or what she was but promised she would remain true to him. Later an unknown lady was found dead in Leicester Fields, whom Gay recognized as his erstwhile friend and managed to identify as the daughter of a Jacobite Irish lord. She had apparently been employed as a spy by the government and assumed occasionally the role of a beggar. When we consider Gay's thesis about the similitude between high life and low, it appears quite possible that he may have derived some inspiration from this early romantic episode.[40]

The eighteenth century was not over-precise in its definition of the ballad, including in the term, as mentioned earlier, almost any short song, lyrical or narrative, which was commonly sung up and down the streets. Like the songs of Gay's opera, it was ordinarily set to a specified old air. "The street ballads sometimes served the same purpose as the sensational newspaper of modern times," writes Irving, "for they found in the executions the pabulum for many a song."[41] Not only were the Tyburn hangings promptly lyricized, but almost any extraordinary event—a fire, a murder, a great frost, a political event, or a social scandal—found its way into the ballads. At times, in their stated or implied comment on the news of the day, the ballad singers were not unlike romantic and perambulating editorial writers arousing public opinion. "Lillibullero" is said to have driven James II out of England,[42] and the "Sturdy Beggars" intended the same compliment, but with less success, to Robert Walpole in 1733. The ballad-singers themselves were often included in the *dramatis personae* of the political ballad operas for the mere purpose of delivering on the stage the political songs that were current on the streets.[43]

An example or two from the printed ballads previous to *The Beggar's Opera* may illustrate some of the foregoing points. Among the Pepys ballads we find this engaging specimen: "A warning for wiues, By the example of one Katherine Francis, alias Stoke, who for killing her husband, Robert Francis, with a paire of sizers, on the 8. of Aprill at night, was burned on Clarkenwell-greene, on Tuesday, the 21 of the same moneth, 1629. To the tune of *Bragandary*." More lyrical in treatment and subject is the broadside ballad "The Thames uncas'd: or, the Waterman's Song upon the Thaw. To the Tune of *Hey Boys up go we*." An attack upon the Puritans in "The Ballad of the Cloak: or, the Cloak's Knavery. To the Tune of, *From Hunger and Cold, or Packington's Pound*," has interest because the music is prefixed to the song. Without indulging in needless repetition of ballad titles, we may quote in full the title of one of Gay's ballads, mentioned previously: "Newgate's Garland: Being a New Ballad. Shewing How Mr. Jonathan Wild's Throat was cut from Ear to Ear with a Penknife, by Mr. Blake, alias Blueskin, the bold Highwayman, as he stood at his Tryal in the Old-Bailey. 1725. To the Tune of *The Cut-purse*."

The ballad form, then, was not the sole property of the anonymous street singers. Not only Gay, but the wits and the courtiers generally might and did take a hand at it. The subject-matter might be purely lyrical, as in Gay's " 'Twas When the Seas Were Roaring," or topical, or political. In the *vers-de-société* manner is the ballad written by Pulteney and Chesterfield, to the tune of *Molly Mog*, on the occasion of John Hervey's marriage to Molly Lepell, one of the attractive members of the Gay and Pope circle. This, of course, came some years before the bitter animosities between Hervey and Pulteney and also the Sporus attacks of Pope. Croker quotes one of the stanzas in his introduction to Hervey's *Memoirs:*

> For Venus had never seen bedded
> So perfect a beau and a belle,
> As when *Hervey the handsome* was wedded
> To the *beautiful Molly Lepell.*"

Hervey himself was a confirmed writer of ballads and occasional verses—frequently of a political nature—and about 1731, before his rupture with the Prince of Wales, helped Frederick to compose ballads and sonnets." The tradition of the political ballad remained prominent throughout the century. One of its chief later exponents, as may be seen in the correspondence of Horace Walpole, was Hanbury Williams. In short, in the employment of songs set to old airs —with political significance or without—Gay was simply introducing into the theatre a perfectly ordinary practice, common both to the street ballad and to the aristocratic social or satirical ballad.

The influences and traditions indicated so far in the present chapter have all been English, and they may in themselves suffice to account for the appearance of ballad opera. In the plays of D'Urfey and other writers, as we have seen, are found anticipations of the formula developed by Gay. The assertions that he invented an absolutely new dramatic form, however, lose some of their force when we glance at the drama across the Channel, for in the *comédies en vaudevilles* the writers of the Fairs had evolved independently a genre almost identical with ballad opera. Even before the full development of this dramatic form at the Théâtres de la Foire, songs set to specified old airs had appeared, prior to 1700, in the repertory of the Théâtre-Italien. The plays of this theatrical company were easily available in England, for the famous Gherardi collection, published in six volumes in 1700, was brought out in London in 1714 by Jacob Tonson. At least a few *vaudevilles* are found in some eight or ten comedies of the Théâtre-Italien: *Ulisse et Circé* (1691), *L'Opéra de campagne* (1692), *La Baguette de Vulcain* (1693), *Le Départ des comédiens* (1694), *La Foire de St. Germain* (1695), and others. In the later plays of the collection references to the ballad singers, especially the "chantres du Pont-Neuf," are numerous. That these characters in real life were not infrequently the dispensers of personal scandal is evident from the following speech of Lenor in one of the comedies:

Où sont-ils ces calomniateurs, qui m'ont mis en mauvaise odeur dans mon quartier, dont ma vertu estoit la cassolette? Que de Vaudevilles, que de *Robins turelure* sur moy! Que de *Vous m'entendez bien!* Il faut que je me vange de tous ces Chansonniers.[46]

The term *vaudeville*, it might be mentioned, is derived from *vau-de-Vire* ("Valley of the Vire") in Normandy, where popular songs were composed by the poet Basselin in the fifteenth century.[47] In any case, by the late seventeenth century the term designated songs set to known airs. With regard to its functions and possibilities in the musical drama, Lesage defines it thus: "...le Vaudeville, espèce de Poësie particulière aux François, estimée des Etrangers, aimée de tout le monde, & la plus propre à faire valoir les saillies de l'esprit, à relever le ridicule, à corriger les mœurs."[48] The term *comédie en vaudevilles* indicates the use of known tunes, as in ballad opera, whereas *comédie à ariettes* implies specially written airs by known composers, as in most of the work of Favart.

In the Comédie-Italienne the *vaudevilles* appeared in a decidedly rudimentary form. Only a very few songs were inserted in a play, as a rule, and these were likely to be grouped together at the end. The development of the regular *comédies en vaudevilles* was an accidental result of the long and bitter struggle between the privileged Comédie-Française and the enterprising showmen of the Foire St. Germain and the Foire St. Laurent, who performed at Paris at a specified time each year—in other words, the mock-heroic battle between the *romains* and the *forains*. When the Comédie-Italienne was banished from France in 1697, its repertoire was appropriated by the companies of the fairs. Filled with jealousy at the success of its humble rivals, the Comédie-Française instituted countless legal actions, which led occasionally to the actual tearing down of the stages of their adversaries, and peremptorily forbade the use of connected acts, of dialogue, even of monologue. The ingenious devices of the *forains*, who reappeared in a Protean variety of new genres, are too numerous to mention here completely. Among the most interesting were parody of scenes from the Comédie-Française in jargon of meaningless sounds scanned like tragic hexameters; *pièces à écriteaux*, in which the actors carried their dialogue on large scrolls to be exhibited to the spectators (later the *écriteaux*, proving cumbersome, were lowered over the stage); and finally the *comédies en vaudevilles*. The last were made possible through the acquisition, in 1708, of the privileges of music, song, and dance from an old enemy, the Académie Royale de Musique, with the addition, in 1714, of the permission to sing vaudevilles. The *forains*, moreover, managed to secure the services of authors of no little importance—Fuzelier, Dorneval, and especially Lesage. The two last collaborated in a ten-volume edition of the *Théâtre de la foire*. In his preface to this collection, Lesage describes briefly the development of the *opéra comique*, by which he means here simply the *comédie en vaudevilles*. Referring to the players of the *foires* he says:

Ils traitèrent avec l'Opéra, qui, en vertu de ses Patentes, leur accorda la permission de chanter. On composa aussitôt des Pièces purement en Vaudevilles, & le Spectacle prit le nom d'OPERA-COMIQUE. On mêla peu-à-peu de la prose avec les vers, pour mieux lier les couplets, ou pour se dispenser d'en trop faire de communs: De sorte qu'insensiblement les Pièces devinrent mixtes. Elles étoient telles, quand L'Opéra-Comique a enfin succombé sous l'effort de ses Ennemis, après en avoir toujours été persecuté.[49]

We see thus that in its final stage the *opéra-comique* of the fairs, instead of being entirely in *vaudevilles* as was required by the terms of the theatrical war, gradually employed dialogue in prose to join the songs. The result is a dramatic form substantially the same as ballad opera.

How convenient it would be at this point to discover a neat little passage in the correspondence or the annals of the eighteenth century proving beyond question that Gay was familiar with the French *comédie en vaudevilles!* But the presiding genius of literary archeology has not been kind, and if documentary proof ever existed, it must have fallen a prey to the non-human bookworms long ago.[50] It can only be said that Gay made one trip to France in 1717 and another in 1719, and that he was no doubt conversant with the French theatre and literature. His *Epistle to William Pulteney*, for example, shows interest in French and Italian opera and refers especially to singing in the audience—a practice common in the Théâtre de la Foire. Several airs in *The Beggar's Opera* are of French origin and one of his musical sources may have been the collection called *Le Clef des chansonniers*.[51] Gay's general treatment of the songs is not unlike what we find in the Parisian plays. The dance in Newgate at the end of Act III is on the general style of the *divertissement* of dance and music which regularly concluded the comic opera of the fairs. The style of printing in the two countries is about the same, except that the French *vaudevilles* were not numbered and the music, when printed, as in the Gherardi collection, was ordinarily appended at the end of each play.

If Gay did not witness any of the French pieces on his trips to the Continent, it was quite possible for him to have seen similar performances in London at some of the playhouses, especially the little theatre in the Haymarket. Numerous companies of French players performed there between 1720 and 1728, their repertoire being listed fully in Appendix C of Allardyce Nicoll's *A History of Early Eighteenth Century Drama*. One example will suffice to show that the *comédie en vaudevilles* was known to the English stage. The *Daily Post* for Monday, May 9, 1726, advertises a play to be given by the French comedians with the addition of a farce, "Le Tableau du Mariage. Never acted here before; composed by Monsieur Lesage. With a new Dance, call'd, Le Cotillon, perform'd by 12 Dancers."

This same play happens to be in the Lesage-Dorneval collection. It is a slight but extremely witty comedy of manners in one act by Lesage and Fuzelier, in which Diamantine, after wavering long on the question of whether to marry or not, decides suddenly in the negative—so that the play ends with "les Contre-fiançailles" instead of the expected wedding. There are fifteen scenes (French style) of prose and songs, with twenty-seven *vaudevilles* to specified airs. Here we have a perfectly good example of ballad opera played in the English capital a year or so before Gay's play.

So far as *The Beggar's Opera* is concerned, the model is, of course, purely one of form. There is little resemblance between the Newgate low-life content and the subject-matter of the average French play of the fairs. Despite the cynical realism of its satire, the *Théâtre-forain*—taken as a whole—indulged far more than English ballad opera in buffoonery, in *lazzi*, in machines, in the use of the exotic. Its concern, as Bernardin well expresses it, was largely with the "merveilleux mythologique, merveilleux magique, merveilleux féerique, ou tout simplement merveilleux oriental et romanesque, et merveilleux allégorique."[52] The plays, it must be remembered, were in part conditioned by the *commedia dell'arte* tradition with its stock characters and situations. But the magic and the horse-play were not all, and both the Comédie-Italienne and the Théâtre de la Foire frequently offer a devastating comedy of manners, Latin in its vivacity, exposing to heartless ridicule the bourgeois types of the day—the lawyers, the judges, the army officers, the financiers, most of all the coquettes. English ballad opera rarely succeeded—even in the work of Gay and Fielding—in this high social comedy, or at least, it did it far less effectively. Another difference may be worthy of note in passing—the Parisian drama of the fairs stooped often to vulgarity, especially before the participation of Lesage, but it remained morally more decent than ballad opera, both in word and in situation. It employed raillery and innuendo rather than the "luscious" song (in the designation of Burnet)[53] and the sensual image, and it brought no low prostitutes on the stage. The English tastes were no doubt attributable in part to the Restoration standards and in part to the alluring pornography of English song.

The indebtedness of Augustan drama to French comedy has never fully been analyzed. In all probability it is far wider than ordinarily supposed, and it is not surprising to find that ideas and situations in English ballad opera have been anticipated in the Comédie-Italienne, the Comédie-Française, and the Théâtre de la Foire. Within the realm of remote possibility, even, may be the discovery some day of a forgotten or unpublished *comédie en vaudevilles* which presents an earlier Harlequin Macheath with an Isabella Polly and a Columbine Lucy; but the likelihood of such an event is small. The fact remains that *The Beggar's Opera* proved, throughout its century, altogether alien to the French mind. Its performance in Paris by a company from London in 1749 was forbidden, nor were its translations ever successful. An illuminating article by Sybil Goulding in the *Modern Language Review* amply proves the point.[54] The author quotes the opinion of César de Saussure, a French traveller in England, who happened to see the twenty-first performance of *The Beggar's Opera:*

C'est une espèce de farce, les décorations représentent une prison et des maisons de débauche; les acteurs sont des voleurs de grand chemin et des libertins fieffés, les actrices sont des catins. Je vous laisse à penser ce qui peut sortir du cœur et de l'esprit de gens de cet ordre. La pièce est remplie de vaudevilles très jolis mais trop libres pour être chantés devant des dames qui ont de la pudeur et de la modestie.[55]

The opinion of Prévost and of later critics was substantially the same. It seems unlikely that Gay could have borrowed from French drama scenes and characters that were so alien and distasteful to it. The Gallic passion for parody and burlesque may very well have impressed him, however, and from the *comédie en vaudevilles* he may easily have derived the use of specified ballad airs within the framework of a prose comedy.

It appears from all this that some qualification must be made to Dr. Johnson's assertion that Gay invented the ballad opera form. The materials stood ready at hand from a number of diversified and more or less independent sources—from Swift's suggestion, from Newgate life and drama, from opera—serious, comic, and burlesque, from contemporary comedy, from the ballad singers and English song, from the Théâtre de la Foire. *The Beggar's Opera* offered a happy combination of already existent elements, but a combination which to the average playgoer of a rather conventional established theatre seemed daring and original. Whatever novelty there was derived emphasis from the applicability of the satire to contemporary politics, from the excellence of the production by Rich, and above all from the happy felicity of Gay's literary style. His various ingredients, in the words of Professor Thorndike, were combined "with a fitness and finality perhaps never equalled in later efforts in comic opera."[56]

CHAPTER THREE

The Beggar's Opera and Polly

THE RELATIVE neglect in scholarly circles of the ballad-opera repertoire as a whole has found some compensation in the minute study of *The Beggar's Opera* and its stage history, a line of research decidedly encouraged by the unforeseen success of Gay's play at the Lyric Theatre, Hammersmith, in the 1920s and its triumphant tours in America, Australia, and elsewhere. An agreeable if not exhaustive survey of *The Beggar's Opera* material, by Kidson, appeared in 1922, to be followed the next year by a more definitive and documented study by William Eben Schultz, which allows little room for further contributions to our knowledge of the subject. To such works, of course, must be added numerous editions of *The Beggar's Opera,* some of them excellent, and Charles E. Pearce's *"Polly Peachum"* (1913), an eminently readable book addressed to the general public. Interesting suggestions have appeared from time to time in the periodicals,[1] but no fresh material of any vital importance has recently come to light. A possible new lead, having reference to the *comédies en vaudevilles* as precursors of *The Beggar's Opera,* has been discussed briefly in the preceding chapter.

While the emphasis of the present work should properly rest on the other and less-known operas, it nevertheless remains imperative —for an understanding of what happened later—to review briefly the pertinent facts about *The Beggar's Opera* and its surprising sequel, *Polly*. It will be remembered that on January 29, 1728, *The Beggar's Opera* appeared at Lincoln's Inn Fields, graced on its debut by "a prodigious Concourse of Nobility and Gentry,"[2] including many of Gay's aristocratic friends and fellow-wits. Just how much earlier the play had been in process of composition is difficult to determine, but from the author's letter to Swift on October 22, 1727, we learn that the opera was at that time completed.[3] Earlier in the same year the *Fables* had been published with a dedication to the young Duke of Cumberland and with evident hope on the part of the author for further court preferment. He had previously received a small sinecure in 1723 as lottery commissioner and had also been granted the privilege of lodgings at Whitehall. But his expectations of substantial patronage were summarily disappointed when he was offered the post of gentleman-usher to the Princess Louisa, an infant of two years. He declined the appointment in October—rather unreasonably, thinks Melville⁴—and undoubtedly determined to gain his revenge by turning his satire more directly and more caustically against the court and the ministry. One may suppose that various changes were made in the course of writing the opera, whether before or after October 22. It is said, for example, that Gay had planned no musical accompaniment for the songs until Rich and the Duchess of Queensberry persuaded him otherwise just before the final rehearsal.⁵ Be that as it may, the opening night found a rather puzzled audience gradually won over to enthusiastic applause before the end of the evening. In a record run of sixty-two performances,⁶ interrupted only by a few benefit nights, *The Beggar's Opera* proved the sensation of the age, reaching all parts of England, traveling to Ireland, Scotland, Wales, and Minorca, and bringing great profit to all concerned. Gay netted £693 13s 6d from the four author's nights and sold the copyright of the play and the *Fables* for ninety guineas.⁷ His total proceeds have been variously computed from £2000 down.⁸ Equally fortunate was the sagacious manager Rich, who had ventured to present the opera after its rejection by Colley Cibber. Almost everyone knows the popular catch of the time that *The Beggar's Opera* made Gay rich and Rich gay. Rich's gaiety may be attributed largely to his profits of £4000 or more.⁹

The popularity of Gay's Newgate pastoral, as is likewise well known, endured for well over a century both in England and America, with occasional but ineffective remonstrances from the moralists—such as the Reverend Thomas Herring and Sir John Fielding—who felt that it tended to encourage crime. Only in the Victorian age did it disappear from the stage, the last important performances of the nineteenth century being those by Sims Reeves in 1878-1879 and in 1886. But the time was propitious in 1920 for the play's resurrection, and with some alterations and musical improvements by Frederic Austin it once more captured the popular fancy, achieving an amazing run of three years in London and traveling overseas as far as Australia and New Zealand. Even the inferior *Polly* was revived with considerable success. During its brilliant career of two centuries *The Beggar's Opera* suffered almost every possible metamorphosis. It was played by Lilliputian companies, by women exclusively, by men taking the women's parts and women taking the men's. It appeared as full-length play and as afterpiece, with or without the addition of hornpipes and other variety; it bore repeatedly the ravages of bowdlerism.[10] Perhaps the most unusual recorded performance was the one at Barnstaple, in 1790, "when Macheath had but one eye—Polly but one arm—the songs supported in the orchestra by a man who whistled the tunes —whilst the manager could not read."[11]

The diversified roles of *The Beggar's Opera* have, since the original performance of the play, proved universal favorites on the stage. Actors and actresses of talent have never failed of success, and the Pollies of the first century discovered in the part an additional measure of good fortune, since no fewer than five of them married into the nobility. For the original Polly, John Rich made a wise selection in Lavinia Fenton, secured for Lincoln's Inn Fields mainly for the part of Cherry in *The Beaux' Stratagem* and now given an increase in salary from fifteen to thirty shillings a week. Her immense success as the heroine of *The Beggar's Opera* brought forth the usual flood of poems, pamphlets, lives, and scandalous histories, the most entertaining of them being *The Life of Lavinia Beswick, alias Fenton, alias Polly Peachum* (1728). Perhaps of greater truth than the colorful accounts of her amorous history— even John Gay having been suggested in one poem as among her lovers—is the report in *The Life of Mr. James Quin, Comedian* that Lavinia was the only actress on record over whom a duel was fought. At the close of *The Beggar's Opera* season, in any event, she was taken off the stage by the Duke of Bolton, who had remained her faithful admirer during the run of the piece. She bore him two children and after the death of the Duke's wife in 1751 became the Duchess of Bolton. In Ireland both Mrs. Sterling and Mrs. Barbier were early interpreters of Polly, and to them must be added Peg Woffington, aged ten, who made her first appearance on any stage in the same part as a member of Mme. Violante's company of children. The second London Polly, Miss Warren, was a sister of Mrs. Mapp, the celebrated bone-setter of Epsom. She, too, was taken off the stage, but unfortunately by an adventurer. Among her successors in the next season or two were Miss Norsa, mistress and later wife of Horace Walpole's brother, and the incomparable Kitty Clive, whose ballad-opera career had started early, in Cibber's ill-fated *Love in a Riddle*. In 1736 the town found great diversion in the dispute between Kitty and Mrs. Cibber over the role of Polly. A complete register of the famous Pollies is impossible here, but with a flying leap to the Hammersmith revival we may mention Sylvia Nelis as the first of a dozen twentieth-century actresses in the part.

For the original Macheath, Rich had intended to employ Quin, who, according to one of the stories, had little relish for the part but went half-heartedly through two rehearsals. Overhearing Thomas Walker humming some of the tunes backstage, however, he promptly yielded to Walker's superior ability. The change proved a happy one, for Walker almost equalled Lavinia Fenton's success and became—to his eventual misfortune—the favorite of the young rakes of the town. Quin eventually did try the role of Macheath in 1730 and also played a singing part in Gay's last opera, *Achilles*. Of the army of later Macheaths we may mention in passing the famous singer Beard, who acted opposite the Polly of Miss Brent. Sims Reeves has already earned mention as the last important Macheath of the nineteenth century. In the Hammersmith revival the ever-popular role fell to Frederick Ranalow. On various occasions, for the sake of novelty, the philandering Captain was played by women. Peg Woffington, still a child, was one of the early female Macheaths. As late as 1820 Mme. Vestris attempted the same role.

Returning to the Rich production of 1728, we find Hippisley and the portly Hall in the character parts of Peachum and Lockit. Both were excellent comedians, particularly skillful in the delineation of old men. Hippisley, whose theatrical career had started in the modest employment of candle-snuffer, achieved considerable success in such roles as Fondlewife, Pandarus, Sir Francis Gripe, and Antonio in *Venice Preserved*. His powers of farcical acting showed to best advantage in his own skit, "Hippisley's drunken man," which delighted audiences for many years. Mrs. Peachum, another broadly comic part, was played by Mrs. Martin, who likewise appeared in the original performance as the unsavory Diana Trapes. For the spirited role of Lucy, Rich selected Mrs. Egleton, wife of "Baron Egleton." She appeared in numerous ballad operas later and is said eventually to have died "enamoured of Bacchus."[12] Filch, Mrs. Peachum's favorite, was acted by Nat Clark and Mat o' the Mint by Spiller, who could always rely on an enthusiastic following of butchers from Clare Market. The robustious highwaymen were played by H. Bullock (brother of Christopher Bullock), Houghton, Smith, Lacy, Pit, Eaton, and Morgan. As for the equally picturesque women of the town, they included such actresses as Mrs. Holiday, Mrs. Lacy, Mrs. Rice, Mrs. Rogers, Mrs. Morgan, Mrs. Palin, and Mrs. Salee. To them must be added Mrs. Clarke as Jenny Diver, the character that has so important a part in Gay's sequel, *Polly*. Chapman and Milward as the Beggar and the Player, respectively, complete the initial cast.

The usual accretion of fable and tradition has not failed to color romantically the history of *The Beggar's Opera*. The stories are usually based upon contemporary gossip and comment, and some of them may well be apocryphal. There is the account, for example —related in Spence—of the faith of the Duke of Argyll in the success of the play: "It will do,—it must do!—I see it in the eyes of them."[13] Or we have the tale about the restlessness of the first audience at the lack of prologue or of introductory music. Whereupon the flustered John Hall—sent in haste to pacify the audience —begged them not to call for the first and second music, "because you all know, that there is never any music in an opera."[14] Contemporary accounts differ somewhat on the line which finally con-

verted the skeptical audience, one place being fixed at Polly's plea
in Scene XII of the first act: "Oh! ponder well! be not severe."[15]
Another tradition of long standing asserts that Robert Walpole
was present in the boxes at the initial performance, when an enthusiastic encore was demanded for Lockit's song in Act II:

> When you censure the Age
> Be cautious and sage,
> Lest the Courtiers offended should be:
> If you mention vice or bribe,
> 'Tis so pat to all the tribe;
> Each cries—That was levell'd at me.

Observing that the words were applied to him with special pointed-
ness and that the eyes of the crowd were focussed upon him, Walpole applauded the song and encored it with his single voice—there-
upon receiving an ovation from the audience for his ready wit and
parry.[16]

In form *The Beggar's Opera* departed somewhat from dramatic
custom in having no prologue and in limiting itself to three acts.
Most farces had one or two acts, while the regular comedies
employed the customary five. Operas, however, frequently made
use of a three-act division and Gay very probably had them in
mind. In lieu of a prologue, a short introduction opens the play
with the Beggar and a Player discussing the forthcoming opera and
calling for the overture. Gay had already employed an introduction
in *The What D'ye Call It*—no novel device if we remember such
plays as *The Taming of the Shrew* and *The Rehearsal*. The three acts
of the opera proper, after the overture, deal with the discovery of
Polly's marriage, her romantic parting from Macheath, his betrayal
by the doxies, his escape from Newgate with the help of the jealous
Lucy, and his prompt recapture. As he is about to pay the customary penalty—an almost inevitable culmination in view of the prevailing dramatic theory of poetic justice—the Player and the
Beggar return to the stage, offer some animadversions on the
absurdity of opera, and call for a reprieve of Macheath. Thus the
plot, while relatively slight, satisfies the minimum requirements
for action, and as Loiseau points out in an excellent critical article,

it is neatly and carefully constructed.[17] It has no vital dependence on either song or music and could proceed very well without their aid, although this omission would greatly diminish the charm and the novelty.

Gay's sixty-nine songs (sixty-eight in the first issues of the first edition) were designed apparently to be sung by the actors without the accompaniment of the orchestra, until Rich and the Duchess of Queensberry suggested the change.[18] Dr. Pepusch, a native of Berlin, at this time musical director at Lincoln's Inn Fields, was employed to prepare the necessary orchestration and to write an overture. In most of the editions the music—as was customary in the operatic pieces published by John Watts—was prefixed to the songs. The overture appeared in the second edition and the simple basses, also prepared by Dr. Pepusch, in the quarto third edition. For the music to his songs Gay seems to have depended mainly upon D'Urfey's *Pills*, Playford's *Dancing Master*, and the other song collections. As was true of later ballad opera—a point mentioned in the first chapter—the tunes show considerable variety in origin and date of composition. Most of them may be assigned to the seventeenth century, but there are some later favorites as well as some traditional airs of considerable antiquity. Among the older tunes we may mention "Chevy Chase," "To Old Sir Simon the King," "Green Sleeves," and "A Lovely Lass to a Friar Came." Where the airs are recent, it is sometimes possible to identify the composer, whether it be Jeremiah Clark, or Purcell, or Handel, or Bononcini. Whatever his sources, Gay showed remarkable skill and artistry in adapting the words to the music, with the result that his songs are usually far superior to the original ones. In addition to the musical features he attempted a few spectacular stage effects in the dance of the prisoners in chains, the drill of the highwaymen, and the cotillon of the ladies of pleasure.

This bare survey of some of the facts of *The Beggar's Opera* does not include, of course, a critical consideration of the reasons for the immense success of the piece. Few plays have received in their own time such enthusiastic notice and acclaim, not appreciably dimmed by the protests of the moralists. Of the thousands of comments we may quote one expressing the critical judgment of the anonymous compiler of the list of plays appended to Whincop's *Scanderbeg,* a writer sometimes identified with John Mottley:

Mr. Gay's *Beggar's Opera* had every Charm in it that could make a Play take, Good-sense, Wit, Satire, and Novelty, an entire new Sett of Characters being introduced in it on the Stage; the Songs were almost every one of them a good Epigram, and it was no Wonder, they should please, when sung to Tunes that most of them had been favorite Airs or Catches, some for an Age past.[19]

While this is high praise, it is generally deserved, although some slight qualification may be made about Gay's use of an "entire new Sett of Characters." We have seen that whores and highwaymen appear frequently enough in Elizabethan and Restoration drama. Gay's satirical treatment of them, however, which invests them with a semi-heroic glamor and a life of their own, seemed essentially different and novel to his contemporaries. The best and most interesting analysis of this phase of Gay's characters is given by Loiseau. Of Macheath, he writes: "C'est le bandit philosophe, mi-épicurien mi-fataliste, allègrement résigné aux risques de son métier." Polly represents "L'amante sentimentale et tendre," in contrast to Lucy who is "toute vivacité et acidité."[20] From the adept characterization, from the satirical intent, from the heightened dialogue, Loiseau concludes that ". . . sous les mœurs des clients de Newgate, nous retrouvons les traits permanents de la nature humaine."[21] Whether or not we share this view entirely, we must agree that Gay's plan was to show the essential similarity between high life and low, to point out that the whore of Vinegar-lane was a recognizable replica of the lady of fashion, that a highwayman was no worse—if not much better—than a statesman, that mankind from the highest to the lowest was motivated by the identical considerations of interest, vanity, and treachery. " 'Tis a plain proof that the world is all alike," exclaims Macheath sadly when he hears that he has been peached by Jemmy Twitcher, "and that even our Gang can no more trust one another than other people."[22] Behind this unusual blending of high life and low, of aristocratic manners and realism, seems to lurk a negative philosophy of disillusion which colors the opera with an all-pervading cynicism. On the other hand, Gay has been called gentle and carefree, and Dr. Johnson has attested to the general spirit of gaiety in the piece, so that we may interpret the mood of *The Beggar's Opera* in almost any way that we like. From one angle, certainly, Gay's indictment of humanity in the play seems scarcely less severe than Swift's in *Gulliver's Travels*. Quite worthy of the Dean of St. Patrick's is Lockit's reflection that "Of all animals of prey, man is the only sociable one."[23] What obscures this basic misanthropy is the brilliancy of Gay's wit, the rapid gusto of his scenes, and the uncertainty of whether to take him seriously or not.

A prominent factor in the play's success was its satire—one of the features mentioned in the quotation from Whincop and one which operates, as we have just seen, in the characterization. From it the opera derives its main vitality. While high life and humanity itself are subjected to constant ridicule, certain specific classes of society are held up to particular scorn both in dialogue and song— the courtiers, the doctors, and the lawyers. Neither are women spared. Macheath, betrayed by Jenny and her companions, reflects, "Women are decoy ducks; who can trust them!"[24] Far from being abashed by their own and Jenny's treachery, the fair doxies almost quarrel for an equal share of the reward for the Captain's betrayal. In the ceremony insisted upon by the prostitutes, in their elaborate and often barbed compliments to one another, in their mode of dress, in their drinking, Gay is obviously aiming at the ladies of fashion. When Jenny Diver asserts that she never drinks strong-waters but when she has the cholic, for example, Macheath comments immediately, "Just the excuse of the fine ladies."[25] Further satire of women concerns the cordials they keep for their private drinking, their fashionable amusement of watching executions at Tyburn, their gushing enthusiasm for music, their mercenary attitude toward marriage and widowhood. Polly escapes relatively unharmed, but her naive romantic viewpoint merely emphasizes the contrast with the others. "I did not marry him (as 'tis the fashion) cooly and deliberately for honour or money. But I love him," she declares to her incredulous and disapproving parents.[26]

Gay's satire seems clearly to have been directed also at Italian opera. Certain writers, including Pearce, however, have attempted to prove that this view is erroneous, that *The Beggar's Opera* offers no travesty of the Italian form but only rivalry of it, attempting merely to capitalize on its success. The point is inconsequential. If Gay's opera does not offer a complete and detailed parody or travesty of its fashionable predecessor, it does indulge in numerous satirical strokes. Everyone will recall immediately the lines of the Beggar in the introduction:

I have introduc'd the Similes that are in all your celebrated Operas: The *Swallow*, the *Moth*, the *Bee*, the *Ship*, the *Flower*, &c. Besides, I have a Prison Scene, which the ladies always reckon charmingly pathetick. As to the parts, I have observ'd such a nice impartiality to our two ladies, that it is impossible for either of them to take offence. I hope I may be forgiven, that I have not made my Opera throughout unnatural, like those in vogue; for I have no Recitative: excepting this, as I have consented to have neither Prologue nor Epilogue, it must be allow'd an Opera in all its forms.

More severe ridicule occurs in Macheath's sudden reprieve at the end of the play. When the Player objects that the catastrophe is manifestly wrong, for an opera must end happily, the Beggar complies at once with the taste of the town. "Your objection, Sir, is very just; and is easily remov'd. For you must allow, that in this kind of Drama, 'tis no matter how absurdly things are brought about."[27] Schultz finds a satirical intent in the mere use of English as opposed to Italian music[28] and believes that the medley of ten songs by Macheath in Scene XIII, Act III, provides a parody of operatic recitative.[29] It is commonly believed that a reference in the Introduction and the quarrel between Polly and Lucy in Newgate were meant as allusions to a heated dispute of 1727 between two opera singers, Faustina and Cuzzoni. In any event, the conclusion seems inescapable that Gay was satirizing certain features of Italian opera, as Fielding and others continued to do in later ballad pieces. Loiseau, in the article already cited, finds evidence in the entire play of a more sustained satirical parody of the kind specifically denied by Pearce.[30] Whichever theory is right, one of the immediate effects of *The Beggar's Opera* was the temporary discomfiture of its Italian rival.

In its real or supposed political satire we discover an even more relevant factor in the prolonged success of the Newgate pastoral.

One Gay, a poet, [states Hervey in his *Memoirs*] had written a ballad opera, which was thought to reflect a little upon the Court and a good deal upon the Minister. It was called the "Beggar's Opera," had a prodigious run, and was so extremely pretty in its kind, that even those who were most glanced at in the satire had prudence enough to disguise their resentment by chiming in with the universal applause with which it was performed.[31]

Satire of Walpole was obviously intended in *The Beggar's Opera*, although even Gay may have been surprised at the numerous allusions read indiscriminately into his lines by the contemporary public. The clearest reference to the minister comes in the name read by Peachum from the register of the gang—Robin of Bagshot, alias Gorgon, alias Bluff Bob, alias Carbuncle, alias Bob Booty. This personage, who does not appear in the play, is described by Peachum as follows: "He spends his life among women, and as soon as his money is gone, one or two of the other ladies will hang him for the reward, and there's forty pound lost to us for-ever."[32] Swift wrote of Walpole as "Bob the Poet's foe," and as we shall find in the later operas, virtually no character could be called Bob, Rob, or Robin without allusion to the minister. Walpole's extravagance, his alleged debauchery, his love of food and wine, his coarseness form the subject of numerous political tracts, poems, plays, and newspaper innuendos. A particularly favorite line of attack dealt with his long connection with Maria Skerrett, who became his mistress at about this time and whom he married a decade later, after the demise of his wife. An early reference to this liaison has been seen in Peachum's assertion that Robin spends his life among women. With or without the intention of Gay, Walpole was associated further with Macheath, depicted likewise as having a weakness for the ladies. Polly and Lucy were even thought to represent Lady Walpole and Maria Skerrett, an identification which would give special point to Macheath's song, "How happy could I be with either, were t'other dear charmer away." Peachum's frequent reference to the Captain as "a great man"—a term often used as a sneering designation of Walpole—would be likely to strengthen the association in the mind of the audience between the highwayman and the minister. A further characterization of Walpole was found at the time in the cynical and double-dealing Peachum, the Jonathan Wild of the play, whose relations with Lockit reveal the *sub rosa* understanding between the forces of crime and the law. It will be recalled that before and after the quarrel between the two men in Act II they call each other "brother," a fact which rightly or wrongly reminded the audiences of a famous dispute between Walpole and his brother-in-law, Townshend. Cooke dates this quarrel in the latter part of 1727;[33] Croker[34] and the *Dictionary of National Biography*, probably on the authority of Coxe, set the occasion in 1729. The fact remains that regardless of the date of its actual occurrence the audiences and readers of later years promptly read in the Peachum-Lockit misunderstanding an allusion to political history. Compared to what happened subsequently, the multiplex attack on Walpole in *The Beggar's Opera* proved relatively mild, but it pointed the way to Fielding and the anonymous writers of political operas. An interesting footnote to this entire question of political satire may be offered in the suggestion of A. E. H. Swaen that the allegro part of the overture is an adaptation of a song known as "Walpole, or The Happy Clown," thus giving us a political allusion even in the music.[35]

Despite its satirical purpose *The Beggar's Opera* is not without its romantic and sentimental elements, modified as these may have been by Gay's humorous intent and his tone of mock seriousness. Here we find the author's nearest approach to the Gilbertian spirit. The affecting passion of Polly, the elegance of many of the lines, the alleged valor and loyalty of the gang, the grand manner of Mrs. Peachum, these and other things give coloring and grace to what might have been a mere sordid representation of low life. Many of the songs—those without a humorous or satirical purpose—are imbued with lyrical sentiment and may be called, in Gay's own words, "charmingly pathetick." In occasional scenes appears an ironical topsy-turvydom—as in the famous one between Polly and her parents where the heroine is roundly berated for her marriage to Macheath—so that we find at times an air of unreality not in accordance with a literal depiction of the Jonathan Wilds of real life, a device illustrative, of course, of Gay's thesis of a similitude of manners in high life and low. *The Beggar's Opera* thus shows a happy combination of realism and fancy, of fact and imagination, done with the same delicate artifice as in *Trivia* or the *Pastorals* and enlivened by a superb power of irony and satire.

Gay's literary style was one of the features which excited the admiration of his contemporaries. The sentence quoted earlier from Whincop asserts that "the Songs were almost all of them a good Epigram." The same might easily be said of the dialogue, which is at once graceful and brilliant, at its best not inferior to that of Congreve or Oscar Wilde or George Bernard Shaw. The best lines are familiar to most readers but it may not be amiss to marshal two or three at random for illustration—"No woman would ever marry, if she had not the chance of mortality for a release"; "Why, thou foolish jade, thou wilt be as ill us'd, and as much neglected, as if thou hadst married a Lord"; "A woman knows how to be mercenary, though she hath never been at a court or an assembly." The "twist" or "punch" at the end of the sentence—often in the form of an unexpected simile or abrupt antithesis—occurs as a frequent device, as in the lines just quoted or the equally neatly expressed, "For a husband hath the absolute power over all a wife's secrets, but her own," or Peachum's line about the lawyers, "They don't care that any body should get a clandestine livelihood but themselves." Multiplication of examples is needless to show that in lucidity and precision and wit Gay's style could scarcely be improved. He was himself unable to equal it in his two later ballad operas. While the epigrammatic nature of the dialogue departs of necessity from the language of life, it fulfills with particular aptness the requirements of the satire and has the further quality of seeming dramatically convincing.

To gauge accurately the wide influence of *The Beggar's Opera* on the ballad plays that followed, it is necessary to remember its perennial revivals, particularly during the first century of its existence. No one could surpass Gay in the exact thing which he had succeeded in doing, although various attempts were made, but it was rather in individual elements and features that *The Beggar's Opera* became the subject of much conscious or unconscious imitation. The title itself, for example, was reproduced in a dozen variations: *The Cobler's Opera, The Sailor's Opera, The Throwster's Opera,* and so on. In the matter of form, there was an early tendency to employ an introduction between one or two players and the alleged author, which would normally end with a request for the overture. Extension of this device through the entire play led to the many ballad "rehearsals," satirical operas modeled after Buckingham's famous play. The sudden reprieve of Macheath at the end had several imitations and inspired occasional allusions. The ballad songs, of course, were universally adopted as the distinguishing marks of the form, and almost the same compliment was paid to the dances. Several scenes made a profound impression upon the minds of subsequent writers and reappear regularly in later operas and plays. A surprising number of stage directions, also, call for a man—like Peachum—sitting at a table with a large book of accounts before him, or else confronted, as in Act III, with an assortment of wine, brandy, pipes, and tobacco. Particularly frequent as a later motif became the bitter rivalry of two women over one man, an obvious reflection of the Polly-Lucy fracas. In style, the dialogue and songs of the later plays were replete with dim and inaccurate echoes of *The Beggar's Opera.* Even the types of song—the similes, the plaints about the power of gold, the sentimental love ballads, the satires on lawyers—reappear with monotonous regularity. In his very first attempt, then, Gay succeeded in crystallizing the form, and his spirit hovered, lightly or uneasily as the case might be, over most of the operas that came after him.

Apart from mere form or superficial imitation, *The Beggar's Opera* determined some of the main tendencies of the genre. While in one direction it pointed the way to low life, in another it led to high life and social satire. *The Cobler's Opera* and *The Patron,* different as they are, have thus an equal indebtedness to the inspiration of Gay. *The Beggar's Opera* initiated a long line of political plays, usually in the form of attacks on Walpole, and gave sanction at the same time to a number of topical pieces on various subjects. It undoubtedly determined the use of satire as one of the main characteristics of ballad opera. In its few romantic elements it may even have had some slight influence on the plays of love and intrigue that followed. There is some danger of inaccuracy, on the other hand, in viewing all later ballad plays merely in terms of *The Beggar's Opera,* for, as we shall see, none of them can be considered as exact copies of the original. Gay performed the task too well to admit of any exact imitation, and the subsequent writers were frequently men of considerable talent, not to be guided unduly by any model. It is amusing in this connection to observe that Gay's own sequel *Polly* belongs among the operas bearing the least resemblance to *The Beggar's Opera.*

For *Polly* is at once more sentimental and more moral, mindful of its duty to dispense poetic justice. While some realistic elements are retained and the songs preserve their sad or satirical burden on the follies of mankind, the atmosphere has become strangely romantic. In deserting the environs of Newgate and Houndsditch for a new world he had never seen, Gay was tossing away his trump cards, for his depiction of the West Indies and the "noble savages" lacks the ring of truth and the power to convince. In turning Macheath into an arrant coward and a villain and in the ridiculous idea of disguising him as a Negro, Gay was furthermore sacrificing the glamor, the charm, and the gallantry of his hero. Morano's infatuated attachment for Jenny Diver, his erstwhile betrayer, strikes a false note which is not in keeping with the earlier philandering character of Macheath and which appears to have been inspired by vague recollections of *Antony and Cleopatra.* The failure of Polly to recognize her husband in blackface and his equal inability to recognize her in boy's clothes, although in keeping with the theatrical conventions of the time, must have seemed unconvincing even to contemporary readers.[36] Even more unnatural must have appeared Polly's capture of Morano during the battle. The height of

absurdity is not reached, however, until the end, with its assurance
that Polly will eventually marry the sententious Indian Prince,
Cawwawkee, and be obliged to listen for the rest of her life to his
moral apothegms. Only in the unreformed Diana Trapes and in the
unattractive figure of Ducat do we have, in an inferior way, something of the flavor of the original opera. There is an element of
unfairness, on the other hand, in the inevitable comparison between
the two pieces. Considered merely by itself, *Polly*, in spite of the
artificiality of its situations, is far from lacking in interest and
charm and compares favorably with romantic pieces on the style of
The Village Opera.

The suppression of *Polly* by the Lord Chamberlain, late in 1728,
merely amplified Gay's good fortune, for it prevented comparison
on the stage with the superior *Beggar's Opera* and it brought him
vast financial returns when the piece was printed by subscription
in 1729. It was because of her ardor in soliciting subscriptions in the
royal apartments that Gay's patroness, the Duchess of Queensberry, incurred the displeasure of George and Caroline and was
banished from the court, her husband taking occasion to resign his
employments at the same time. When *Polly*, with alterations by
Colman, came out finally in 1777, the aged Duchess was able to
attend some of the performances. The play did not prove a success
on the stage, although it fared considerably better during its revival
in the 1920s. No doubt the naive picture of the Indians and the
improved music and dance, as well as the impetus of *The Beggar's
Opera* success, had a large share in the twentieth-century approval.

Most modern commentators have wondered at the suppression
of *Polly*, considering the piece inferior and inoffensive and a mere
victim of Robert Walpole's spite. One should note the different
feeling on this score sometimes expressed in the eighteenth century.
Hervey, for example, gives the following account in the *Memoirs:*

Gay, who had attached himself to Mrs. Howard, and had been disappointed of preferment at Court, finding this couched satire upon those to
whom he imputed his disappointment succeed so well, wrote a second
part to this opera, less pretty, but more abusive, and so little disguised,
that Sir Robert Walpole resolved, rather than suffer himself to be pro-

duced for thirty nights together upon the stage in the person of a highwayman, to make use of his friend the Duke of Grafton's authority as
Lord Chamberlain to put a stop to the representation of it.[37]

While *Polly* seems free enough from specific political allusion, something must certainly have led to the current opinion about the play
and to its suppression. One perfectly obvious fact mentioned by
Hervey has been generally disregarded by the critics, namely that
Macheath had become fully identified in the popular mind with
Walpole. The debasement of the Captain into the pirate Morano
would correspondingly magnify the abuse of the first minister, who
could scarcely relish being represented as poltroon and blackguard
and unceremoniously hanged at the end—a consummation ear-
nestly hoped for by the Opposition. The desertion of Polly, the
faithful wife, for the dissolute Jenny Diver could only relate to
Walpole's connection with Molly Skerrett. In view of what was
done in the later operas there may be a remote possibility that the
miserly Ducat, who attempts to introduce Polly into his household
as his mistress despite the protests of his jealous wife, was meant
as a hit—if not a very clear or successful one—at the royal family.
If so—and this is merely a matter of conjecture—Gay was considerably surpassed in satire of George and Caroline by Fielding and by
the anonymous author of *The Wedding, or The Country House-
Wife.*

Like its predecessor, *Polly* has three acts with an introduction
and an overture. In all, seventy-one songs appear, some of them
with tunes from the French. None can compare with the best in
The Beggar's Opera. Somehow Gay seems to have lost the bite or
sharpness of his satire and we wonder whether there may not be
something in the contemporary belief—denied, however, by Pope
—that he was aided in the earlier piece by the junto of wits at
Twickenham. Cooke in his *Memoirs of Macklin* repeats a story,
based on the testimony of the Dowager Lady Townshend, that four
of the songs in *The Beggar's Opera* were written by Swift, Chesterfield, Charles Hanbury Williams, and Fortescue—a report that
Schultz tends to disbelieve.[38] The fact remains that Gay's three
ballad operas show a steady decline in excellence, with *Polly* inferior

to *The Beggar's Opera* and *Achilles* inferior to *Polly*. A possible and simple explanation of this may lie simply in the failing health of the poet.

When *Polly* made its belated appearance at the Haymarket on June 19, 1777, Colman replaced a few songs by new ones and made some minor omissions in the dialogue. Bannister played the part of Macheath opposite the Jenny Diver of Mrs. Hitchcock. Polly was acted by "a Gentlewoman, her first appearance."[39] The noble Indians, Pohetohee and his equally moralizing son Cawwawkee, were entrusted to the acting of Fearon and Du-Bellamy. The play was revived for three performances at the Haymarket in 1782 and once in 1818 at Drury Lane, then consigned to oblivion until the present century. Unlike its distinguished predecessor, it had practically no influence on the ballad opera repertoire.

CHAPTER FOUR

Other Continental and English Influences

THE RISE of ballad opera has been viewed thus far primarily in relation to its immediate literary antecedents, both French and English. In them we may find, in part, an explanation for the surprising popularity of Gay's opera and its progeny. The exploitation of ballad songs, for example, fell definitely in line with the lively interest—during the Restoration and after—in ballad literature and popular song. The concern with low life and the passion for satire, likewise, were characteristic literary manifestations of the age. To account fully for the sustained popularity of the form, however, we must look for other reasons as well. Obviously ballad opera fell on receptive literary soil in a favorable intellectual climate. In the eighteenth-century phrase, it hit the taste of the town. Before we proceed to trace the development of the genre through the various forms which it assumed, therefore, we shall consider some of the intellectual and literary fashions which formed the taste of the age and determined the expectations of the audience.

One of these fashions we shall find in the whole tradition of burlesque. The seventeenth century in France saw an efflorescence of what Brunetière calls "la maladie du burlesque." With the publication of *Le Virgile travesti* in 1648 Scarron initiated in French literature a kind of gay and learned fooling which proved to be congenial to the spirit of the time. In this poem was offered a witty and systematic degradation of the heroes and actions of antiquity, presided over by the "petite Muse au nez camard." The humor lay partly in the vulgarity of the diction, partly in the unexpected allusions to low life, and partly in the cynical device of representing the Roman gods and heroes in terms of seventeenth-century French society. As Charles Whibley expresses it, he "did an ill thing supremely well."[1] The fashion of burlesque established by *Le Virgile travesti* swept over France and England. Among the immediate imitations were Furetière's *Les Amours d'Enée et de Didon* (1649), Perrault's

L'Enfer burlesque (1649), Richer's *L'Ovide buffon* (1649), and
Picon's *L'Odyssée d'Homère* (1650). In the decades that followed,
Ovid, Juvenal, Ariosto, Virgil, and Homer all suffered the indignities of parody. In 1716 Marivaux was tempted to try his hand at
Homère travesti, ou l'Iliade en vers burlesques, to be followed in
1726 by l'Abbé Faure in *Homère, danseur de corde, ou l'Iliade fu-
nambulaire.*

The impulse set in motion by Scarron was bound to find its way
into the theatre, so that it is not surprising to find the gods, goddesses, and heroes of antiquity transported with little dignity to
the stages of the Comédie-Italienne. Ten or twelve plays of the
Gherardi collection of scenarios, to which reference has been made
earlier, deal with classic themes or personages, the latter being frequently interpreted, for purposes of humor, by Harlequin, Mezzetin, or the other Zanni. Most important among these plays are *La
Descente de Mezzetin aux enfers* (1689), *Ulisse et Circé* (1691),
Arlequin Phaéton (1692), and *La Baguette de Vulcain* (1693). The
treatment of the gods in these pieces is witty rather than vulgar,
one purpose of the comedies being to satirize the manners of contemporary society. Helen of Troy is called "une petite impertinente
et une coquette fieffée,"[2] Arlequin wants to capture Cerberus in
order to exhibit him at the Foire St. Germain,[3] and Pluto is
astounded when Mezzetin and Orpheus, "soy-disant musiciens de
l'opéra," visit Hades to plead for the return of their wives—so
astounded, in fact, that he tells them to take back all the women in
Hades, not even excepting Proserpine![4] Not content to burlesque
the Roman gods and heroes, the authors of the Comédie-Italienne
frequently employed the same methods in travesties of contemporary tragedies and operas. *Arlequin Phaéton* is a parody of the
opera by Quinault and Lully. Several pieces include travesties of
operatic airs, and *L'Opéra de campagne* goes to the extent of paro-
dying two of the opera singers—M. du Mesnil and Mlle. Rochois.
All in all, serious opera fares rather badly in the Comédie-Italienne;
what satirical thrust by Gay can rival the line from *Ulisse et Circé*
—"L'Opéra, c'est un hermaphrodite entre le bon sens et le mauvais?"

To trace the history of burlesque and parody in French drama would require a book in itself. It should suffice to add that the tradition was continued and developed in the Théâtre de la Foire. Carolet, in such plays as *Le Cocher maladroit, ou Polichinelle Phaéton,* portrays the gods in "le genre poissard." Lesage, in a parody of the Abbé Pellegrin's *Télémaque,* depicts the son of Ulysses as a superlative booby and in another well-known parody, *Arlequin Thétis,* writes in the form of a *comédie en vaudevilles.*

Meanwhile the furore for burlesque initiated by Scarron had made its way in England. To Charles Cotton fell the rather doubtful honor of writing the first imitation of *Le Virgile travesti,* the first part of his *Scarronides, or Virgil Travestie* appearing in 1664.[5] The same author, a decade later, subjected some of Lucian's dialogues to similar treatment. Cotton, however, went considerably beyond Scarron in the vulgarization and degradation of his classic personages, failing to imitate the elegant wit and critical intent of his Gallic model. Numerous devotees of the Grub-Street muse were happy to tread in Cotton's footsteps. Monsey, in 1665, published a *Scarronides* of his own, and John Phillips, a few years later, followed it with a *Maronides.* Travesties of Ovid appeared in 1673 and 1680; in 1719 Breval, one of the ballad-opera authors, wrote *Ovid in Masquerade,* a burlesque of the thirteenth book of the *Metamorphoses.* The *Iliad* did not escape in England any more than in France, an early travesty of the first book, by James Scudamore, appearing in 1664 under the title of *Homer a la Mode.* Few of these numerous poems, however, have any literary significance. Their relative unimportance was partly due to the rivalry of the more native burlesque tradition of *Hudibras,* although both of these modes yielded in time to the mock-epic as developed by Dryden and Pope—a story which need not be told here.

The general influence of Scarron and French parody made itself felt in drama as well as in poetry. In such seventeenth-century works as *Prunella* and *Harlequin-Hydaspes,* discussed earlier, may be seen the methods of Gherardi and of the *forains,* even to the parody of operatic airs. Carey later employed the burlesque mode in *The Dragon of Wantley* and *Margery,* both ridiculing Italian opera. Burlesque of tragedy proved equally popular in plays like

Hurlothrumbo, Chrononhotonthologos, Tom Thumb, and *The Co-vent-Garden Tragedy.* Degradation of the Roman deities found its way in ballad opera itself, in Mottley's *Penelope,* Breval's *Rape of Helen,* Fielding's *Tumble-Down Dick, or Phaeton in the Suds,* and other pieces. To the extent that *The Beggar's Opera* degrades the characters of grand opera to the level of highwaymen and whores, it also belongs to the tradition of burlesque. It is impossible to trace with absolute finality the influence of French parody and burlesque on the ballad plays, but one cannot read Gherardi without feeling that Fielding, at least, was familiar with the collection. The interested reader might well compare such plays as *La Descente de Mezzetin aux enfers* and *Arlequin Phaéton* with *The Author's Farce* and *Tumble-Down Dick.* In short, while there exists some direct, formal influence, French burlesque exerted a wider and far more important intellectual influence, not only on the irreverent point of view of the authors but on the tastes and expectations of the audiences as well. The spectators could be relied upon to recognize travesty when they saw it, and to appreciate it.

Further, the native tradition of burlesque reaching back to the Elizabethans reinforced the appeal which the Continental models made to the vivacious critical temper of the audiences who gathered to see the first performances of *The Beggar's Opera.* The chief model for many of the subsequent ballad operas was the Duke of Buckingham's *Rehearsal.* At times, in such pieces as Ralph's *Fashionable Lady* or Fielding's *Tumble-Down Dick,* we have a merging of the "rehearsal" form with the methods of French burlesque. In any event, regardless of where ballad opera derived its inspiration, a complete explanation of the popular reception of the works of Breval, Ralph, Fielding, Gay, and other authors is not possible without some knowledge of the general background of European parody and travesty.

The ribald ghost of Scarron having been laid for the present, we may turn to confront another spirit which haunted both the authors and the audiences of ballad opera—that which presided over the fortunes of the *commedia dell'arte.* In Elizabethan drama, certain references, characters, and plots indicate some direct indebted-

Lane with Mrs. Booth as Andromeda, Catherine Raftor as Diana, and Theophilus Cibber as Harlequin, but to John Rich as "Lun," playing at Lincoln's Inn Fields, must be given the major share of credit for acclimatizing Harlequin on British soil. So great was his success that prices of admission to his harlequinades had to be raised, fashionable society flocked to his performances, and a thousand squibs and diatribes were directed at him in vain by rival authors and sundry critics. Fielding's ironical preface to *Tumble-Down Dick,* for example, is addressed to him.

From the *commedia dell'arte* English drama, whether in the pantomimes or in other dramatic forms, borrowed a good deal. In the first place, it took over a number of the traditional character types, including especially Harlequin and Columbine. Then, primarily through French sources, it appropriated or adapted various scenes, plots, and situations, as well as *lazzi* and stage "business." In the pantomimes, for instance, Harlequin is depicted always as making marvelous escapes, sometimes with the aid of "machines," sometimes with the aid of acrobatic tricks. The old *commedia dell'arte* depended largely on improvised action and business, the actors learning only the general scenario of the play and extemporizing during the stage performance. To what extent "Lun" and the other English Harlequins followed this custom is difficult to say; in the pantomimes, of course, such improvisation would necessarily be limited to the stage business. In a general way, finally, the Italian and Franco-Italian pieces gave added impetus to the tendencies toward spectacle, dance, music, and burlesque that take possession of English drama in the seventeenth and eighteenth centuries. On the other hand, one must be wary of ascribing too much to Italian influence. Allardyce Nicoll emphasizes this point in his book on Restoration drama:

Thus many of the lovers, astute servants and cheated parents, while obviously owing their ultimate being to the dramatic art of Rome, might have been taken not only from the plays of Molière or from plays of the *commedia dell'arte,* but from those of native English dramatists.[8]

The *commedia dell'arte* tradition exerted a formative influence on the construction of certain ballad operas, particularly on those which attempted to form a coalition between ballad play and pantomime. These hybrid performances introduced both the Zanni and the farcical tricks and incidents of pantomime. The conventions already familiar to the audiences were thus employed in connection with the musical and dramatic effects of ballad opera. The best of the negligible performances that resulted was Cibber's *The Harlot's Progress, or The Ridotto al'Fresco.* The same experimentation appears in *Cupid and Psyche, or Columbine-Courtezan, The Songs in Harlequin Restor'd, or Taste Alamode,* and Ward's *Prisoner's Opera,* all of which include one or more of the Zanni. Indebtedness at second hand is apparent in Robert Drury's *The Devil of a Duke, or Trapolin's Vagaries,* and comparison of the Gherardi plays with the farcical ballad operas reveals a number of similarities in situation and incident. In form itself, as we may recall from Chapter II, ballad opera may have been influenced by such plays as *La Baguette de Vulcain,* which contains several songs set to specified popular airs. For a quite opposite purpose, also, English authors assumed that their audience possessed a knowledge of the *commedia dell'arte* devices, for they used the conventions as a method of ridiculing the rage for pantomime and Harlequin's part in it. Three ballad operas of 1730 provided excellent travesties—Odingsells's *Bays's Opera,* Ralph's *Fashionable Lady,* and Fielding's *Author's Farce.* In 1736 Fielding returned to the assault on pantomime in *Tumble-Down Dick,* one of his liveliest burlesques. Ballad opera, in relation to the *commedia dell'arte,* then, adopts some of the characters and scenes of the Italian plays as they were developed in France but acts primarily as a counter-irritant to the numerous pantomimes appearing at Covent Garden and at some of the other theatres.

The two traditions considered so far, which may have had a share in the reception of ballad opera, are Continental in their origin, but in order to explain the popularity of Gay and Fielding, as well as the appearance of numerous political pamphlets in ballad-opera form, we need not search outside of England. Ballad opera merely capitalized the popular interest in political controversy and veiled lampoon which had been aroused for half a century by the rising flood of political literature. The development of effective political writing depends upon reasonable freedom of publication and upon the existence of strong opposing parties. Hence France, for example, because of its absolute monarchy, unimpeded by parliamentary government, and because of its drastic censorship of printed matter, remained far behind England in the open discussion of political problems. The struggle between the Roundheads and the Cavaliers in the seventeenth century allowed plentiful opportunity for the expansion of two political forms—the ballad and the pamphlet. Both wielded considerable influence. Occasionally, like Martin Parker's royalist ballad "When the King Shall Enjoy His Own Again," they might even attain a certain measure of permanence. For a full development of these literary forms, however, we must await the rise of the Whig and Tory parties in the late seventeenth century, especially after the Stuarts had been driven from England. As Beljame brings out in *Le Public et les hommes de lettres en Angleterre au dixhuitième siècle,*[9] the gradual ascendancy of parliament and the division into parties brought about the necessity of organizing public opinion. The men of letters, as a result, were catapulted into a position of dignity and importance, sought and patronized by the Whig or Tory leaders. The Augustan authors— Addison, Steele, Prior, Swift, Arbuthnot—found themselves, with few exceptions, in one camp or another and were expected to contribute their share of political writing. They discovered a ready and enthusiastic public. Swift's *Conduct of the Allies,* we are informed, reached a sale of a thousand copies in two days and eleven thousand in a month.[10] Some forty thousand copies of Sacheverell's famous sermon were sold in a few days. From Arbuthnot's *History of John Bull* and many other pamphlets we may assert that the political writing of the age of Queen Anne attained a high excellence. While both the prose tracts and the political ballads were normally brought out anonymously and might be of popular authorship, they were frequently composed by lords or by authors of high repute.

The long administration of Robert Walpole brought to an abrupt end the wholesale patronage of men of letters, but political writing itself continued. The struggle now became one between Ministry and Opposition, or.as a catchword of the time expresses it, between "Court" and "Country." This was no mere guerrilla warfare but a concerted campaign on a number of literary fronts. Percival, in the introduction to his *Political Ballads Illustrating the Administration of Sir Robert Walpole,* gives an excellent résumé of the situation. The political ballad retained its importance. It might be composed by the anonymous street singer or by Chesterfield, Pulteney, or Hervey, but in it are reflected all the important issues of the time. The political pamphlet, with its cousin, the political sermon, proved perhaps the most important literary weapon. The registers of published books in the newspapers and magazines of the period are filled with anonymous attacks and answers. In its appeals to the reading public, the Opposition might command the pens of Bolingbroke, Pulteney, Amhurst, and, at times, of Pope, Fielding, Lyttelton, and Henry Brooke among many others. The Court would have to depend on Lord Hervey, Bishop Hoadly, Sir William Yonge, and Horace Walpole—a less brilliant, but a not inconsiderable, array of political pamphleteers. They, as well as the Opposition, could count on a vast circle of readers, for the Ministerial *Enquiry into the Reasons for the Conduct of Great Britain* is alleged to have sold over twenty thousand copies in three weeks, and the *Defense of the Enquiry* even more.[1] It should be noted that the famous duel between Hervey and Pulteney resulted from an exchange of pamphlets.

If in the pamphlet the two opposing political forces seem fairly evenly matched, in the allied field of journalism the Opposition had a clear advantage. *The Craftsman,* established in 1726, proved an innovation in its singleness of purpose and its polemic brilliancy. Under the editorship of Nicholas Amhurst, with the active aid of Pulteney, Bolingbroke, and other members of the Country party, it remained a continual thorn in the side of the Ministry. Allied with *The Craftsman* in opposition were *Fog's Weekly Journal* and, later, *The Daily Post, Common Sense, The Champion,* and *The London Evening Post.* On the side of Walpole we find *The Free Briton, The Daily Courant,* Orator Henley's *Hyp-Doctor,* and, in 1735, Ralph Courteville's *Daily Gazetteer.* Most notorious among the "hired scribblers" of the government were William Arnall and James Pitt (writing under the pseudonyms of Francis Walsingham and Francis Osborne), who appear in the political ballad operas, as does, of course, Orator Henley. To Francis Osborne, the Opposition wits gave the unkindly nickname of Mother Osborne. At their best the Walpole journalists could not approach, much less rival, the wit and brilliance of the authors of *The Craftsman*. Since the coffee-houses carried all the important newspapers, they became local foci for political discussion and activity, and gave to the journals of both parties a far greater influence than their actual circulation would suggest. An amusing satire of the coffee-house politician, by the way, appeared in *The Tatler*[12] and later in Fielding's *Rape upon Rape, or The Justice Caught in his Own Trap*.

The ballad, the pamphlet, and the newspaper proved important weapons in political warfare, but they were not alone. Caricature, as Percival points out, played a minor but important role, especially in connection with the Excise agitation of 1733. The frontispieces of the first seven volumes of *The Craftsman* were collected and published together as *Robin's Reign, or Seven's the Main*. The importance attached to them by the government is indicated by the fact that the printer was prosecuted. These and other political cartoons aided the Opposition, but in the theatre with its opportunities for effective propaganda the Country party found a considerably more formidable ally. The ballad operas took an important place in the development of this dramatic pamphleteering. They were, however, only one phase of this movement upon the stage. Tragedy was enlisted against Walpole. In *The Fate of Villainy* (1730), in *The Fall of the Earl of Essex* (1731), and especially in *The Fall of Mortimer* (1731), a play closed by the Ministry, the audiences were regaled with veiled but obvious parallels to the present political situation, in which Sir Robert was depicted in all the knavery attributed to him by his enemies and was brought to a miserable end. These plays, along with the satirical pieces by Fielding, such as *Pasquin* and *The Historical Register for 1736,* encouraged bolder attacks in the theatre and eventually gave Walpole an excuse for the passing of the Licensing Act of 1737.

The Beggar's Opera exploited this widespread interest in political warfare and fired the opening gun in the dramatic assault on Walpole. To its satirical representation of the first minister it added the full force of the ballad tradition. The suppression of *Polly* helped to establish the political mission of ballad opera. It remained for the unacted pieces of the Excise year—and some of the acted ones—to merge in a novel form several of the important lines of attack against Walpole: the pamphlet, the political ballad, the political play, and, to a certain extent, the newspaper article and political caricature. In ballad opera, therefore, we find an interesting manifestation of the party spirit which dominates much of English literature in the eighteenth century and which finds its roots in the seventeenth.

The relations of ballad opera to burlesque, to the *commedia dell'arte,* to political writing, and to some of the other types mentioned elsewhere help to emphasize its heterogeneous character. This strange amalgam of conflicting forms was as much due to the confused expectations of the audiences as to the dramatic ineptitude of the authors. Ballad opera has itself been accused of being a factor in the degeneration of drama in the eighteenth century. How to define degeneration and trace the causes for it brings one to dangerous ground and to reckless conjecture. Certainly the comedies of the eighteenth century, as a whole, do not compare favorably with the best of the Restoration or of the Elizabethan age. Fewer full-length comedies make their debut on the stage, particularly in the years between 1730 and 1760. Drama apparently ceased to be a dominant literary force and attracted fewer first-class writers, perhaps because of the rise of the novel, perhaps because of the excellence of the actors and their dependence upon a traditional repertory. The triumph of sentimentalism; the tendencies toward show, spectacle, music, and dance starting in the Restoration and increasing during the eighteenth century; the popularity of farcical afterpieces; the growth of a wider and less critical dramatic public; the closing of the little theatres—all may have contributed to the decline of the comic spirit. Allardyce Nicoll feels that the degeneration arose from the confusion of motives, the lack of a dominant purpose and faith in any one form of the drama, the complexity of standards and aims.[13] On the other hand, we may perhaps consider the feverish desire for novelty in the eighteenth century as a sign of life rather than decline. Whether for good or bad, drama was moving forward, it reflected the changing times, it ridiculed the pomposities of heroic tragedy and of opera, and in the domestic plays of writers like Lillo it gave some intimations of the drama of the future. Ballad opera played its part in this hectic evolution, not always a distinguished part but often an interesting one. It started, in England at least, a general tradition of musical comedy which was continued in the comic opera of the second half of the century and which led eventually to Gilbert and Sullivan and to the modern revue, perhaps even to the musical "talkies" of the present day. And in Kitty Clive it discovered the first of the musical comedy "stars." An idea of these various contributions will be given in the pages that follow.

CHAPTER FIVE

Low-Life Operas

So UNUSUAL and popular a dramatic innovation as *The Beggar's Opera* could not remain long without competition, nor is it surprising to find the early rivals imitative in form, situation, and phraseology. The Grub-Streeters seem to have been impressed first by the low-life milieu and they hastened to resurrect one or two old plays dealing with criminals in a Newgate setting.[1] In the next few years, they searched for new realistic material to exploit and soon produced a chimney-sweeper's opera, a "throwster's" opera, a sailor's opera, and a trooper's opera—all of them, unfortunately, unpublished. In the meantime, the dramatic scribblers began to realize the possibilities of ballad opera for topical reference. What Gay had achieved in his veiled allusions to Walpole could be done with greater impunity for persons of little or no importance, particularly for the disreputable characters of London night life, the Jenny Divers and Mrs. Coaxers of the real world. London itself, in 1728, it must be remembered, was still a relatively small place. Within it existed certain small interrelated groups of varying degrees of respectability—the rakes, the libertines, the gamblers, the prostitutes, the Lucklesses, and the Mother Punchbowls—all of them engaged in providing or in pursuing "the pleasures of the town." The members of these groups were all known to each other, their names were bandied about in the coffee-houses, and their adventures or misadventures reported with a smirk in the pages of the newspapers. Because their activities were so vivid and varied, they offered inspiration to Hogarth, as we shall see, and to the writers of ballad opera.

As it happens, the first imitation, *The Cobler's Opera*, held no topical interest. It was a one-act piece by Lacy Ryan, the actor, who had been selected by Addison sixteen years before to play Marcus for the initial run of *Cato*. Ryan's opera was presented by Rich at Lincoln's Inn Fields, where it interrupted the original run of *The*

Beggar's Opera.[2] Between 1728 and 1739 it appeared some dozen times, in 1731 under another title as *The Amours of Billingsgate.* The first performance was for the benefit of Hippisley, the Peachum of *The Beggar's Opera,* who appeared in it, as did other members of Gay's cast—Hall, Mrs. Egleton, and several minor players. *The Cobler's Opera* is Ryan's only recorded play, although Chetwood says he made "several Excursions in the Region of Poetry."[3]

Decidedly second-rate, *The Cobler's Opera* continued the low-life tradition in its representation of Billingsgate and the Gun Tavern, with a motley crew of fishwives, sailors, and "oyster-meeters." Gay's influence on the piece was obviously very strong. It appears in the introduction and request for the overture; in the rascally old men, Melton and Pyefleet, who quarrel and make up as in the Peachum-Lockit scenes (played by the same actors); in the unexpected order releasing the pressed seamen and providing a happy ending; in the charge of Ap-leek,[4] Welsh oyster-woman, that she is with child by Harry Pyefleet; and in the bitter rivalry between Jenny Melton and the jealous Peg Welfleet for the love of Harry. Peg, who has plenty of fire, reminds us of Lucy. For that matter, the entire play sounds definitely second-hand, as is likely to be true of plays written by professional actors of long standing.

In spite of the many resemblances, however, *The Cobler's Opera* taken as a whole does not give us the impression of being merely an abbreviated copy of its more distinguished predecessor. It is inferior, it lacks the satire and elegance of Gay; it is sentimental in plot and artificial in dialogue; even its representation of low life seems superficial and fabricated. A pleasant realism appears in some of the speeches, as when Peg exclaims: "O *Harry Pyefleet!* shall I see thee take her Arm, and every *Sunday,* in thy best Attire, lead her to *Hornsey, Islington,* or *Tottenham,* to revel with thee over Cakes and Ale?"[5] But not equally convincing, although rather delightful, is the speech by the same character: ". . . Nay, Knights and 'Squires have come on Purpose to *Billingsgate,* to see how neatly, and how like a Gentlewoman, *Peg Welfleet* open'd an Oyster."[6] And for rococo sentimentality—perhaps designed for humor —consider Harry Pyefleet's sailor-like speech regarding the tears of

Jenny Melton, who—thinks Peg—has taken on airs since she was put to that oyster-woman in St. James's Street: "How like a *Lilly*, o'ercharg'd with Dew, she now declines her Head; and with what haste those trickling Drops speed to their soft Retreat, as if they knew her tender Bosom would enfold and warm 'em.'" Despite the differences in treatment many of the elements of nineteenth-century melodrama are already present in *The Cobler's Opera*—the attempted seduction of Jenny by the villainous lieutenant, her sentimental and dramatic insistence on the preservation of her virtue, the suspense over the pressing of Harry into the royal navy with its ultimately happy ending, the strong note of patriotism in Harry's desire to serve his country and his final resolution to beget willing sailors for the king.[8]

   The Quaker's Opera, performed at Lee's and Harper's Great Theatrical Booth in Bartholomew Fair (September, 1728), is more convincing in its depiction of low life. One of three dramatic pieces by Thomas Walker, the original Macheath, it is a ballad-operatized version of the anonymous *The Prison-Breaker* (1725), which has been mentioned as a possible influence on Gay. Nicoll calls it a poor adaptation;[9] Baker, an indifferent piece[10]—but it is nevertheless not without interest, although slow and dull considered merely as a play. Like *The Cobler's Opera*, it shares many features with its mendicant predecessor—the introduction leading to the overture, the Newgate setting, the sinister entente between the master-gaoler (Rust) and Jonathan Wile (Wild), the gang of thieves, the women of the town, the jealousy of Mrs. Hackabout and Mrs. Frisky over Shepard, his final betrayal by Mrs. Hackabout, the activities of Coaxthief and Mrs. Coaxthief, and so on. That Walker kept his eye on *The Beggar's Opera* is evident in the third act, where the gang of robbers drink to Polly Peachum and the women of the town to Macheath. But here again, the mood and treatment show little similarity to Gay's. The stress is all on the physical action—the escapes and robberies of Shepard and his eventual recapture. Amusingly enough, the romantic—if such they can be called—passages between Shepard and his two doxies are sometimes written in blank verse, a practice that appears in a number of the later ballad operas.

Among the stock characters in the play we find the lascivious, hypocritical Quaker—so common to the eighteenth-century stage—who likes his wine and his women. "Thou art as round as a Full Moon," he tells Mrs. Poorlean, "and as fleshy as the Goats that wanton upon the delectable Mountains, thy Tabernacle is surrounded with Mammon."[11] Some interesting realistic characters make their appearance, such as Dr. Anatomy, who is seeking bodies to dissect, and Mrs. Poorlean, who sells drinks within the prison. Customers are too sparse, the latter complains, and when the Quaker inquires what she has to sell, she replies:

Sir, you may have what you please; *Wind,* or *right* Nantz, or *South-Sea,* or *Cock-my-lap,* or *Kill-Grief,* or *Comfort,* or *White-tape,* or *Poverty,* or *Bunter's-Tea,* or *Apricock-Water,* or *Roll-me-in-the-Kennel,* or *Diddle,* or *Meat-Drink-Washing-and Lodging,* or *Kill-Cobler,* or in plain English, *Geneva.*[12]

No doubt because of the opportunities for farcical acting, local dialects won considerable recognition on the ballad-opera stage. In the Welsh lawyer and in the Irishman Blunder, Thomas Walker has followed a general practice. But in spite of his efforts to hit the taste of the town, *The Quaker's Opera* with its twenty-six uninspired songs remains insipid and helps to prove how far Gay soared beyond the mere representation of Newgate low life.

Another three-act adaptation, *Love and Revenge, or The Vintner Outwitted,* appeared in 1729 at the Haymarket in ballad-opera form. The original play, Marston's *Dutch Courtezan,* proved its enduring popularity by suffering a variety of alterations by Betterton, by Christopher Bullock, by the unknown author of the 1729 opera, and was finally abbreviated into one of the drolls published in 1742 in the collection "The Strolers Pacquet Open'd. Containing Seven Jovial Drolls or Farces, Calculated for the Meridian of Bartholomew and Southwark Fairs. Representing the Comical Humours of Designing Usurers, Sly Pettifoggers, Cunning Sharpers, Cowardly Bullies, Wild Rakes, Finical Fops, Shrewd Clowns, Testy Masters, Arch Footmen, Forward Widows, Stale Maids, and Melting Lasses." As a droll, the play is reduced to the farcical scenes only and makes no use of songs.[13]

Love and Revenge satirizes mankind and the professions in the manner of *The Beggar's Opera*. It combines a curious plot of passion and revenge involving Rovewell, Bellamira, and Trueman with a series of hilarious farcical episodes in which Brainworm, a cheat, is able to rob and deceive repeatedly an equally villainous vintner, Mulligrub. All the main characters manage to meet in Newgate for the last scenes, where the play ends amid wholesale repentance and marriage.

As with Walker's adaptation, the songs are mere decoration included for extra measure; the plot and characterization could manage just as well without them. The more serious scenes are realistic and cynical but not always effective. The farcical portions, however, are undeniably good fun and must have made the audience hold their sides with laughter, as when the grieving Mrs. Mulligrub brings a rope to Newgate for the hanging of her husband, in the belief that she was supposed to supply one. Mother Pierce belongs to a long line of pious bawds. "Ah, Marry, there's Logick!" she exclaims in Act I, Scene III, "there's an Argument to encourage Trading in our way. If I had not left my Pocket-Book and Pencil at Church last Sabbath-Day, I would have taken it down in Shorthand."[14] And later, facing execution in Newgate, she consoles herself with the reflection, "Well, well, if I am to be hang'd I can't help it; but my Comfort is, I shall die a good Protestant, and a High-Church Woman."[15] Her part was played by a man, Mr. Reynolds, in accordance with seventeenth- and eighteenth-century custom in roles of low and vulgar humor. Bellamira, the passionate woman of Restoration drama, expresses herself in blank verse in an ecstasy of revenge. There is a suggestion of the sentimental drama in Louisa's romantic devotion to Rovewell and in his belated reform and repentance: "Farewell all youthful Follies, I have been wild and roving in my Time; long tost on the dangerous Ocean of loose Desires, but am now resolv'd to rest contented with a virtuous Love."[16] In Mr. Heartfree we have one of the few kindly and understanding fathers in the drama of the period. But all things considered, *Love and Revenge* with its disguises and deceptions remains a pot-pourri of earlier dramatic elements dressed up for the occasion in song and dance.

The part of Mulligrub is ascribed in the *dramatis personae* to a Mr. Fielding. This undoubtedly was Timothy Fielding, actor and keeper of a booth in Bartholomew Fair,[17] and not the future author of *Tom Jones*, whose career as a dramatist had begun in 1728.

The title-page of a brief publication of 1730 shows considerable promise of entertainment and refreshment: "The Prisoner's Opera. To which is added Several Other Entertainments, Interchangably [*sic*] perform'd at Sadler's Wells. During the Summer Season. Where also the best of Wines, excellent Ale, brew'd of the Well-Water, and all other Liquors may be had in perfection." Only the songs, with a scattering of stage directions, are printed, and we are left to guess at the nature of the entertainment, if we may assume that it was actually performed. The twelve songs of the "opera" specify no ballad tunes. Among the features indicated in the text are a chorus of prisoners, a song by the Head-Turnkey, a country dance, and a song by Punch. In addition to these, the inclusion of Harlequin and "a Scaramouch dance" would suggest an element of pantomime in a piece concerned mainly with prison and low life.[18]

We now come to the several operas inspired by London night life. For a key to the characters represented it may be advisable to glance at the pages of the *Grub-street Journal* for 1730 and 1731, where may be found numerous items of disreputable nature—about a certain Kate Hackabout, for instance, whose indomitable spirit offered considerable violence to a constabulary intent upon securing her permanently in Bridewell:

A woman [says the journalist] noted in and about the Hundreds of Drury, for being a very terror, not only to the civil part of the neighborhood by her frequent fighting, noise, and swearing in the streets in the night-time, but also to the other women of her own profession, who presume to pay or pick up men in her district, which is half one side of the way in Bridges-street.[19]

Among the other nymphs of the theatrical district and the purlieus of Mother Needham was the noted Moll Harvey—a true virago, it seems—who on one occasion set upon Michael Willis as he was conducting a prisoner to the Gatehouse and knocked him down with a certain pewter article "with which she beat him so violently that his life is in danger."[20] Likewise we may include in this select company one Mary Muffet who, having been committed to Bridewell, is described as beating hemp in a gown very richly laced with silver.[21]

The Kate Hackabouts and Mary Muffets, unfortunately, received neither mercy nor respite from Sir John Gonson, stern moralist and justice of the peace—the harlot-hunting justice, as he was called—who ferreted them out of their lodgings and drove them to prison or exile. Gonson earned mention in Pope's *Satires of Dr. Donne, Versified* (Satire IV)[22] and was noted for his learned charges to the grand juries, which were said to have been written by the much-ridiculed Orator Henley.[23]

In the same environs of pleasure moved the rakes of the town—most notorious of whom, at this time, was the goatish Colonel Charteris, or Chartres, a Scotchman of years and fortune, always accompanied in his nocturnal rambles by his man John Gourly, known as Trusty Jack. The Colonel finally met his match in Ann Bond, his servant maid, who—to the Homeric laughter of the town—brought him to trial at the Sessions House in the Old Bailey on a charge of rape. He was found guilty, locked up in Newgate, deprived of his estates, and sentenced to death. Eventually, through the efforts of his son-in-law, the Earl of Weems, doubtlessly with the liberal aid of political influence and vast expenditure, Colonel Charteris escaped the gallows and returned to Scotland. It was reported, in the meantime, that the undaunted Ann Bond, basking in the sunlight of publicity and forgetful of her moral distress, married Charles Heather, a drawer at a tavern in Smithfield, "and that they have since taken a Tavern in Bloomsbury, and design to set up a well painted Head of Col. Chartres for their sign!"[24]

Before long these varied characters and scenes of London low life were appropriated by art and literature. Probably the main artistic achievement was Hogarth's first series of "moral paintings," *The Harlot's Progress,* finished in 1731, if we may judge by the date inscribed on the coffin in Plate VI.[25] Perhaps Hogarth's long relations with the stage and the actors induced him to invent and develop a form that, in its telling of a complete story, might be called dramatic. The characters in this pictorial narrative were largely "drawn from nature." Colonel Francis Charteris himself appears in Plate I with his confidant Gourly and Mother Needham, a famous procuress. The name of the heroine, Mary Hackabout, not only recalls the real Kate Hackabout, mentioned previously, but recurs commonly in the plays and poems of the time. Fielding, for example, has a character called Hackabouta in *The Covent-Garden Tragedy*.[26] The harlot-hunting justice, Sir John Gonson, is drawn with striking likeness in Plate III of *The Harlot's Progress*.[27] The portrait of Macheath in the same print gives us a connecting link with *The Beggar's Opera*, which, indeed, may have helped to inspire Hogarth's choice of subject. The wig-box on the tester of Mary Hackabout's bed bears as superscription the name of James Dalton, a street-robber, who was executed on May 12, 1730.[28] More characters from London life are represented in the last two plates: the "beggar-coupling" clergyman from the Fleet; Dr. Misaubin, the celebrated quack; Elizabeth Adams, a woman of the town; and the infamous Mother Bentley.[29] Some of the other figures in the series, also, may have been identifiable in their day. All this is mentioned here merely to emphasize the extreme literalness of the Hogarthian treatment—a literalness which figured also in the contemporary drama far more than we might suspect at first glance.

The Harlot's Progress very soon inspired three long poems, published in 1732, which exploited with full details and some obscenity the contents of the Hogarth series. The topical interest of the subject and the popularity of the Hogarth prints were bound to attract the dramatic scribblers. Thus we find that in 1733 Mary Hackabout and her disastrous career reached the stage of Drury Lane in Theophilus Cibber's *The Harlot's Progress, or The Ridotto al 'Fresco*. This "Grotesque Pantomime Entertainment," as the author calls it, was printed for the benefit of Richard Cross, the prompter. It is graced by two engravings—one of Theophilus "in the Character of Antient Pistol" and one of Hogarth, to whom the piece is dedicated. Credit is indeed due to the painter, for Cibber did little more than present the Hogarth prints in pantomime with occasional songs and the addition of Harlequin and his mates from the *commedia dell'arte*. The end illustrates admirably the spectacular hodge-podge so characteristic of pantomime:

—Scene changes to the Street. A great Number of People pass over the Stage, as going to the *Ridotto,* among whom appears the Marquis *de Fresco,* perform'd by the little Harlequin Dog. The Scene changes to the *Ridotto al Fresco,* illuminated with several Glass Lustres, (the Scene taken from the place at *Vaux-Hall.*) Variety of People appear in Masquerade, and a grand Comic Ballad is perform'd by different Characters to *English, Scotch, Irish* and *French* Tunes, which concludes the whole. Then follows the Masque of the *Judgment of Paris,* &c.[30]

The title-page informs us that the six songs were "made (to old Ballad Tunes) by a Friend." Whoever the friend was, his verse has the required qualities of lightness and wit. Particularly appropriate are the words for Air V, sung by Miss Raftor to the tune of "Lad's a Dunce." In composing the pantomime, Cibber no doubt had this particular actress in mind, as the harlot (whom she played) is appropriately called Miss Kitty.

The Harlot's Progress belongs to the strange hybrid classification of pantomime ballad opera, but a three-act play of more conventional form was published in 1733 also, under the name of *The Jew Decoy'd, or The Progress of a Harlot,* with a frontispiece after Hogarth and the usual complement of ballad airs. No record exists of any performance on the stage. If one has any relish for low realism presented with some power and with a brutal frankness scarcely surpassed by de Maupassant or any of the other nineteenth-century realists, one might bestow a brief glance on *The Jew Decoy'd.* In an introductory scene in *The Beggar's Opera* manner, the author defends the subject with the reflection that comedy must always be drawn from life. Primarily is his material drawn from *The Harlot's Progress,* with extraordinary literalness. The principal characters appear under the relevant names of Colonel Goatish, Squire Spruce, Ben Israel, Justice Mittimus, Parson Smirk, Mr. Smellcorps (an undertaker), Mother Lurewell, and Moll Hackabout. Colonel Goatish speaks with a Scotch, and Ben Israel with a Portuguese, dialect. The main episodes are those represented in the Hogarth prints, the most sordid and powerful scene being undoubtedly the final one in Act III at Moll Hackabout's funeral.

A supremely ironical moment occurs in this scene when Mother

Lurewell is urged to sing a tune of the days of Charles II. At first she demurs with the assertion, "That's impossible; besides, the loss of teeth will not permit me." But the ancient bawd finally obliges the company with the lovely song "Gather Ye Rosebuds While Ye May," taken bodily from Herrick but with no mention of authorship. The words of the poem, in view of the singer, assume a truly gruesome significance.

One curious device of the anonymous author deserves notice in passing. Obviously disturbed by the impossibility of preserving the unities, he explains in the Introduction that

the stage is quite altered, ballad opera's are an invention of our own times, and as they are compounded of comedy and farce, I have to solve this difficulty made free with the chorus of ancient tragedy, and introduced something like it between the scenes, in order to acquaint the audience with what length of time is supposed to be taken up, while they are shifting them.[31]

This extraordinary descendant of the Greek chorus is none other than the *Time-Teller*, who appears at regular intervals and explains in heroic verse all the chronological lapses:

> .... my office is to shew
> What has been done, the manner, when, and how,
> Between the scenes of the ensuing piece,
> Farce, Opera, Comedy, or what you please.[32]

While the device may have its uses, the author was obviously no poet.

In still another play was poor Moll Hackabout to find resurrection, though here she appears under a different name. Henry Potter's *The Decoy*, a long and mediocre ballad opera of three acts and fifty-two songs, was presented four times at Goodman's Fields in February of 1733.[33] It made some slight pretense at originality by disregarding the plot and the sequence of *The Harlot's Progress*, though it deals with the same general material. Colonel Charteris appears as Sir Francis Firebriecks, Justice Gonson as Sir Ralph Reformage, and the harlot as Jenny Ogle. Two well-known comedians, Stoppelear and Penkethman, gave performances as Mr. Xenodochy, a Grecian merchant, and Justice Hamper. Two aged bawds were impersonated, as usual, by men. Here again we have scenes in Bridewell and the customary women of the town. In an ill-motivated happy ending, Squire Spendthrift learns that his uncle, Sir Thomas Pairnails, has died of apoplexy and left him a fortune on condition he marries a poor girl, whereupon he promptly forsakes Jenny Ogle for Miss Arabella Lovely, who otherwise has no part in the play. *The Decoy* and Henry Potter, whoever he was, may well remain buried in obscurity.

With the passing of years ballad opera tended to develop in other directions, but it usually retained at least some characters and scenes of low life. In the ballad farces of Fielding, for example, we find realistic reflection of the life and events of the day, but it is usually modified and caricatured by a strong admixture of burlesque. Fielding's comic spirit lacks subtlety but makes up for that deficiency in a dashing, animal exuberance. It departs from a mere representation of low life, furthermore, as a result of the extensive literary acquaintanceship of the author, among whose favorites were Lucian, Cervantes, and Molière. Fielding's efforts in ballad opera, therefore, will be considered in the chapters on satire, burlesque, and intrigue rather than here.

Sometimes the low life was presented in a mock-heroic vein, as in Robert Drury's *The Rival Milliners, or The Humours of Covent-Garden,* performed at the Haymarket in 1736. While the opera seems very slight, it must have enjoyed some measure of popularity; it was played several times in 1736 and 1737 and reached its fourth edition in the year 1761. Of the author little is known except that he was an attorney's clerk and that he wrote several "potboilers" in the ballad-opera form; on both counts he earned scornful mention in the *Grub-street Journal.*[34] *The Rival Milliners* marks the height of his modest achievements. The mock-heroic verse is passable and sometimes sprightly, and the numerous farcical situations involving the milliners (Sukey Ogle and Molly Wheedle), their mistress (Mrs. Plainstitch), and their various suitors (Trim, Staytape, and Hunks), prove mildly amusing. Reminiscence of *The Beggar's Opera* appears in the jealousy of Sukey and Molly over the young Templar, Pleadwell. Interestingly enough, the part of the hero was taken by Mrs. Talbot.

In the philandering Pleadwell, whose chambers afforded an unexpected meeting of the three ladies of the play, we may perhaps imagine that Robert Drury, the young attorney's clerk, was presenting an idealized portrait of himself. With considerable diplomacy and legal dexterity he contrives to marry off the three women to their low-life suitors, promising to visit the wives in case of trouble. His address to Sukey, early in the play, will offer in two lines a sample of Drury's verse:

> My pretty Girl, whose Industry prepares,
> The neatest Linnen that her Pleadwell wears.[35]

A preface by the author complains of indignities received from several managers, especially from "the Grand Seignior of Drury-Lane," as a result of which *The Rival Milliners,* although approved, was not given production. It fared little better at Covent Garden, but Robert Drury admits that by two other managers he was treated in a very "kind and genteel" manner. The printed play employs inverted commas to indicate passages omitted on the stage, from which it is apparent that when it did eventually secure representation it was abbreviated to almost half its original length. By 1736, of course, new full-length operas had become increasingly rare, the form having been reduced generally to the meaner uses of afterpiece.

The representation of low life, then, introduced into ballad opera at the suggestion of Swift, manifested itself in several important ways: in the selection of realistic milieus, in the revival in musical form of Newgate comedies of the past, in the presentation on the stage of current personages and motifs of London night life. More than that, the realistic tradition permeated, in some degree at least, virtually all ballad opera, even though the main features might be something else. The plays in this chapter have all dealt with London and urban life; those of the next chapter will take us to the country village, to the open country, or to Arcadia—where much low life is to be found among the clowns and the rustics, but where the treatment and the general atmosphere are considerably more idyllic and romantic.[36]

CHAPTER SIX

Pastoral and Village Operas

IN HIS "rehearsal," *The Fashionable Lady, or Harlequin's Opera,*
James Ralph in 1730 satirized the prevailing tastes for entertainment through the theatrical criteria of Mr. Ballad.

Oons! *Mr. Drama* [exclaims this interesting character], I don't like these
Merits, and *Sprightlys,* and *Smooths,* and *Foibles,* they are not the proper
Subjects of an Opera—I tell you, High-way-men and Whores, Beggars,
and Rusticks are your only People, 'tis they raise the loud Laugh,—I
say, Sir, let us have some Whores, a *Chorus* of Whores, or a Gang of
Street-Robbers, it does my Heart good to see them.[1]

While some of the attractions thus designated belong to the low-
life operas of the preceding chapter, in the Beggars and Rusticks
of Mr. Ballad we find two of the main concerns of the early operatic
pieces that lead us from the city to the English countryside. Both
of these groups had long been familiar to metropolitan audiences,
but interest in beggars as dramatic material undoubtedly received
considerable impetus from the success of Gay's play.

As the earliest of the "plein air" operas was a pastoral, it may be
advisable to consider first the representatives in ballad opera of
that conventional, artificial, and singularly persistent form. The
popularity of the pastoral on the stage does seem to the modern
reader something of a mystery—certainly the poetical diction ordinarily employed is trite and unnatural, the plots are of the most
patent simplicity, and the characters are delineated as general and
colorless types. The eighteenth century, however, was thoroughly
steeped in pastoral literature, Latin and English, in prose as well
as in verse, and took its conventions for granted. For a sophisti-
cated London audience there may have been added enjoyment in
the realization that the idyllic goodness, simplicity, or rustic humor of the characters on the stage were being portrayed by the
players of Drury Lane and Covent Garden, who were certainly
neither simple nor pastoral.

In any event, in 1729, as related later in *An Apology for his Life,* Colley Cibber attempted an imitation of *The Beggar's Opera,* but

upon a quite different Foundation, that of recommending Virtue, and Innocence; which I ignorantly thought, might not have a less pretence to Favour, than setting Greatness, and Authority, in a contemptible, and the most vulgar Vice, and Wickedness, in an amiable Light.[2]

Despite his high moral intentions, *Love in a Riddle* was interrupted by such serious disturbances and riots that on the second night (January 8, 1729), when Frederick, Prince of Wales, was present at Drury Lane, Cibber could pacify the audience only by promising that if the opera were permitted to go on that night it should never be acted again. The damning of the play, it must be admitted, occurred on political rather than on moral or artistic grounds, as Colley's staunch Whiggism had long earned the enmity of the Jacobite party and of the Tory wits. Cibber himself ascribes the rioting to a report, with no foundation in fact, that he had been instrumental in suppressing the performance of *Polly* so that his own opera might suffer no competition. Perhaps the failure of *Love in a Riddle* proved eventually a benefit to the play, however, for in the one-act condensation as *Damon and Phillida,* played and printed later the same year with the authorship anonymous, Cibber vastly improved his pastoral and produced one of the successful afterpieces of the century.

An amusing study remains yet to be made of the seventeenth- and eighteenth-century father in drama and fiction. When he was not a choleric disciplinarian, bemoaning his having a romantic daughter of sixteen with a mind to matrimony and a dozen unworthy suitors, he was likely to appear as a glorified Peeping Tom, spying incognito on his son and helping to guide the latter's destiny, usually for purposes of character-building and moral instruction. It must have been embarrassing to the average lad of good family to realize that any bearded stranger might be his father in disguise or one of his father's agents. A favorite, if hoary, device of the "good" father was to interchange children with a poor neighbor in order to emphasize the advantages of wealth or poverty, as the case might be. *Love in a Riddle* presents such a pair of fathers—Arcas and

Aegon—whose two sons and daughters are transplanted and subjected to the necessity of proving their virtue through a considerable amount of prompting and spying. In this serious part of the
play Cibber has decidedly earned his promotion by Pope to the
throne of Dullness. The experiment, needless to say, turns out quite
satisfactorily—Pastora, in love with the supposedly poor Amyntas,
refuses a match with Philautus, a vain and polished fop from the
neighboring Corinthian court, who was acted by Cibber himself.
The other daughter, Ianthe, refuses to terminate a lovers' quarrel
with the other son, Iphis, until he has solved a riddle from the shrine
of Diana. The poor shepherd's crime had been merely the "sensual
Insult" of stealing a kiss from Ianthe by deception, but it requires
a fit of madness on his part—as well it might—to solve the riddle
and earn his forgiveness.

The humor of the play is derived from an underplot in which
Phillida, courted by two booby brothers—the weeping Cimon and
the laughing Mopsus—shows her preference for the roving Damon
but refuses to surrender on any terms but matrimony—

> Call first the Priest and name the Day;
> Then, then name the Day.

The lively underplot forms the basis of *Damon and Phillida*, which
appeared July 16, 1729, at the little theatre in the Haymarket. A
reworking by Theophilus Cibber of the same play was published
in 1730 under the title *Damon and Phillida, or The Rover Re-
claimed*. Another revision by Charles Dibdin in 1768, turned the
ever-popular afterpiece into a comic opera. Baker in his *Companion
to the Playhouse* has high—perhaps too high—praise for *Damon
and Phillida:*

.... Indeed amongst all our Ballad Farces I scarcely know any thing that
lay a juster Claim to Applause, the Words of all the Songs being happily
adapted to the Music, the Music to the Words, and the whole mingled
with a Simplicity of Manners and Uniformity of Conduct that render it
most perfectly and truly pastoral.[3]

Love in a Riddle forgets the simplicity of the pastoral in its prologue and epilogue, both of which are excellent and far wittier than

the text. Harper in the role of Aegon followed the new mode of singing instead of reciting the epilogue, part of which runs as follows:

> Since Songs, to Plays, are now-a-days,
>   Like to your Meals, a Sallad;
> Permit us then, kind Gentlemen,
>   To try our Skill by Ballad.

The songs throughout the play, while more sentimental than Gay's
and less inclined to satire, are generally pleasing. Their original
number of fifty-five was reduced to fifteen in *Damon and Phillida*.
A fair sample of their quality may be shown in the first stanza of
Phillida's song about the inconstant Damon, rendered to the tune
of "O Mother! A Hoop."

> What Woman could do, I have try'd, to be free,
>   Yet do all I can,
> I find I love him, and tho' he flies me,
>   Still, still he's the Man.
> They tell me, at once, he to twenty will swear:
> When Vows are so sweet, who the Falsehood can fear?
>   So, when you have said all you can,
>   Still—still he's the man.⁴

The failure of *Love in a Riddle* did not prevent the attractive
Catherine Raftor (later Mrs. Clive) from winning admiration and
applause in the part of Phillida, one of her first great successes.
Kitty's fine singing and pert impudence of manner must have been
very effective in this role, which she played also in the shortened
version of the play. She is represented as Phillida in a well-known
portrait painted by Schalken and engraved by Faber. From the
date of Cibber's ballad opera until her retirement forty years later
to "Clive-den," the small house presented to her by Horace Walpole at Strawberry Hill, Kitty Clive was the main actress of comic
musical drama in England.

Of far greater poetical merit is another pastoral opera of 1729,
Allan Ramsay's *Gentle Shepherd*. As we have seen, the original version of the poem in 1725 was not designed for stage production.⁵ It
has only four songs, with one lyric to a specified tune, whereas in

its later and more familiar form it has twenty-one songs set to
Scotch airs. The renovated *Gentle Shepherd* was presented by
schoolboys[6] in Taylor's Hall, Edinburgh, on January 22, 1729, and
by the Haddington boys on August 27 of the same year. Numerous
performances were given thereafter in Scotland by schoolboys, amateurs, villagers, and professional players.

The Gentle Shepherd nevertheless remains a hybrid product,
more pastoral poem than ballad opera. Its title comes from a line
by Spenser. There are five acts in rhymed couplets and songs, with
a short prologue of six or eight verses introducing each scene. With
due attention to the unities, the author gives the duration of the
action as twenty-four hours and specifies carefully the chronology
and place for each act. While he preserves the classic style of the
pastoral, the locale is not a nebulous Arcadia or Greece but Scotland. The names of the characters, their sentiments, their dialects
are all pronouncedly Scotch and to that extent realistic. The discovery that Sir William Worthy originally bore the name of Sir
Colin MacAndre leads Martin to suggest a possible historical basis
for the play.[7] There are implications, also, of a slight political
coloring.

The conventional elements of the plot, with its revelations and
discoveries, do not succeed in detracting from the graceful charm
of the work as a whole. Sir William Worthy, restored to his lands
after the death of Cromwell and returning to his decayed estates in
disguise, is another of the good but spying parents. Like Richard
Feverel's father, he has a definite plan for his son's future, which
threatens Patie's happiness with Jenny until the revelation that
she also is of gentle blood—in fact, that she is the laird's own niece.
Before this happy discovery, however, the plight of the lovers at
Patie's sudden elevation is genuinely affecting. In Mause, reputed
to be a witch, in the comic hind Bauldy, and in the other rustics
we have excellent—though not highly individualized—characterization of Scotch types.

Burns Martin believes that the 1729 revision of *The Gentle Shepherd* is not altogether fortunate,[8] but be that as it may, the verse
must be judged superior—both in text and songs—to that usually

found in ballad opera. Far from detracting from the enjoyment, the dialect offers added pleasure and on the printed page is rarely obscure, though to an unaccustomed ear it no doubt would seem so on the stage. One of the songs, "By the Delicious Warmness of Thy Mouth," is set "to its ain Tune"; the others depend for their music upon familiar Scotch ballad airs. As the songs are easily available, it will not be necessary to quote from them here. "My Peggy Is a Young Thing" is no doubt the most familiar; it is considered the best of Allan Ramsay's lyrics.[9]

In 1730 Theophilus Cibber turned Ramsay's pastoral into a one-act ballad opera, *Patie and Peggy,* for representation at Drury Lane, where it was played several times that year and in 1731. He admits in the preface that it was planned and finished in one day, "his Benefit being fixed before he had laid his Design." The speed of his labors, of course, proved of no advantage to the verse, which he translated into English with considerable butchery. Curiously enough, Theophilus states that he added to the number of the songs, an incomprehensible assertion in view of the fact that he has twenty-two songs, only one more than *The Gentle Shepherd,* and that this modest addition results merely from his splitting Air XI of Ramsay into two songs. Examination reveals that Cibber altered considerably the order of the songs, occasionally substituted a different tune, paraphrased the words into English, embodied a few stanzas of Ramsay's lyrics into his dialogue, and omitted two of the original songs for which he substituted words of his own. The result is paltry enough, but quite in accordance with the practice of the times. The only possible advantage of the revision lies in the reduction of Ramsay's sprawling five acts to one.

Theophilus concludes his preface with a certain condescension, not truly justified in view of the subject-matter of English ballad opera: ". . . I shall therefore only add, tho' the CHARACTERS in this OPERA are *low,* I flatter myself, they'll not appear distasteful to the politest Circle of our ENGLISH BEAUTIES."

Several of the characters, including Mause and Bauldy, do not appear at all in the Cibber version. In the performance Theophilus played the relatively minor role of Roger. Kitty Raftor represented

Peggy opposite the Patie of Mrs. Roberts, who frequently, like
Charlotte Charke, impersonated men on the stage. A prologue was
spoken by Theophilus and an epilogue by Mrs. Cibber, "dress'd
like a Petit-Maître." Mrs. Cibber, the first wife of Theophilus, had
no other part in the play.

The next pastoral ballad opera appeared in 1731 at Lincoln's Inn
Fields with the title of *The Judgment of Paris, or The Triumph of
Beauty*. The authorship is not indicated on the title-page. G. H.
Tufts, in his list of ballad operas in the *Musical Antiquary*, warns
against confusing this play with other pieces bearing a similar title.[10]
The Judgment of Paris takes place, as we might anticipate, in the
vicinity of Mount Ida. Three of the characters are rustics—a miller,
his wife, and his son—who argue heatedly about attending the pastoral revelries in honor of Paris, but finally decide to go. The miller's wife has some mildly amusing Dogberryisms. When her son
describes the sports, revellings, and new devices that are to take
place, she exclaims:

How! Revilings, and new Vices, and not let the Boy come in for his
Snack of them!—Let every one speak their Opinion freely, as far as their
own Want of Discretion shall direct them, is this Reasonable? 'Tis a
Parent's Business, sure, to shew their Son all the Contempt they can:
And unless we are reconcil'd, and perfectly divided among ourselves in
this Point, how can he ever hope to find Disrespect from the Neighbourhood?[11]

The more serious part of the play shows Paris presenting the
"golden ball" to Venus and being rewarded by her, in return, with
the love of a nymph. After this there is a dance of shepherds and
shepherdesses. From all this it may be seen that *The Judgment of
Paris* resembles the masque in its slight plot and its scenic effects.
The various gods descend in machines and speak in blank verse.
The appeal to the audience, without question, rested mainly in song
and spectacle. Paris was played by Walker and Juno by Mrs. Egleton—in roles somewhat more elevated if less colorful than those
that fell to their lot in *The Beggar's Opera*. Mrs. Cantrell enjoyed
the distinction of having been selected for Venus.

The pastoral drama continued, but luckily not in the ballad-

opera form, to which it was decidedly not fitted. It enjoyed considerable popularity in the "musical entertainments" of the second
half of the century with specially composed music, such as *The
Chaplet* (1749) and *The Shepherd's Lottery* (1751) by Moses Mendez, a wealthy Jew.[12] Kitty Clive sang in both, but they are not
ballad operas and need not detain us here.

The village or country operas do not differ materially from the
pastorals except in their greater realism, their more definitely English localization, and their use of prose instead of verse. The first
and best example of this type, Charles Johnson's *Village Opera,*
was performed at Drury Lane in February, 1729. It is one of a veritable family of plays—English and French—on the same theme.
In its romantic mood and setting, in its simple but well-organized
plot, in its gay dialogue and charming songs, it comes very close to
modern musical comedy, eschewing entirely the grimmer realism
and the destructive satire of Gay. It reflects, no doubt, the jovial
good humor of Charles Johnson himself, a person of social habits
with extensive acquaintance at Will's and Button's, which "ensured
him great Emoluments on his Benefit Night, by which Means, being a Man of Oeconomy, he was abled to subsist very genteely."[13]
Unfortunately, however, a few lines in the prologue to *The Sul-
taness* won him a place in the *Dunciad.*[14]

The Village Opera deals with a young man who has himself hired
as a gardener so that he may court the maid of the heiress he is supposed to marry. Eventually he is forced to reveal his identity when
a former servant impersonates him in order to win the heiress and
the dowry. The maid, of course, turns out to be a gentlewoman and
not a domestic, and a happy ending is provided for the lovers. The
Biographia Dramatica states that Johnson's plots are seldom original, but that he made many additions of his own and presented his
plays in a pleasing dress. No source is mentioned for *The Village
Opera,* but I have found two French plays to which Johnson seems
to have been indebted, whether directly or indirectly, for much of
his material. One, a comedy by Dancourt, *Le Galant Jardinier*
(1705), contains the very important disguise of the hero as a gardener. The finding of the locket by Lucile on the sleeping gardener,

and his explanation, when M. Dubuisson discovers him at the girl's feet, that he was merely showing her how the *potager* could be turned into a *parterre*, have been retained by Johnson. In fact, *Le Galant Jardinier* accounts for most of the Betty-Freeman plot in *The Village Opera*, although much modified and on the whole improved in Johnson's handling. With this, the English author has seemingly combined the situation of a one-act play by Lesage, *Crispin rival de son maître* (1707). In this extremely witty farce, Crispin, with the aid of a fellow-valet, La Branche, impersonates M. Oronte's future son-in-law in order to secure Angelique's *dot*. One marked similarity to *The Village Opera* is found in the lavish compliments paid by Crispin to the foolish and vacillating Mme. Oronte, who probably suggested the characterization of Lady Wiseacre. As in Johnson's play the valets are eventually discovered and pardoned, although their efforts to extricate themselves from their predicament are wittier than those of their English counterparts. While *Le Galant Jardinier* has some singing and dancing at the end, neither French play is a *comédie en vaudevilles*. In any event, unless Johnson borrowed from some intervening source, much credit must be granted him for his skillful adaptation of the two plots, his omission of much unimportant or irrelevant material, and his successful Anglicizing of the characters and setting so that one would scarcely surmise a French origin.

The Village Opera introduces us to characteristically English scenes: Sir Nicholas Wiseacre's country seat; his garden, where Freeman has been metamorphosed into the gardener Colin; a village "mop" or "statute"—a fair for the hiring of servants; a green, where the country folk are assembled for a wedding and a sheepshearing. "I am a Romantick, you see, by this Habit and this Place," declares Colin,[15] and so far is he from the Restoration lover that after a long debate on whether he should marry Betty or not he rejects the thought of making her his mistress as Reason and Honor forbid it. Romantic also are most of the other characters, especially Rosella and her supposed maid Betty who read novels and believe in love at first sight. Even the testy Sir Nicholas and the scoundrelly footmen, Brush and File, have a pleasant, musical-comedy air about them. Not the least amusing incident occurs when Brush, impersonating Freeman, takes or pretends to take the foolish Lady Wiseacre for the bride-to-be. As severe satire as Johnson allows himself—and that more in good fun than in malice—appears in the passage where Sir Nicholas questions the two culprits:

SIR NICH. . . . Sirrah, where did you learn to lye thus?
FILE. I was two Days and a half in Lady *How-d'ye's* Service.
SIR NICH. And where did you get this Trick of Forging Persons and Letters?
BRUSH. I was once, Sir, a great Dealer in Stock, Sir.
SIR NICH. Impudent Dog! 5000 *l.* at one Main, where had you Courage?
BRUSH. I always hated piddling Play; and as to my Courage, Sir, I was once Captain to a Pharaoh-Table.[16]

Johnson possessed a happy knack of writing agreeable songs, with humor and pleasing sentiment. Particularly amusing are Air XIV ("I Am Paul Pillage, I Live in Yon Village") and Air XLI ("Let Ralph in Beer His Pleasure Take"). A recurrent type of comical song in ballad opera is illustrated in Air I—what we might call a vegetable simile song:

> My Dolly was the Snow-drop fair,
> Curling Endive was her Hair;
> The fragrant Jessamine, her Breath;
> White Kidney-Beans, her even Teeth.
>
> Two Daisies were her Eyes;
> Her Breasts in swelling Mushrooms rise;
> Her Waist, the straight and upright Fir;
> But all her Heart was Cucumber.[17]

An excellent cast interpreted *The Village Opera* at Drury Lane, with the popular Catherine Raftor as Rosella. The comedians Miller and Oates took the parts of the two footmen. In spite of the acting and all its natural attractiveness the play made no great success in the Charles Johnson version, appearing four times at Drury Lane in 1729 and three times at the Haymarket in 1730.

All things considered, *The Village Opera*, utterly different as it was from *The Beggar's Opera*, may be considered as second in excellence only to the latter in the ballad-opera repertoire. Theatrical, artificial in its rusticity, romantic and sentimental, it never falls into bathos or over-sentimentality and it has just a little of the fresh gracefulness of Farquhar. Its intrinsic excellence is evidenced by its many adaptations. A version by Edward Phillips, reduced to one long act, appeared at Drury Lane in February, 1730, under the title of *The Chamber-maid.* The cast omits a few of the rustics of *The Village Opera* but the principals are practically the same as in the 1729 production, the only changes being in the parts of Freeman and Lady Wiseacre. The play is shortened, but otherwise little altered. There are twenty-eight songs instead of the original fifty-three. By all rights, the name of Charles Johnson, not that of Edward Phillips, should appear on the title-page.

The next reincarnation, a one-act ballad opera by James Wilder called *The Gentleman Gardener,* was offered at Covent Garden in 1749 with the author—an erstwhile painter—in the part of Colin, "his first attempt in the dramatic way."[18] The printed opera (Dublin, 1751) gives the cast for the Smock Alley production and makes the assertion that the piece was taken from Dancourt. This direct indebtedness seems limited to the title, for in reality the text was taken from *The Village Opera,* as an examination of the plot, the songs, and the names of some of the characters will readily show. This, at least, balances with some slight poetic justice Johnson's own failure to mention Dancourt or Lesage. A certain Mr. Pasquali set the last of the twelve songs; the words and airs of the others are borrowed verbatim from *The Village Opera.*

A further efflorescence of this ever-popular play came on December 8, 1762, when Bickerstaffe's *Love in a Village* made its debut at Covent Garden. Taking the plot mainly from *The Village Opera,* Bickerstaffe revised and rewrote the work as a comic opera with songs by various composers and considerable alteration and addition. He corrected the main defect of *The Village Opera,* namely the failure to bring Rosella's lover on the stage, by adding the part of Eustace, and he modified Johnson's other characters to suit his own purposes, changing their names as well. The one plot in which File and Brush attempt to win Rosella by impersonation of Freeman he omits entirely. The resulting play is an artificial but agree-

ably sentimental comic opera, with the added spice of a few *risqué*
lines of a mild sort. It may be remarked that by the 1760s English
drama had turned genteel and proper, so that we find Francis
Gentleman, for example, somewhat exercised over Lucinda's words
to Rosetta—"This libidinous father of yours, he follows me about
the house like a tame goat."[19] In a dedication to Beard, the singer,
Bickerstaffe states that the songs are not common ballads. Arne, it
seems, contributed most of the music and compiled the rest from
the works of Handel, Boyce, Gallupi, Giardini, and others. *Love in
a Village* cannot be characterized as a ballad opera, but, except for
the music, it bears a close resemblance to the form. It marks the
first step in the transition to comic opera and in many ways foreshadows musical comedy of today.

Genest finds a striking similarity between the underplot of *The
Village Opera* and a farce by Garrick, *Neck or Nothing* (Drury
Lane, 1766).[20] The indebtedness, interestingly enough, is not to
Johnson, but to Lesage, as the piece is a fairly close translation of
Crispin rival de son maître with the usual failure to mention the
source. Schultz suggests that *The Villagers* (Drury Lane, 1756) is
another descendant of *The Village Opera*.[21] While neither this nor
Garrick's play falls under the heading of ballad opera, the two
pieces show the continued vitality of the plot.

We return to 1729 to consider several plays dealing with beggars,
who, it must be remembered, were considerably more mysterious
and romantic figures in the eighteenth century than they seem
today. The *Grub-street Journal,* for example, has occasional interesting items about them, such as the incarceration of an impudent
individual with a long periwig who called himself the king of the
beggars.[22] Of even greater interest is the account of the wedding in
1732 of two beggars whose combined age was 160 years. Among the
thirty attendants there were seven bagpipers and "one who played
a bladder-marine." The gargantuan wedding feast included a roast
mutton, thirty pounds of potatoes, a large salmon, thirty pounds of
cheese, eight pounds of butter, bread, and one gallon of strong beer
per person! The marriage, as we are told by the journalist, was
consummated in a barn, but unfortunately some hay fell over the

couple during the night and they had to be dragged out naked, almost smothered.[23] Such news reports as these will serve to show that the exploits of the mendicant tribe on the stage were probably not wildly exaggerated. Or perhaps the beggars were merely living up to their theatrical reputation.

In 1729, a three-act ballad opera by Charles Coffey, *The Beggar's Wedding,* made a very modest appearance of three performances at Smock Alley, Dublin. As one of the contributions of the Irish stage, it is discussed in an interesting article by W. J. Lawrence in the *Musical Quarterly.*[24] On its arrival in London, however, it had an astonishing run of some thirty nights, as a full-length and as a one-act play, and won a hearing also at Bartholomew and South-wark Fairs. Little is known about the author except that he was a native of Ireland and that he had a hand in the even more popular *Devil to Pay.* Baker says he was considerably deformed—he was, in fact, a hunchback—but so little sensitive about his person that he performed the character of Aesop for his own benefit in Dublin.[25] When he died, in 1745, he was buried in the parish of St. Clement Danes. His importance to us lies in the fact that he wrote no less than eight ballad operas.

The Beggar's Wedding starts briskly with a clever prologue commenting upon the popularity of "Sing-song" and upon the tastes of the times:

> All Sense in Entertainments we disown.
> What, please the Mind! No, rather take the Eye,
> On Carpenters, not Poets we rely,
> For what are Morals to a Sink or Fly?[26]

It cannot be said, however, that Coffey's play relied largely upon carpentry, or for that matter upon highly spectacular effects other than a beggars' wedding and dances. Like *The Beggar's Opera* it shows a tacit understanding—though a less sinister one—between the law, as embodied in Alderman Quorum, and the mendicant underworld, as represented by Chaunter, king of the beggars. Here also, as in Gay's play, the two old men have a quarrel which ends in the admission that they were both in the wrong. Quorum is "a kind of a Virtuoso," that common character of seventeenth- and eighteenth-century drama whose salient passion is the collection of useless oddities and curiosities. While some of the songs and the scenes are realistic, the general tone of the play remains one of gaiety and romance, of the outdoors in spring. The plot itself seems to us flimsy and ill-motivated, a common defect of the time, but its weakness obviously did not prove a bar to the play's success. It ends with the unexpected discoveries and revelations that Quorum is Mrs. Chaunter's brother; that Hunter is really Quorum's son, carried off in youth by gypsies; and that Phebe is not Quorum's daughter, but an orphan left in his care. With these dizzy changes of relationship, all is thus cleared for the wedding of Hunter and Phebe. Chaunter, the king of the beggars, is asked to alter his way of life but he refuses, not caring to change his condition even with the greatest prince in Europe.

In an amusing passage the author seems to endorse the prehistoric state of man:

Right—[says Chaunter] how happy was the primitive World, when there were no other Laws to govern by, than those of Nature? when Men enjoy'd every thing in common; and no such Crimes were heard of as Robbery or petty Larceny: When if a poor Man wanted any thing his rich Neighbour possess'd, he might take it without farther Ceremony, and be in no Danger of a Goal [sic]; but it was look'd upon as a Loan, which he was again to repay in some other kind—But Hospitality is long since banish'd the World, and the Laws of Nature quite perverted.[27]

Even the beggar lasses are devotees of Nature, as indicated in the following stanza:

> We scorn all Ladies Washes,
>   With which they spoil each Feature;
> No Patch or Paint, our Beauties taint,
>   We live in simple Nature.[28]

The Beggar's Wedding, with a total of fifty-five songs, opened at the little theatre in the Haymarket on May 5. The one-act version, not much reduced except in the number of songs, now thirty, appeared at Drury Lane under the title of *Phebe, or The Beggar's Wedding* with Mrs. Roberts as Hunter and Catherine Raftor as Phebe. Quorum was played by Fielding—Timothy Fielding, no doubt. In August what was seemingly an alteration came out at Bartholomew Fair with a new title, *The Hunter, or The Beggar's Wedding.*

Another important contribution to the "begging" drama came in 1731 as a ballad-operatization of Richard Brome's *A Jovial Crew, or The Merry Beggars* (1641), already discussed briefly in Chapter II. The new version, *The Jovial Crew: a Comic Opera,* published anonymously and presented successfully at Drury Lane, was ascribed by the *Biographia Dramatica* to Roome, Concanen, and Sir William Yonge. From an "Advertisement" asserting that the songs were written about three years previously by a gentleman since dead, a circumstance mentioned now "only to obviate some Idle Rumours that have been spread about relating to the Author," Sonneck conjectures that the rumors perhaps refer to the ascribed authorship to Roome, Concanen, and Yonge.[29] A one-act version is recorded by Genest for April 5, 1731, at which—quite in accordance with modern practice—"books of the Play and Opera will be sold at the Theatre."[30] The popularity of the original comedy continued in the ballad-opera alteration, which enjoyed frequent revivals and reprintings. Baker grudgingly records that it brought crowded houses despite what he considers its many absurdities and indelicacies.[31]

The anonymous author or authors followed Brome's play rather closely except for the modernization of the language and the interpolation of songs. The five acts were reduced to three, according to the operatic custom, and prose was substituted for passages written originally in a kind of irregular verse. The only change in the *dramatis personae,* the omission of Talboy, was deplored by Genest, who, by the way, has considerable praise for the songs.[32]

The Jovial Crew is something of an open-air epic, in which Oldrents' two daughters with their respective lovers disguise themselves as beggars, for a lark, and join a band under the leadership of Springlove. This last person acts as Oldrents' steward during the winter, but every spring, when the cuckoos and nightingales (which obviously figured prominently among the "sound effects" backstage) begin to sing, he feels an irrepressible urge to go a-vagabonding. His present venture occasions a meeting with Amie, the runaway niece of Justice Clack, whom he courts in a "genteel Way." The beggars are eventually brought before Justice Clack and Old-rents, where by means of a play within the play they bring the various matters to a happy termination. In one of the usual unexpected revelations, Springlove is discovered to be Oldrents' son.

The plot may therefore be described as slight but pleasant enough. As in Coffey's play we have much disporting and dancing of the beggars, evidently a popular feature. The characterization, which is excellent, follows in general the Jonsonian formula of "humours" but within its limitations the various persons are drawn with skill and spirit. The girls, though their language is toned down slightly from the breezy frankness of Brome's play, manage to retain their wit and vivacity. In the hands of a good actor, the portrayal of Justice Clack must have been very amusing, as for example in his scene with Martin, where he monopolizes the conversation and at every effort of the poor clerk to edge in a word sternly inquires, "Nay, if we both speak together, how shall we hear one another?"[33] He employs legal phraseology with humorous effect, and since he is a devotee of the theatre, he knows his stage jargon as well. The role at Drury Lane was taken by Griffin. Mrs. Heron (whom poor Letitia Pilkington found to be a rival)[34] played Rachel, and Mrs. Cibber, Meriel. Opposite the ubiquitous Kitty Raftor as Amie we find Mills playing the part of Springlove.

Concerned in the main with the three hedonistic topics of love, springtime, and wine, the songs by the unknown author provide one of the main attractions of the play. They have a lyric spirit and freshness that we associate rather with D'Urfey or with the Elizabethans than with the more formal age of George II. Consider Rachel's little begging song in the second act:

> My Daddy is gone to his Grave;
>   My Mother lies under a Stone:
> And never a Penny I have,
>   Alas! I am quite undone.
> My Lodging is in the cold Air,
>   And Hunger is sharp, and bites;
> A little Sir, good Sir, spare,
>   To keep me warm o'Nights.[35]

An attractive duet by the two girls is offered earlier in the play:

RACHEL. Abroad we must wander to hear the Birds sing,
         T' enjoy the fresh Air, and the Charms of the Spring.
MERIEL. We'll beg for our Bread, then if the Night's raw,
         We'll keep ourselves warm on a Bed of clean Straw.
RACHEL. How blest is the Beggar, who takes the fresh Air!
MERIEL. Tho' hard is his Lodging, and coarse is his Fare.
RACHEL. Confinement is hateful————
MERIEL. ————————————And Pleasure destroys.
BOTH.   'Tis Freedom alone is the Parent of Joys.[36]

Numerous other songs could bear quotation, but these will suffice to show, I believe, that *The Jovial Crew* should not be dismissed too quickly and that Nicoll's characterization of the 1731 adaptation as undistinguished may not be altogether just. The author's poetry never reaches the heights, but it makes no pretense at doing so and for its own particular purpose it is more than adequate.

The inevitable problem of classification arises in connection with such pieces as *Flora* (1729) and *A Sequel to the Opera of Flora* (1732), two very free adaptations of Doggett's *Country Wake*, a hilarious and not over-decent farce of deception written over thirty years before and played by a distinguished cast including Betterton, Doggett, Mrs. Barry, and Mrs. Bracegirdle. The two ballad operas were published anonymously, but ascribed at first to Colley Cibber,[37] then in the later editions and the *Biographia Dramatica* to John Hippisley, the comedian. In plot, they are comedies of deception and intrigue, in which Sir Testy loses his niece Flora to Friendly, his daughter Lucia to Truelove, and his wife—who remains incognita to her lover—to Woodville. One may include the plays here, however, because of the Somersetshire[38] setting and dialect and the background of the country wake with its rustic dancing and its bouts at cudgels. The spirit of the two pieces is purely farcical, with the laughter arising chiefly from the predicaments and the horseplay of Hob, certainly one of the funniest of the country clowns. The intrepid scholar would gladly offer a small fortune to be transported back suddenly to the pit of the Haymarket and behold Hob's mother straining to pull the bucket up from the well only to discover her son Hob in the bucket, then to hear the roars of the groundlings when she thinks he's a ghost and lets him drop down again. Her maternal solicitude when he is finally rescued touches the heart: "Oh, poor Hob, come along, Child, and I'll get thee a little Zugar-zops to comfort thy Bowels."[39] Almost equally mirthful episodes show Hob misdelivering a letter, beating Sir Testy at cudgels, and saying farewell on what he thinks is his death-bed. In spite of its farcical scenes the *Sequel* proved a failure, but *Flora* belongs to the outstanding successes of the century in the one-act ballad-opera form. Nicoll records some two hundred per-formances between 1729 and 1749.

A short burlesque pastoral by Essex Hawker belongs to 1729, which was apparently a banner year for village and country operas. Two slightly different editions of 1729 are entitled respectively *The Wedding: A Tragi-Comi-Pastoral-Farcical Opera...With an Hudi-brastick Skimmington* and *The Country-Wedding and Skimming-ton,* the former as acted at Lincoln's Inn Fields, the latter at Drury Lane. A print from *Hudibras* represents the Skimmington—defined in the *New English Dictionary* as "a ludicrous procession, formerly common in villages and country districts, usually intended to bring ridicule or odium upon a woman or her husband in cases where the one was unfaithful to, or ill-treated, the other." A ceremony of this sort was likewise presented on the stage, probably as the main feature of the piece. There are twenty-three songs with incidental music and an overture by Dr. Pepusch. The theme of the playlet is simply the rivalry between Peartree (a gardener), Ply (a water-man), and Razoir (a French barber) for the hand of the fair Margery. As in the regular pastorals, verse is employed in lieu of prose, and for light mock-heroic it succeeds well enough.

The rustic operas considered so far have been characterized generally by light and romantic treatment. Quite different in im-pression is George Lillo's *Silvia, or the Country Burial,* his first dramatic work. It came out at Lincoln's Inn Fields in 1730 for three performances beginning November 10. Its reception is recorded in the *Grub-street Journal* with special reference to

a sett of people who seemed to damn the whole performance if it had been in their power (by their continual hissing and catcalls) notwithstanding which, the same was performed with applause by the general approbation of the pit and boxes.[40]

Lillo was a Dissenter, although Davies hastens to add, "not of that sour cast which distinguishes some of our sectaries."[41] In view of this fact and on recalling his famous *London Merchant,* we need not be surprised to find a strong moral purpose even in so frivolous a medium as ballad opera. *Silvia* presents an object-lesson in morality, driven home by means of a melodramatic plot with the rather strange assistance of sixty-three ballad airs. In Welford, torn by the pangs of a guilty conscience, and in Sir John Freeman, tortured both by his love for the virtuous Silvia and by his determination to continue his evil ways of life, we have apparently reflections from the tragic drama, perhaps very distantly from Marlowe's *Faustus.* Rebuffed by Silvia's refusal of his indecent proposal, Sir John finds a "less scrupulous Female" in Lettice and readily persuades her to become his mistress. "This Girl," he exclaims, "is as much a Libertine in the Affairs of Love, as my self. . . . It's pure Nature in her."[42] But he still loves Silvia, and angered by her father's admonitions, threatens to ruin Welford by way of revenge. This gives Welford an opportunity to disburden his conscience. With the help of the aged midwives, Goody Busy and Goody Costive, he proves that Sir John is really his own son, exchanged in infancy by Mrs. Welford at the death of the real Freeman boy, and that Silvia is rightfully the present heir to the Freeman estates. Welford had hoped to right the injustice by the marriage of the two but was prevented by the improper proposal to Silvia. Previously, Sir John had been much moved by the visit of Lettice's parents and had attempted to make amends for the loss of her virtue. The way is now clear for him and Silvia to marry anyway, once her moral scruples have been satisfied.

Silvia would make an effective and pathetic heroine were it not for her utter perfection and her smug predilection for moralizing, which leads her into aphorisms and into stilted and unnatural language. "Imprecate no more," she tells Sir John in Act I. "Wave [*sic*] this Discourse, and I am satisfied."[43] Later, she announces Sir John's proposal to her father in the following terms: "Vain of his Wealth, and his superior Birth, with bold, licentious Freedom he rail'd on Marriage; then talk'd to me of Love, Enjoyment, and eternal Truth; endeavouring, by imposing on my Simplicity, to render me vile as his own Ends."[44] These represent fair samples of her speeches throughout the play, but one must admit that she has been placed by the author under rather trying circumstances. Like most moralists, Lillo does much better with the depiction of sin; both Lettice and her predecessor Betty are excellently characterized. Lettice's downfall has convincing motivation, with rather unusual social consciousness for the time, in her hatred of poverty, work, and confinement.

Along with the serious action we have the "country" portion of the opera, the chief connecting link being Lettice. At the funeral of her mother, Dorothy Stitch, all the country folk have gathered. Their comments are sympathetic if not altogether flattering. They agree that Dorothy was a good woman in the main but add that she was proud, lazy, thievish, impudent, whorish, and above all a sad drunkard, having even died in her drink. Timothy, her husband, insists upon fulfilling his promise to her that, in the event of her death, he would stay all night by her uncovered coffin. Despite the objections of the rustics, he remains in the graveyard. As we readily expect from the situation, Dorothy comes back to life—she had been in a drunken fit—and she and the terror-stricken Timothy are happily reunited. Lettice, in the meantime, has listened to Sir John's solicitations. The search of the parents for her bring them in contact with Welford and Freeman, and the country people *en masse* are again presented at the testimony of the midwives in the last act. The rustic scenes are handled with considerable humor and give the ballad opera its chief merit.

Silvia must be judged a mediocre but a very interesting play. The morality rests rather uneasily on a form initiated by the biting wit and cynical satire of Gay. The main defect of the opera lies in its undue length and its oversupply of songs, none of which are particularly memorable. The theme, however, has the advantage of being forceful, unusual, and in many ways original. The names of the cast do not appear in the printed play, but are given by Genest.[45] In 1736 *Silvia* was reduced to two acts and presented at Covent Garden as afterpiece to *The Merry Wives of Windsor*.

Numerous farcical and intrigue operas have a country setting or at least some country yokels for purposes of humor, such as Carey's *Betty, or The Country Bumpkins* (1732). While it might be possible to include such works here, most of them will be reserved for the next chapter. The rustic operas fell mainly in the years 1729–1731. For a number of years after 1731 ballad opera tended to develop into other directions, but the best of the "plein air" pieces were, of course, subject to continued revival and adaptation. By the 1740s and 1750s, when ballad opera became somewhat passé, it fell into the hands of amateurs whose efforts were ordinarily limited to a single play, which might or might not be unspeakably bad. Not of the worst is a "pastoral ballad farce" of 1749, *The Country-Wedding, or the Cocknies Bit* by name, said on the title-page to have been played at the Haymarket. The author's name does not appear, but the epilogue refers to the opera as the first production of his rustic muse. It is a realistic little play, rather misnamed a pastoral, in which Dolly, "an innocent young girl," pretends pregnancy so that she will be forced to marry Roger, her country suitor, instead of Mr. Easy, a Londoner, whom her father has designed for her. The father, strangely enough, becomes overjoyed when he is finally told of the deceit. It is a slight performance with a few not over-delicate lines. Peggy and Dick provide the low rustic humor.

The "female pens" that contributed so much to the novels and romances of the time seem to have been relatively inactive in ballad opera. Letitia Pilkington, it is true, says she was employed by Worsdale to write operas,[46] but we have no further record of them. There is one unpublished ballad piece by Mrs. Egleton, in all probability the actress who first played Lucy and who is described by W. Cooke as having "died enamoured of Bacchus,"[47] and a published one by a certain Mrs. Elizabeth Boyd. A third—which belongs as much in this chapter as elsewhere—was published in 1755 with a notation on the title-page of a possibility (no doubt remote) that it might be performed at Drury Lane. It was written "By a Young Lady" whose identity is modestly withheld. The opus of the "Virgin-Authoress" bears the title of *The Country Coquet, or Miss in Her Breeches* and has a dedication to the Ladies of Great Britain.

One must reveal with regret, however, that *The Country Coquet* is an inexpert medley of all the trite effects of the pastoral, the country opera, the play of intrigue, and the satirical piece. It resurrects, among others, the ancient device of the "breeches part" with the usual result that not even her father and her suitor can recognize the heroine in male attire and that they accept her as an actual rake. The pastoral scenes between Alexis and Nanny are brought in with little justification. Even the attempt to satirize the Prude, the Coquet, the *"Man* of *Pleasure* in the Character of an artful *Villain,"* and other types fails in its purpose because of the utter incoherence of the whole performance. In short, the play has nothing to recommend it. The most charitable procedure will be to dismiss *The Country Coquet* and record the hope expressed in the prologue regarding the authoress, that "When grown adult, she'll form a better Play."

All things considered, the village and country operas contributed nothing particularly new or unusual to ballad opera. We may regret that Gay, who wrote with so much freshness and originality in *The Shepherd's Week,* did not attempt a true rustic opera in addition to his Newgate pastoral. The authors of the country pieces, however, were usually content to alter earlier English plays or to borrow situations and characters from the French drama. Nevertheless, in their tendencies—however slight—toward romance and the outdoors, they offer an occasional relief from the cynicism and unpleasant realism found in most of the ballad plays.[48]

CHAPTER SEVEN

Farce and Intrigue

THE POPULARITY of *The Beggar's Opera* did not suffice to guarantee even moderate success for the full-length operas that trailed in its wake. The relative failure on the stage of pieces of three acts or more[1] was due in part to the inimitable perfection of Gay's play, in part to the inability of ballad opera to attract other authors of the first rank. For that matter, in spite of the excellence of the actors, the age of George II was not oversupplied with dramatic writers of genius. Fielding, who had not yet found his real talent, attempted ballad opera in passing, but in it he limited himself to broad farce or burlesque. Other playwrights, most of them professional men of the theatre, were content to capitalize the vogue for ballad opera by the simple expedient of sprinkling ballad songs, like so many raisins, into the text of any old plays they could lay their hands upon. Sometimes the result was excellent. But the form itself had its element of sterility in the inevitable repetition of ballad tunes. As early as 1729 Chetwood apologizes for the use of airs in *The Lover's Opera* which had appeared in other productions—as he claims, without his knowledge.[2] The writers of the more ambitious operas, furthermore, showed a peculiar lack of judgment in their insistence on having an overflowing measure of song. *Silvia* calls for sixty-three airs, *The Fashionable Lady* for sixty-eight. While a plethora of music might be expected of a musical piece, it should not be overlooked that—unlike later comic opera—ballad opera employed the songs as *décor* and not as the main concern. The music was always secondary; too much of it would obscure and retard the action of the play. As time went on, fewer full-length operas were attempted and the ones produced were usually mediocre.

Since the beginning of the century, however, the afterpiece had become virtually a necessary appendix to all stage production. It was here that, along with the non-musical farces, ballad opera found a real mission and *raison d'être*. Not only were short pieces constantly being written and produced to satisfy the demand, but many of the longer operas, as we have seen, were promptly reduced to one or two acts. Short, simple in plot, not usually overburdened with songs, the musical afterpiece made no pretense at originality or at any purpose other than entertainment. It employed farcical situation and drew heavily on the drama of the past, particularly on the old comedy of intrigue. Shakespeare, the Restoration dramatists, the French writers, all were cordially plagiarized. James Worsdale, in the prologue to *A Cure for a Scold*, objects to the practice of borrowing from France:

> Long has our Stage with Foreign Wit been cloy'd,
> And British Authors annually employ'd,
> To alter, mend, transpose, translate and fit
>   Moliere's gay Scenes to please an English Pit,
> Like Botching Taylors, whose whole Merit lies
>   In changing Suits to different Shapes and Size.

But in the play that follows, Worsdale (or was it Mr. Pilkington?)[3] pays the identical compliment to Shakespeare and *Sauney the Scot* with little to commend his procedure beyond the patriotism of using an English source.

The eighteenth century made a broad and rather careless distinction between pieces of three acts, which were called ballad operas, and pieces of one or two acts, which were labeled ballad farces.[4] From a modern standpoint this nomenclature is both inaccurate and misleading, for virtually all of the ballad plays—regardless of length—are farcical or at least have some farcical features. The present chapter will not be limited to afterpieces but will deal mainly with operas of any length that represent, in ballad opera, the degeneration of the old comedy of intrigue and deception. In it will be considered any otherwise unclassifiable pieces of a farcical nature, but with some attempt to exclude such well-defined groups as the "rehearsals" or the *pièces de circonstance*, which deserve special review. In spite of the great popularity of some of the productions in farce and intrigue, the goddess of Dullness will rule over most of the pages that immediately follow, for we find here ballad opera at

its most ephemeral and often at its worst. Yet, making due allow-
ance for the fine acting of the century, there must have been a spark
of genuine merit in such pieces as *The Devil to Pay* and *The Mock
Doctor* to account for their striking and continued success.

A composite picture of the ballad farce of intrigue reveals that
little originality was demanded in plot. The formula unfolds with
monotonous regularity. At its simplest the ingredients were as follows: an heiress of sixteen; a gallant; an aged or foppish or boorish
rival; an opinionated father or avaricious guardian; a clever valet;
an intriguing chambermaid; a stratagem; a marriage. While variations naturally occur, the basic pattern remains the same. Suspense
arises from the discovery of the deception and its apparent failure,
but in the nick of time some new trick is devised and the lover wins
the heiress, to the discomfiture of the parent or the rivals. Disguises
by the hero, heroine, valet, or maid play a vital part in the stratagem and undoubtedly gave the actors an excellent opportunity to
display their powers of mimicry and impersonation. While the
lovers offer occasion for sentiment and pathos, the servants usually
provide the wit and the trickery, so that the title of Fielding's *The
Intriguing Chambermaid* could equally well be applied to a vast
number of farces. In an age when the parents ordinarily determined
the matches with an eye to estates and interest rather than love,
the young girls show a commendable independence in their desire
to marry the men of their choice and in their utter refusal to lead
apes in hell. The other personages—the multitude of fops, of cruel
fathers, of amorous captains—are drawn on a standard plan, with
little attempt at individual characterization. They are all familiar
from Restoration comedy and from Molière.

This précis of the ballad opera of intrigue does not take into
account certain other occasional elements, such as the magical
transformations in *The Devil to Pay* and *The Devil of a Duke*,
which will be discussed in connection with the individual operas. In
view of their large number, the representatives of farce and intrigue
will be taken in strictly chronological order. Unpublished ballad
pieces will be mentioned only when definite information about
them is available.[5]

By virtue of the Flora-Friendly plot, Hippisley's *Flora* (1729), already listed among the country operas, belongs here as well. Beside the lovers, the characters include the avaricious uncle, the intriguing chambermaid, and, in Hob, the very antithesis of the clever servant.

Opening at Drury Lane in May 1729, *The Lover's Opera* by William Rufus Chetwood, prompter at Drury and writer of several plays, comes closer to the norm. Justice Dalton, however, has two daughters instead of one and consequently a double burden of worry. His efforts to marry them off, for a consideration, to unacceptable suitors come to nought through the machinations of Lucy, the intriguing chambermaid, who brings all the stratagems to a satisfactory conclusion. It is a conventional and stupid performance, with the incredible defect of an overhead soliloquy in which Dalton reveals his mercenary plans for his daughters. But the play proved a success nonetheless, earning over sixty performances at the various theatres between 1729 and 1738. The original Drury Lane cast indicates Mrs. Thurmond as the maid Lucy, and Mrs. Cibber and Catherine Raftor as the two daughters, with Mr. Charke and Mrs. Roberts as the lovers. For the music, Chetwood has thirty-two songs in mediocre verse.

Equally unoriginal but slightly more convincing is *The Contrivances, or More Ways than One*, a farce by Henry Carey, author of the celebrated song "Sally in our Alley," who—like another ballad-opera writer, Odingsells—ended his career by suicide.[6] In 1729 Carey revised for Drury Lane his own farce of 1715 with the addition of thirteen airs, the music for which, however, was composed by himself. Technically, as Sonneck points out,[7] the music rules the piece out of the category of strict ballad opera, but Carey seems to have adopted the style of the street ballads and his contemporaries all speak of *The Contrivances* as a ballad farce. That the music and the play were neither pretentious nor burlesque on the style of *The Dragon of Wantley* appears evident from the lines delivered by Theophilus Cibber in the prologue:

> To Night we show, no high-flown Love or Rage,
> But simple Nature's brought upon the Stage,
> A Hemskirk Piece of Poetry at best,
> And calculated merely for a Jest.

The Contrivances has both the avaricious father in Argus and the "good" but spying father in Hearty. The humor arises chiefly from the disguise of Rovewell as Squire Cuckoo's sister and of the servant Robin as "a Country-Putt." The stratagem and its failure must have proved duly hilarious, besides allowing Carey to satirize the country gentry as Fielding did later. Of the Squire, Robin says: "—He has drunk down six Fox-hunters sin last *Lammas*—He holds his old Course still, twenty Pipes a Day, a Cup of Mum in the Morning, a Tankard of Ale at Noon, and three Bottles of Stingo at Night."[8] A good sentimental duet was sung by Rovewell in the street and Arethusa above at the window of her home. All the songs, as a matter of fact, reveal Carey's aptitude for smooth and pleasing lyrics. Needless to say, Rovewell carries out successfully his elopement with Arethusa, and when Hearty—long absent in the Indies—reveals himself and bestows a fortune on his son, Argus becomes reconciled to the match. The intriguing maid is present as usual in the character of Betty. Catherine Raftor appeared as Arethusa and no less a personage than Theophilus Cibber as Robin, the clever servant.

Southwark Fair, or The Sheep-Shearing, by the Irish hunchback Charles Coffey, a ballad farce presented at Reynolds' booth in Southwark Fair, combines intrigue with pastoral low life. Disguises abound—Roger as herdsman and as astrologer, Sally as highwayman and as gamester—until the eventual wedding of the lovers. Squire Mumps, Sally's uncle, is victim of all the trickery. The third scene, no doubt, constitutes the *pièce de résistance* as it appropriately represents Southwark Fair itself with the attendant street cries and sheep-shearing celebrations.

The Devil upon Two Sticks, or The Country Beau, also from the facile pen of Coffey, appeared at Drury Lane in April of 1729 for a single performance. Mottley, the supposed compiler of the list of plays appended to Whincop's *Scanderbeg*, says it was an alteration for the worse of Vanbrugh's *Country Squire*. No such play by Vanbrugh is recorded, although he did write an adaptation of Molière's *Monsieur de Pourceaugnac* under the title of *The Cornish Squire*. Baker, dating the play in 1744,[9] mentions one performance at Shepheard's Wells, May Fair, and ascribes the original play to Giles Jacob. In any event, Coffey's piece falls most probably among the farces of intrigue.

The year 1729 marks the first ballad opera composed and produced initially in Ireland, a slight play called *Chuck, or The School-Boy's Opera,* given at Smock Alley on January 27, 1729, for the benefit of Lewis Layfield, the original Irish Macheath. On being published in London in 1736, it was ascribed to Colley Cibber, probably—thinks Lawrence[10]—because it was based on one of his comedies. As early as 1702 Cibber did write an adaptation, *The School Boy,* in which he himself acted the part of the booby Master Johnny. This slight farce was founded on Colley's own comedy, *Woman's Wit, or The Lady in Fashion* (1697).

The following year, 1730, saw several ballad operas of intrigue, the first being a three-act piece by the prolific Charles Coffey, *The Female Parson, or Beau in the Sudds,* presented at the Haymarket on April 27. Essentially realistic and with an admixture of low life, it departs considerably from the customary intrigue formula. Captain Noble is pursuing, not a maid of sixteen, but the wife of Sir Quible Quibus, "an old debauch'd Justice of the Peace." Even this good Restoration situation, however, shows the infusion of the new sentimentality. When the Captain almost reaches success in his amour, Lady Quibus reveals that her wedding ceremony was performed by her maid Pinner disguised as a parson and that because of her aversion to Quibus the marriage was never consummated. On learning this deception—which we may properly call retroactive —Captain Noble realizes that Lady Quibus loves him and promptly sublimates his passion.

Amazement!—she has stung me to the Soul with just and merited Reproach; her Virtue, like her beauty, is transcendant, and ne'er displayed its Lustre to these misty Eyes, 'till this auspicious Moment. Already I begin to feel the Symptoms of a pure and lasting Flame blaze round my Soul with irresistless Power.[11]

Virtue proves more than its own reward, for the lady reveals further that she has just inherited an estate. Like Squire Sullen, the Justice is overjoyed at an immediate separation and the lovers are united.

The servants, Comick and the sprightly Pinner, who scorns men of her own station, provide some excellent comedy. In Scene IV, Act II, easily the most attractive of the play, Comick—disguised in a riding-habit as Sir Theophilus No-land from Wales—proposes to Pinner, disguised as a lady of quality, and cleverly tricks her into accepting him. She does not discover the deception until the end of the play. The realistic angle of the opera concerns Miss Lure, "a Jilt of the Town" and mistress to the Justice, who with the assistance of two "Bravos" succeeds in gulling the foppish Modely. He is eventually "plumped into the Sudds," hence the subtitle. All things considered, *The Female Parson* does not seem altogether the poor play that Genest calls it[12] and deserved, perhaps, a slightly better fate than its two performances at the Haymarket.

One competitor for the title of the worst ballad opera belongs to 1730—*The Jealous Clown, or The Lucky Mistake,* by Thomas Gataker, Gentleman, who was quite obviously an amateur. The plot is of the thinnest, with the usual stratagem and elopement theme but has no pretense at motivation. Some slapstick humor and the title of the play depend upon a double portion of mistaken identity whereby a jealous clown is twice mistaken for the hero. As the songs are likewise mediocre, the performance may be judged from every angle as puerile. In the Goodman's Fields production, Mrs. Thomas as Friendly joined the august company of ladies who acted men's parts.

The Stage-Coach Opera, a moderately popular piece, was merely a ballad-operatization of the farce *The Stage Coach* (1704) by Farquhar and Motteux, who themselves adapted the play from en earlier source, La Chappelle's *Les Carosses d'Orléans.* Almost a score of performances of the ballad opera are recorded by Nicoll between 1730 and 1732, the earliest being at Drury Lane on May 13 and May 27 of the former year. Lawrence, however, mentions an earlier presentation at Smock Alley, Dublin, on April 2, 1730, for the combined benefit of Widow Eastham and Mr. Le Roux. In an interesting article in the *Modern Language Review*[13] he expresses his belief that the London and Dublin productions were not independent and tentatively ascribes the adaptation to William Rufus

Chetwood. Lawrence has made the interesting discovery, also, that the ballad opera, believed previously to have been unpublished, was printed by error in the old Dublin edition of Farquhar's works. No alteration of the original text appears except for the addition of fifteen ballad songs. Like its model, therefore, *The Stage-Coach Opera* is an entertaining farce of intrigue, dealing with the unexpected meeting at a country inn between a captain who is rushing to London to elope with the heiress and the girl in question who is being rushed away from London by her uncle in order to foil the captain. Complications naturally follow, to which are added the "humours" of travel by coach and the vicissitudes of a stay at a provincial inn.[14]

No dearth of information exists regarding the next ballad farce, *The Devil to Pay, or The Wives Metamorphos'd*, which opened at Drury Lane on August 6, 1731. Not only did it prove Charles Coffey's greatest success but in its reduced form it became probably the most popular ballad afterpiece of the century, with only one or two rivals for that honor. The long career of the piece on the stage began—without music—in Jevon's *A Comical Transformation, or The Devil of a Wife* (1686), in the writing of which Whincop says the author was probably assisted by his brother-in-law, Shadwell.[15] Coffey and Mottley were responsible for the 1731 conversion into a three-act ballad opera. Theophilus Cibber—according to the account in Whincop (apparently written by Mottley)—shortened the piece to a single act, omitting the offending role of a non-conforming pastor and adding two songs, by Colley Cibber and Rochester[16] respectively. For the first half of the century this abbreviated version secured an average of twenty-five performances yearly in London alone and continued in public favor for many decades later, both in England and America, one late adaptation being *The Basket-Maker's Wife* at Niblo's Garden, New York, in December 1852. In Germany, as mentioned earlier,[17] *The Devil to Pay* had an important part in the introduction of the *Singspiel*. A translation of 1743 by Herr von Borck[18]—*Der Teufel ist los*—appeared at Berlin and Hamburg, and a new one by Christian Felix Weisse, partly set to music by Standfuss, met with great success at

Leipzig in 1752 and 1753, in spite of bitter attacks by the critic Gottsched.[19] In France also did Coffey's farce find a generous welcome. It was included by Patu in his translations from the English theatre and adapted in 1756 by Sedaine for the *Théâtre de la Foire* as *Le Diable à quatre,* with music by Philidor. Perhaps indebted to this French piece was a new German version by Weisse, produced in 1766 with J. A. Hiller as composer. Various other adaptations followed.[20]

The writer of the prefatory remarks of the Oxberry edition of 1824 has a decidedly condescending view of the popularity of Coffey's play. "There is, 'tis true," he admits, "an air of rude nature about it, which captivates the vulgar, who are delighted with the romps and revelries of the kitchen, while the songs, being adapted to favourite old airs, can never fail to please." We must admit, with this supercilious critic, that *The Devil to Pay* is far from caviar to the general. It is decidedly "lowbrow," it indulges in boisterous horseplay, but even in the reading it possesses life and vitality, and above all it has those two attributes of permanence on the stage—universality of appeal and simplicity of theme. Poor Nell, the cobbler's wife, is beaten and abused by her brutish husband, Jobson. Lady Loverule, on the other hand, combines the shrew and the virago, tyrannizing over her husband and proving a very terror to the servants and tenants. An astrologer, ill-treated by Lady Loverule and by Jobson, secures his revenge by transposing Nell and Lady Loverule in their opposite stations, with the result that the cobbler's wife is exalted to the luxury of the manor and the shrew is properly beaten and tamed by Jobson. When the two husbands have been assured that the proprieties have not been violated, the wives are promptly exchanged again, and as a result of the experience Lady Loverule promises to mend her ways. As one may see at a glance, the formula is simple, but here we find all the ingredients of success—the taming of a shrew, the unexpected exaltation of a Cinderella, a taste of magic, and more than a taste of farcical action, as when Lady Loverule smashes the fiddle over the blind musician's head and when she herself is beaten by Jobson.

As any one who has witnessed amateur performances knows,

good farcical acting is in many ways more exacting than the playing of tragedy; hence a determining factor in the success of such a piece as *The Devil to Pay* would necessarily be the skill of the actors. At a time plentifully supplied with capable comedians, the Drury Lane company was nevertheless fortunate in having Harper as well as the matchless Raftor to play the parts of Jobson and Nell, which they performed with such éclat that Harper's salary was raised and Kitty's doubled as material recognition of their acting. In the 1731 full-length version Stoppelear played Sir John Loverule, with Mrs. Mills as his lady. The latter was supplanted in the abbreviated opera by Mrs. Grace. The parts of Ananias and Gaffer Dungfork, which were then eliminated, had been acted by Charke and Theophilus Cibber. Catherine Raftor remained the most popular of all Nells, but among later able actresses in the role we may list Miss Pope and Mrs. Jordan.

The original forty-two airs are reduced to sixteen in the afterpiece. Two of the songs in the latter have no indicated tunes and a third was set by Mr. Seedo, whose odd name appears also in connection with several of Fielding's lyrics. One of the tunes, "Charming Sally," was apparently Carey's famous song. Interestingly enough, the astrologer casts his spell to "the Spirit's Song in Macbeth," perhaps from the opera composed by Locke. The songs have a fair amount of gusto but are not particularly distinguished. A short lyric sung by Nell will offer an adequate sample of their worth:

> My Swelling Heart now leaps with Joy,
> And Riches all my Thoughts employ;
> No more shall People call me Nell,
> Her ladyship will do as well,
> Deck'd in my golden rich Array,
> I'll in my Chariot roll away,
> And shine at Ring, at Ball, and Play.[21]

The next year proved, like its predecessors, a happy period for farcical and intrigue operas. Of two pieces that might very well be included among them, one—the *Sequel to Flora*—has been mentioned earlier. The other, Fielding's *The Lottery*, has farcical features and an intrigue that failed, but like so much of the same author's work, has a satirical intent as well and will be reserved for discussion in a succeeding chapter.

In January of 1731, another ballad farce of Irish origin was offered at Madame Violante's booth in Dame Street, Dublin, acted by a company of children. The piece, a two-act operatization of Charles Johnson's *The Cobbler of Preston* (1716), itself taken from the Christopher Sly episode in *The Taming of the Shrew,* was published anonymously.[22] Lawrence suggests that the author of the operatic *Cobbler of Preston* may have been William Dunkin, a student at Trinity, who contributed some prologues for Madame Violante's farces and wrote plays for Stretch's puppet-show.[23] Merely amplifying the situation in Shakespeare, the farce has in common with *The Devil to Pay, The Devil of a Duke,* and others the sudden elevation of a low-life character into high life, evidently a popular theme. There is no record of a presentation of the opera in London, but it achieved considerable success in Dublin as given by the "Lilliputian" company. Master Peters appeared as Kit Sly, Madame Violante's daughter as his wife, and no other than Peg Woffington as the ale-wife Cicely Gundy.

Along with Shakespeare, Molière was to be resurrected the same season—though far more successfully—in Fielding's adaptation of *Le Médecin malgré lui* as *The Mock Doctor, or The Dumb Lady Cur'd,* which proved in popularity a serious rival to *The Devil to Pay.* In London alone over 250 performances in the three-act and afterpiece form are recorded up to the middle of the century. Fielding wrote the farce in great haste to substitute for *The Covent-Garden Tragedy,* which had been hissed off the stage. *The Mock Doctor,* opening at Drury Lane on June 23, is a rather free translation in the eighteenth-century manner with changes and additions to make the play more suitable for an English audience. Fielding's main contribution was the insertion of several scenes, quite justifiable for their comic effect, in which Gregory secures revenge by having his wife committed to the care of a "mad-doctor." The original part of the nurse is altered materially and nine ballad airs have been added, but substantially the play remains Molière. Three of the songs were set by Mr. Seedo. The ironic dedication to the quack Misaubin and the epilogue both serve to emphasize the ridicule of the medical profession that underlies the play. In the way of farce the possibilities arising from Gregory's sudden elevation to the medical faculty are unlimited but far too familiar to deserve specific mention here. In Theophilus Cibber as Gregory, and, opposite him, Kitty Raftor as Dorcas, Fielding had two comedians ideally suited to their roles.

That Fielding entered readily into the cynical spirit of his great predecessor is evident from the songs, one of which, sung by Dorcas, runs as follows:

> A woman's ware, like china,
> Now cheap, now dear is bought;
> When whole, though worth a guinea,
> When broke's not worth a groat.

> A woman at St. James's,
> With hundreds you obtain;
> But stay 'till lost her fame is,
> She'll be cheap in Drury-Lane.[24]

Nicoll records an unpublished ballad opera acted at Drury Lane on May 2 and May 12, 1732, thus antedating by more than a month the opening of *The Mock Doctor* on June 23. The title, *A Comical Revenge, or a Doctor in Spight of His Teeth,* certainly suggests the same original by Molière, but whether it was and whether the adaptation was by Fielding or some other hand does not appear.

To Shakespeare and Molière we now join a third inspiration from the past—remotely from Italy via the Restoration—in Drury's *The Devil of a Duke, or Trapolin's Vagaries,* based on Nahum Tate's *A Duke and No Duke* (1685), itself from Sir Aston Cokain's *Trappolin Suppos'd a Prince* (1658), which came in turn from an Italian tragi-comedy witnessed twice by Cokain at Venice. Baker asserts further that Trapolin's amusing but rather indelicate judicial decisions found their origin in the *Contes d'Ouville,*[25] although for generally similar material, of course, we need not search beyond Sancho's governorship in Barataria. *The Devil of a Duke* deals with another magical transformation, Trapolin—a banished procurer—being invested by Mago with the form and dress of Lavinio, Duke

of Florence. Most of the slapstick humor depends on the presence
of two dukes, each countermanding the orders of the other, so that
we find Brunetto in prison one minute and out of it the next, to the
natural consternation of everybody concerned. The more dignified
portions of the dialogue are accorded blank verse, in lieu of the
prose found in the comic passages. Various stage properties and effects are employed in the physical metamorphosis of Trapolin into
the Duke's "double"—music in the air, thunder, demons, an in-
cantation in blank verse suggestive of Milton's *Comus*. Mago "flies
down" to enter into conversation with Trapolin, who in a little
while "sinks"—although the printed play does not reveal the *modus
operandi* for either stage direction. Here we find ballad opera aban-
doning her ordinarily humble ways and stealing a few leaves from
dramatic opera.

The Devil of a Duke, despite some humorous portions, leaves a
confused impression and falls far short of the excellence of *The
Mock Doctor*. It enjoyed two editions in 1732 but had, in its first
form, only one performance at Drury Lane, in which Catherine
Raftor—as usual—took part. It was then considerably shortened
and given three more times. The author was the attorney's clerk,
Robert Drury, who earned scorn and ridicule from the writers of
the *Grub-street Journal* for his theatrical pretensions. His songs,
which at least are his own and not borrowed from an earlier source,
have a goodly share of the sensuous cynicism so common in ballad
opera. Several were set by the active Mr. Seedo.[26]

The same theatre, in December, produced another ballad farce,
Betty, or The Country Bumpkins, written by Carey. Only the songs
were published, but a satirical letter by "Some-body" in the *Grub-
street Journal*[27] ridicules and incidentally summarizes what he calls
the fable. The criticism is interesting in showing that the absurd
features of the current farces did not escape the notice of the more
serious-minded playgoers. Carey's piece, according to the summary,
presents a "rustic Machiavel" who contrives a wedding between his
supposed ghost and the heroine in order to circumvent her marriage
to a rival. "Here's a plot for you!" exclaims the critic. "Egad, Mr.
Bay's silent whisper is a fool to it!" As in *The Contrivances* Carey

himself composed the tunes for the songs, some of which—thinks
"Some-body"—are very pretty. Examination of the choruses indicates that at least two songs may have been set to ballad tunes.
The words for all of them were printed on large sheets and distributed gratis at the theatre, a device which makes us wonder whether
the audience, as in the Théâtre de la Foire, was expected to join in
the singing. Like Gay and Charles Johnson, Carey had a definite
knack for flowing, sprightly verse that fairly trips along. Two of the
shorter airs, numbers II and IV, may give an idea of their quality:

AIR II

Pr'ythee Fellow take Denial,
   Go at once thy way,
Vain is any farther Trial,
   Han't I said thee nay?
Needless 'tis to tarry here,
For thou shalt never marry here.
   Then make no pother,
   Get another,
For I'm not thy Lot,
   Go try thy Fortune,
   And importune
Those that know thee not.
   But I've more Wit
   Than to be bit
By such a hairbrain'd Sot.

AIR IV

BET. Audacious Intruder
   If thus you grow ruder
   I'll raise all the House. [*Very softly.*
RICH. And where's the Man shall curb me,
   If any dares disturb me.
   I'll ha——sh him as small as a Mouse.

It should be hastily added that "Some-body" does not concur
with any favorable opinion of Carey's words. "His every song is like
a painted well-dressed whore, who divested of her attire, is but the
wrinkled, meagre, gastly [*sic*], and forbidding image of a woman."
And from the free distribution of songs at the theatre, adds the acid

commentator, "we may reasonably think he had a sense of their worth." After which, "Some-body" apologizes for sinking so low as to take notice of such worthless pieces of writing.

The Disappointment, last farcical opera of 1732, came out at the Haymarket[28] and was published the same year. John Randall, who merely operatized Mrs. Centlivre's *A Wife Well Manag'd*, mentions in his dedication to the play that this is his first attempt "in the kind." F. T. Wood, however, believes that the author may have been Henry Carey.[29] In any event, *The Disappointment* is a witty but perfectly regular farce of intrigue, set in Madrid, in which Don Pedro intercepts a compromising letter from his wife to an amorous priest and punishes both by the use of the conventional Spanish trickery. Warwell not only acted Father Bernardo but composed the music for four of the twelve mediocre songs. Except for the lyrics there is really no dispute about the authorship, Mrs. Centlivre's dialogue having been retained practically unchanged.

Several ballad operas, including the first one for 1733, Coffey's *The Boarding-School, or The Sham Captain,* deserve the designation of middle-class operas, steering as they do midway between high life and low. Coffey's play, of course, is merely an operatic version of D'Urfey's *Love for Money, or The Boarding-School,* written in 1691. Whincop calls the play a bad alteration of a bad original and we need not quarrel too much about the characterization, although there are a few amusing scenes, particularly those in the boarding-school with the hoydenish young "romps" who devour bread and butter while they are learning to trill a song or dance a new Chacoon. As for the ballroom scene, where the girls show awkwardly their supposed progress in the terpsichorean art before an assemblage of admiring parents, it is excellent and not without its share of malice. The characters belong to the "City," not the court, though Lady Termagant has some slight pretensions to a higher social sphere which lead her not only to bully her husband, Alderman Nincompoop, "a sneaking uxorious citizen," but to cuckold him as well. Stratagems abound, but eventually the parasitic Ned Bragg is exposed and the two boarding-school "romps"— Jenny and Molly—elope with their teachers. D'Urfey is said to have spent some time in a boarding-school for purposes of observation. Though he denied this vehemently, there is enough "local color" in the play to make his treatment realistic as well as satirical. Coupee's song, to the tune of which he demonstrates a dance and at the same time proposes to Jenny, was written by D'Urfey himself; it appeared in the original play and in *Pills to Purge Melancholy*. Three airs in the opera were set by Mr. Seedo. In song, situation, and dialogue the play has a distinctly Restoration flavor and an abundance of double entendres. The last song, as often happens in ballad opera, gives a little sermon on the manners of the age. The first stanza will suffice to illustrate the type:

> The World's like a Boarding-school, common to all,
>   And so ev'n let it pass;
> Where great Knaves are brib'd to devour the Small,
>   Which is daily the Case;
> And each one contributes to heighten the Droll,
>   In this whimsical Age;
> Ranting and Swearing, Pride overbearing,
>   O rare Work for the Stage![30]

The Boarding-School has a dedication to the Duchess of Queensberry, the patron and champion of Gay who retired from court as a result of her zeal in securing subscribers for *Polly*. This would seem to set Coffey, politically, in the camp of the Opposition.

Catherine Raftor played Miss Jenny at Drury Lane, where her entrance "in a Bib and Apron, with a prickt Song in one hand, and a large piece of Bread and Butter in the other" must have provoked much laughter. The part of Molly fell to Mrs. Charke, Colley Cibber's youngest daughter, whose epic adventures form the subject of her own *A Narrative of the Life of Mrs. Charlotte Charke*. Lady Termagant was acted by a man—Harper—and Alderman Nincompoop by Griffin.

Coffey's opera appeared in January and February for a total of four performances. Slightly more successful was a one-act play at Goodman's Fields by Robert Drury. *The Mad Captain* came out on March 5; having been in the players' hands for over a year before securing representation, it was probably the first play by the young attorney's clerk. The apologia in the prologue, written by Drury himself, deserves quotation for its delightful ingenuousness. It ends as follows:

> So I, e're Years or solid Thought began
> To bid me leave the Boy, and rate me Man;
> Without Experience, to direct my Pen,
> Unskill'd in Politicks, unread in Men;
> Without Court Ladies to support my Cause,
> (As Int'rest judges by DRAMATIC LAWS;)
> In these Hard Times, not Eighteen Years of Age,
> Have form'd this little Trifle for the Stage.
> Then let my Youth excuse the many Faults,
> Nor think where Words are cramp'd, that Fancy halts.
> Youth is too giddy, to do always well;
> For Age itself is not infalible.

From the innuendos in both dialogue and songs, however, we must conclude that for a lad of seventeen Drury was more than well versed in the ways of the world. *The Mad Captain* follows the regular intrigue formula, with the hero feigning insanity to marry the heiress and avoid paying his debts. In Betty we have the usual intriguing chambermaid. By an ancient device from the Comédie-Italienne,[31] Sly and Captain Attall trick the two citizens— Pinch and Snip—into enlistment in the army when they each accept a guinea, which they believe is merely in payment of debts. The motivation throughout the play is either wretched or entirely lacking, but some of the lines with their cynical implications are passable. "Why Reputation," says Sly, "is nothing—but invented for Women of the first Rank to be proud of what they never had—But 'tis now like all other Fashions, when the Quality are going to relinquish it, taken up by the Vulgar."[32] Despite its deficiencies *The Mad Captain* had a respectable run of eleven performances in 1733 and two in 1734.

A second innocuous opera by the youthful Drury—*The Fancy'd Queen* by name—appeared at Covent Garden in August, with no success. The author boasts that no scenes were translated from the French, but he did not hesitate, according to Genest, to steal the plot of Shirley's *Sisters*.[33] The theft was scarcely worth the trouble, for *The Fancy'd Queen* deserves few kind words. Confused in situations and ridiculous in the sudden revelations at the end, the piece has no merit other than a few acceptable lines. Flirtilla, who lives under delusions of grandeur, scorns her lover Bellamy for the King of Pawpau,[34] who turns out to be, first, King of the Gypsies; second, an impoverished gentleman named Wildblood; and so on and on. Flirtilla was played by Mrs. Cantrell; her supposed sister, Aureola, by Miss Norsa—the young Jewish actress who became later the mistress of Horace Walpole's brother, with a curious contract promising marriage in the event of his lady's death.

An unpublished adaptation from Molière, *The Imaginary Cuckold,* appeared at Drury Lane for several nights in April and May, with Catherine Raftor as Mrs. Fancifull. In 1733, also, two farces of intrigue by Edward Phillips were performed—*The Mock Lawyer* at Covent Garden in April and *The Livery Rake and Country Lass* at Drury Lane in May. As suggested by the title, the first piece unfolds a plot of deception in which Feignwell, one of the clever servants, forwards his master's amour by impersonating a counsellor. The other familiar ingredients are present—the intriguing chambermaid, the obdurate father, the forgiveness at the end. Laetitia, unlike most of her predecessors, however, remains throughout the obedient daughter and will not marry Valentine without her father's approbation. In the entire play the tone of the old Restoration comedy of intrigue has suffered a modification and become sentimental and genteel, with the spirit of modesty brooding over the dialogue. The background of the law courts, however, enables the author to indulge in many jibes at the law and lawyers on the general order of the attacks found in Swift and Gay, but with decided increase in good-nature. Something akin to Gilbertian humor may be detected in Justice Lovelaw's song in the second scene about the necessity of preserving the proper form in the law. His clerk, Dash, is an interesting character who has been a religious enthusiast in a country conventicle, practiced physic as a Merry-Andrew, served as poet, and has now turned to law as the safest and best of all possible professions. Despite the play's triteness and its many verbal resemblances to *The Beggar's Opera, The Mock Lawyer* proved fairly popular on the stage for a number of years until 1745.

Phillips's other play of the same year, *The Livery Rake and Country Lass*, considerably less proper in song and dialogue, earned from Genest the commendation, "It is a pleasing trifle."[35] The main characters are domestics, and as in *The Footman* (1732)—but in a milder way—we have satire of servants who ape their masters. Tom, the footman, is tricked into marrying one of two heroines who are both named Phillis. Phillips develops this simple plot with some liveliness and one or two current allusions—one to the Charitable Corporation, another to the 1733 political battlecry of "Liberty and Property," the author apparently aligning himself with the anti-Walpole faction. There are jibes also at Senesino and Italian opera. All in all, the piece deserved a better fate than the eight performances recorded between 1733 and 1736. Genest informs us that Miss Norris, granddaughter of Jubilee Dicky, spoke an epilogue at the original performance.[36] As in most comic productions at Drury Lane, Catherine Raftor appeared in the cast, here in a part of the Miss Prue type, the country Phillis. Her chambermaid namesake was acted by Mrs. Mullart.

For April 30, 1733, Genest records a performance at Drury Lane of an unpublished ballad opera, *The Mock Countess*, an afterpiece concocted seemingly from Breval's *Play is the Plot* and Mrs. Centlivre's *Love's Contrivance*.[37] The most vivid personage in Breval's play is the Countess of Kiltankard—in reality my hostess, Betty Kimbow—who in a scene of broad farcical humor attempts to carry out a stratagem. No doubt the ballad farce had similarly a plot of intrigue.

A final ballad farce for 1733, also unpublished, appeared at Fielding and Hippisley's booth at Bartholomew Fair. Its name, *A Cure for Covetousness, or The Cheats of Scapin*, would indicate indebtedness to Molière. Mrs. Pritchard won considerable praise for her performance in the piece, especially for a duet with Salway.

With 1734 the tide of farcical operas began gradually to ebb. In that year the main representative of the type was the successful play by Henry Fielding, *The Intriguing Chambermaid*, adapted in two acts from *Le Retour imprévu* (1700) by the French dramatist

Regnard, who was himself indebted to the *Mostellaria* of Plautus. A version of Regnard's play had already appeared in England, before the advent of ballad opera, in *The Lucky Prodigal* (Lincoln's Inn Fields, 1715). Fielding's farce ran through a number of editions and remained popular on the stage for many years. Here again, as in *The Boarding-School,* we have a middle-class background but with the essential difference that it is not ridiculed. On the contrary, Fielding condemns the parasitic upper classes which have no scruples about encouraging the son of a London citizen to dissipate his fortune. When the father—Goodall—returns from the Cape of Good Hope, he drives out the insolent intruders but is compelled to bear their insults. The chief farcical scenes result from the attempts of the chambermaid, Lettice, to hide the true state of affairs from Goodall. Also, she assists Valentine in carrying out his intrigue with Charlotte, and herself indulges in spirited flirtation with the footman Rakeit. The engaging role of Lettice, as a matter of fact, was created specifically for the erstwhile Miss Raftor, now Kitty Clive, as the original character in Regnard was a male servant. On the occasion of the revolt of the Drury Lane players against the patentees Mrs. Clive had remained faithful to the interests of Highmore and Mrs. Wilks—not animated, as Fielding says, by any motive of interest but merely by her sense of justice. Fielding, who had likewise supported the patentees, prefixed to the printed play a warm tribute to the actress in the form of a dedicatory epistle, written with the straightforward sincerity so characteristic of his prose.

While the entire epistle deserves quotation, space will not permit us here to present more than a single, if rather long, passage. After a few scathing remarks on the disputes among the players and the follies of the town, Fielding writes as follows:

And here I cannot help reflecting with some Pleasure, that the Town, that Part of it, at least, which is not quite *Italianized,* have one Obligation to me, who made the first Discovery of your great Capacity, and brought you earlier forward on the Theatre, than the Ignorance of some and the Envy of others would have otherwise permitted. I shall not here dwell on any thing so well known as your Theatrical Merit, which one of the finest Judges and the greatest Man of his Age hath acknowledg'd to exceed in Humour that of any of your Predecessors in his Time.

But as great a Favourite as you at present are with the Audience, you would be much more so, were they acquainted with your private Character; cou'd they see you laying out great part of the Profits which arise to you from entertaining them so well, in the Support of an aged Father; did they see you who can charm them on the Stage with personating the foolish and vitious Characters of your Sex, acting in real Life the Part of the best Wife, the best Daughter, the best Sister, and the best Friend.

Don Quixote in England, written by Fielding in the same year, will be discussed among the satirical operas, although—as usual—it includes farcical episodes.

The only other ballad farce for 1734 had, like *The Intriguing Chambermaid,* a French original. *The Whim, or The Miser's Retreat,* played at Goodman's Fields and published anonymously, is merely a faithful reworking of Dancourt's *La Maison de campagne* (1688), which had already appeared in English dress, without songs, in Vanbrugh's *The Country House.* Rich in farcical possibilities is the central idea of the miserly bourgeois who retires to the country for economy but whose wife entertains visitors with such lavish prodigality that in desperation he turns his house into a public inn. This situation is developed with the aid of a simple plot of intrigue whereby Beaulove eventually wins Mariana when he intervenes in behalf of Cavil, who has fallen into difficulties over the killing of one of the king's stags. While the two plots are not merged with any particular skill, the play no doubt provided a pleasant evening's entertainment.

A highly entertaining but libertine portrait of James Worsdale, poet and painter, has come down to us in Letitia Pilkington's delightful *Memoirs.* If we are to believe Letitia, Worsdale relied for his more literary achievements on the ingenious practice, widely extant today, of employing "ghost-writers" who performed the labor while Jemmy received the credit. The loquacious authoress of the *Memoirs* mentions specifically three such scribbling assistants— Carey, Mr. Pilkington, and herself. Letitia's own experiences as a virtual prisoner in Worsdale's employ have a true picaresque flavor, as when she describes the four play-bills used for a tablecloth, the butter—when they had any—confined in an old shoe, and her lone coffee-pot which served indiscriminately for coffee, tea, small beer, and less noble uses.[38] In 1735, in any event, came out Worsdale's *A Cure for a Scold,* a ballad opera of two acts founded on *The Taming of the Shrew,* which Letitia says was actually written by Mr. Pilkington and to which she added "a flaming Prologue . . . in honour of my fair country-women."[39] This description of the prologue does not match the contents of the one in the London edition of 1735, but it may nevertheless have been spoken at some of the performances. As concerns the authorship of the play, Jemmy Worsdale seems to have had a plurality of "ghosts," for in addition to Shakespeare and Mr. Pilkington he employed the author of *Sauney the Scot* as well—John Lacy, from whom many passages were taken verbatim or only slightly altered.

In spite of the collaboration the ballad opera, which appeared at Drury Lane on February 25, 1735, remains mediocre, not to mention wretchedly printed, but if one forgets Shakespeare, it has its share of amusing moments—such as are inherent in the situation. A dedication to Edward Walpole, Esq., older brother of the celebrated Horace, implies Worsdale's association with the Court rather than the Country party. Be that as it may, Worsdale received later a considerable place in the government as master-painter to the board of ordnance. The first act of *A Cure for a Scold* ends with Manly's wedding to Peg, the Shrew. The second act takes us to Manly's home and, of course, back again to Sir William Worthy's, where Peg is tamed finally into submission. The text shows twenty-three songs, one of which was printed twice in error. Macklin[40] played the part of Manly, the Petruchio of Shakespeare, while Mrs. Clive—no doubt very convincingly—acted the shrewish Peg.

Charles Coffey's *The Merry Cobler, or The Second Part of The Devil to Pay* was presented at Drury Lane on May 5, 1735, but justly damned on the first night. It abandons the rough-and-tumble gaiety of the first part for a more sentimental situation, in which Sir John Loverule attempts the virtue of Nell only to be repulsed and reformed for his pains. "Let me alone, my Lord," she harangues, "to eat the Bread of Labour, and know no other Finery, but what I earn from honest Pains and the daily Sweat of my Brow."[41] Various low-life characters, including a tinker and his trull, are introduced for no good reason except perhaps to deliver one or two indecent lines. The mediocrity of the play, however, did not suffice to discourage several German adaptations, including *Der lustige Schuster,* presented by Koch in 1759 with music by Standfuss.[42] Coffey's piece has a dedication to Lady Walpole, possibly as a bid for political favor. In the Drury Lane performance Harper and Kitty Clive were called upon to repeat their success in the parts of Jobson and Nell.

The next ballad opera, acted only once, has a definitely tragic association. On the occasion of its single performance—at Drury Lane on May 10, 1735—Macklin, in a petty quarrel over a wig, accidentally killed a fellow-player, Hallam, by running a stick through his eye. *Trick for Trick,* the opera, was written by one R. Fabian, erstwhile footman to George II when Prince of Wales. Genest says the bulk of the plot came from the story of the Prince of Mousel in the *Persian Tales.*[43] In the character of Sancho and the episode of the pretended dinner there seems to be some slight inspiration also from *Don Quixote.* It would not be surprising, however, to discover a more immediate French or Spanish model, for in neatness of plot and skill of construction the play appears considerably superior to most native operas. Two tricks form the basis of the piece—first, Don Lopes engineers the marriage of Elvira to an apparent beggar (but in reality Don Fernand), and then Don Lopes is himself deceived into wedding the deformed Estifania. Against the background of vindictive and aristocratic Spanish passion, it comes as a definite surprise to find the songs set to such characteristically Scotch tunes as "Quoth Jockey to Jenny, Can'st Love" or "As Jockey and Jenny Together Were Laid." Neither aristocratic nor particularly vindictive is Sancho, the most interesting character of the play, who has in common with his namesake in Cervantes a mundane wit, a good practical sense, and a great love for food and the bottle. Within the limits of the Spanish comedy of intrigue, *Trick for Trick* is an expert and adequate performance, and if it is original with Fabian—which remains open to doubt—he deserves commendation for his dramatic flights and his rise from the liveried gentry.

With unusual restraint Fabian has limited the number of songs to ten in the two acts. That they are pleasing but not particularly unusual may be seen from Air VI, sung by Elvira to the tune of "Trip to the Landry":

> O how pleasing 'tis to languish,
>   When soft Wishes warm the Breast!
> Sighs, in part, disclose our Anguish,
>   And our Blushes speak the rest:
> Gay Desires, that fondly please us,
>   Prove by Day our dearest Themes;
> But when Midnight Slumbers seize us,
>   O the charming, charming Dreams!

The Honest Yorkshire-Man, another of Henry Carey's farces of deception, made its appearance at the Haymarket and elsewhere in the summer of 1735. It had first been offered to Drury Lane, where despite promises concerning production it was kept for nine months —so Carey complains—and returned to him in a very ungenerous manner at the end of the season." When the piece finally enjoyed a hearing, it proved fairly popular; it is, in fact, attractive in song and situation, although perfectly usual according to the intrigue formula. Gaylove, a young barrister, circumvents his countrified rival from Yorkshire, Sapscull, by having the clever servant impersonate the heiress while he weds the real Arbella. Sapscull and his servant, Blunder, provide the real fun of the play with their Yorkshire dialect and their wonderment at the ways of London. In describing the marvels of the town, Blunder says, ". . . and ye go to the *Tower*, ye mun see great hugeous Ships as tall as Housen: Then you mun go to Play-Housen, there you'll see your Comical Tragedies and your Uproars, and Roarataribusses, and hear *Fardinello*, that sings *Solfa* better nor our Minster Choir-Men."[45]

Two intrigue operas saw the light of publication in 1736. One of them, *The Lover His Own Rival*, came out at Goodman's Fields on February 10 and enjoyed a total of ten performances in 1736. It was revived in 1740 at Punch's Theatre and was played in 1743 at May Fair.[46] One may find some slight interest in the fact that it was written by Abraham Langford, called by D. E. Baker the most celebrated auctioneer of his age and successor to the great Mr. Cock. The *Biographia Dramatica* states that because of the intimacy between Langford and the manager Rich the play was given every season at Covent Garden in spite of its demerits,[47] but no further record of such performances exists. The opera, in any event, must be adjudged sentimental and trite, with such customary features as the aged rival, the intriguing chambermaid, the disguise of the hero—first as a physician and later as the rival, and so on. Two songs bemoan the power of gold and others have resemblances in wording or theme to Gay's lyrics. In addition to the seventeen ballad airs the prologue and epilogue both were set to music; they were sung by Mrs. Roberts, who played the part of Lucy, the former to the "Second Part of the Dutch Skipper," the latter to "Sir Thomas, I Cannot."

Wretched as it was, *The Lover His Own Rival* shines with the high excellence of a Shakespeare when compared to *The Happy Lovers, or The Beau Metamorphosed* by Henry Ward, one of the unfortunate maiden-efforts of the time. According to the title-page it was acted at Lincoln's Inn Fields, but no record of its performance appears in Nicoll or Genest.[48] The rival in the opera happens to be a fop, who is delineated and exposed as a coward while the hero Constant weds the lady. Very obligingly, at a critical moment, the stern father sets out for the Exchange, thereby allowing Constant to enter the house. Even weaker in motivation is a sudden love scene between two of the servants, who achieve marriage and forgiveness along with their masters. The weakness of the prose is rivaled only by the utter worthlessness of the verse, a sample of which from Air II should suffice to convince the skeptical:

> Women are like the Wind,
>   That is always a changing;
> Some to Lewdness are inclin'd,
>   Some to Roving and Ranging:
> He's the happiest that has least to do
>   With all such fickle Creatures;
> Yet, if we fly them, they'll pursue,
>   'Tis like their simple Natures.

The next year, that of the Licensing Act and of the death of

Queen Caroline, produced few ballad farces, although an operatic piece of a different kind won much acclaim and notoriety.[49] This was Carey's burlesque opera, *The Dragon of Wantley,* founded upon a popular ballad but quite different from ballad opera in form and music, the latter having been composed by Lampe to parody Italian recitative and "sing-song." The only representative of intrigue came out at York, not London, although it secured production at Covent Garden during the succeeding season and reappeared fitfully for several years. *The Lucky Discovery, or The Tanner of York,* as the opera was entitled, combines the old with the new, as it gives us within a single act a Restoration bedroom farce properly interlarded with sentiment and morality. As in some of our modern novels the author, John Arthur, disclaims in a preface any intention of satirizing "particular persons" or "exposing occurrences of private families." His desire, he says, was merely to entertain, although it seems that what he meant as innocent amusement was misconstrued by the gentlemen and ladies of York. We have no way of judging the sincerity of his statement, but apparently the play, if not based upon local scandal at York,[50] seemed so to his contemporary audience.

The Lucky Discovery opens somewhat as does *The Devil to Pay,* with Bark, the tanner, setting out churlishly for the alehouse in spite of the remonstrances of his wife. Left alone, the wife is visited by Mrs. Modish, whose husband, the Squire, has been attempting to philander with the faithful Mrs. Bark, and the two women determine forthwith to reform their wandering husbands. Their intrigue culminates in the ancient device—perhaps more convincing in the days anterior to Edison and the electric switch—of sending the Squire to an assignation with his own wife in Mrs. Bark's chamber. The plot almost miscarries, however, when it is the tanner and not the Squire who enters the bed, under the natural supposition that he is cuckolding himself. The bedroom, which is represented on the stage with the actors presumably groping about in the dark, offers much opportunity for farcical byplay until the situation is eventually cleared up to everyone's satisfaction and reformation, as appears in the following sentimental reflection by the Squire:

How like a Knave do I look now! Who, not content with the large Benevolence my affluent Fortune has bestow'd on me, must meanly descend to rob my poor Neighbour of that valuable Little she has scantily dealt him. 'S death! had I been taken picking a Pocket, I might have pleaded my Necessity.—But here, I can urge no Motive to excuse me, but my Ease and Luxury. Sir, I have but intended you an Injury, for which I heartily beg your pardon.— But here, [referring to his wife] I may blush to say it, I have done a Real One, in neglecting so much Goodness and Virtue.[51]

The sentimental passages, such as the above, are in no wise displeasing, and in other respects as well the play must be considered witty and attractive. Consider one of the lyrics—Air I, sung by Mrs. Bark to the tune of "Tit for Tat":

> A surly, sottish, peevish Booby,
>   Once possest a lovely Wife,
> Yet the sordid sulky Looby,
>   Made her weary of her Life:
>   Always glum,
>   Ever dumb;
>   Never cheary, gay or airy;
> A snarling, crabbed drousy Elf,
>   Just such another as yourself.
> An easy, sprightly, sparkish Wag, Sir,
>   Long had sought her Heart to move;
> So she gave the Sot the Bag, Sir,
>   And return'd him Love for Love:
>   Tit, for Tat,
>   Pit, for Pat,
>   Ever cheary, gay and airy;
> Which gain'd Admission to her Bed,
> And branchify'd the Husband's Head.

The author himself appeared in the original cast as Simon, the drunken tanner's man. We learn from the *Biographia Dramatica* that he was a player of eminence in the character of old men. His connection with the provincial theatres is important, for after acting several years at Covent Garden he became manager of the playhouse at Bath, where he died in 1772. When *The Lucky Discovery* came out in London in 1738, the part of Simon was taken by Hippisley, who, in view of his famous acting skit, "the Drunken Man," must have been excellently cast.

While ballad opera, except in revivals, had lost most of its vitality by 1737, there is no doubt that its demise was further accelerated by the Licensing Act, as many of the new pieces had reached the boards in the smaller theatres. With the silencing of Fielding at the Haymarket we note that few authors of note perpetuated the form, although it still had its devotees among amateur authors and writers for the provincial theatres. It remained for Bickerstaffe and his followers to revive and develop the genre in the direction of comic opera by dressing up the simple ballad music and laying greater emphasis upon the operatic score.

London, in any event, saw no new ballad operas in 1738 other than Arthur's *Lucky Discovery* at Covent Garden, and that one, of course, had appeared earlier at York. Several of the new London plays did employ musical effects: Miller's *Coffee-House* at Drury Lane, a very interesting play in which Theophilus Cibber was cast as himself and which included six songs set by Carey and Burgess; Dodsley's *Sir John Cockle at Court* at Drury Lane, a democratic, sentimental, and patriotic piece termed by the author a "dramatick tale" and designed as sequel to *The King and the Miller of Mansfield;* and Carey's *Margery, or A Worse Plague than the Devil* at Covent Garden, a burlesque opera with music by Lampe which was offered as sequel to *The Dragon of Wantley*. At Edinburgh, however, came out a ballad opera of intrigue in three acts, *The Disappointed Gallant, or Buckram in Armour,* written by a young Scotch gentleman, Adam Thomson. Here we find innumerable deceptions and impersonations, with the usual interrupted infidelities and mock marriages. Sandy Buckram, a Scotch tailor who is induced at one point to fight a duel in armor, proves an excellent low-comedy character. Despite the conventional situations and the dullness of some of the episodes the play reads well, but its multiplicity of stratagems may easily have made it confusing on the stage.

In finding music for his forty-three songs, Adam Thomson would seem to have exhausted too soon his supply of popular airs, for five songs—IX to XIII inclusive—are set to the same tune, namely the "Prince of Orange's Rant." Airs XXII and XXIII also were forced

to share a common tune. One song, "Buckram's Own Tune," had its
music composed by Matthew Briggs. For some reason, four additional songs are printed immediately after the epilogue but with no
indication as to whether they were used in the course of the play.

Although several were published, few ballad operas reached the
London stage in 1739. Covent Garden and Drury Lane were not
without their musical offerings, but two of these were very slight
interludes with original music—*Roger and Joan, or The Country
Wedding* and Carey's *Nancy, or The Parting Lovers*—and another,
Miller's *An Hospital for Fools,* was merely a "dramatic fable" with
four songs set by Arne. At least two of the 1739 pieces are farces of
intrigue, and a third, John Maxwell's *The Trepan, or Virtue Rewarded,* published at York, would seem from its title to belong to
the same category.[52]

A collection of *Dramatic Pieces, and Other Miscellaneous Works
in Prose and Verse,* printed in London, might boast of highly
learned authorship as well as of an interesting father-son collaboration. The joint authors were Daniel Bellamy, Sr., formerly of St.
John's College, Oxford, and Daniel Bellamy, Jr., of Trinity College,
Cambridge. Baker tells us in a delightful passage that the plays

were expressly written to be performed by the young Ladies of Mrs.
Bellamy's Boarding-School at *Chelsea,* at the stated Periods of breaking
up for the Holidays, for the Improvement of themselves, and the Amusement of their Parents and Friends.— They are well adapted to the
Purpose, being short and concise, the Plots simple and familiar, and the
Language, tho' not remarkably poetical, nor adorn'd with any very extraordinary Beauty, yet, on the whole, far from contemptible.— They are
calculated for the shewing the peculiar Talents of the Young Ladies, who
were to appear in them, and to set forth the Improvements they had
acquired in their Education, especially in Music, to which End Songs are
pretty lavishly dispersed through them all.

Whereupon Baker concludes that such public exhibitions should be
practiced in more of the "Seminaries of Education both Male and
Female."[53]

The collection includes one ballad opera of two acts, *The Rival
Priests, or The Female Politician,* which was published separately
in 1741. In a preface by the Trinity Bellamy, public thanks are ex-

tended to the actor Milward for his good offices in recommending
the play to Fleetwood, although it was not accepted for production.
Conscious of the moral obligations of the theatre and perhaps with
an eye to the boarding-school connections, the author goes on to
deny that there is any

single Poem, or Passage, throughout the Whole, that can give any just
Occasion for Offence, or raise a Blush in the most modest even of the Fair
Sex. If, in the amorous Character of old Antonio in the Farce, there may
be an Expression or two introduc'd, that may appear to some rigid Per-
,sons a little too warm or luscious, let them consider, that they were
complied with upon no other Account, than to aggravate his Folly, and
render him the juster Object of Contempt and Ridicule.

In spite of this apologia it must be confessed that many of the
lines do appear "a little too warm or luscious," especially if they
were delivered by the young ladies of Mrs. Bellamy's boarding-
school at Chelsea. Except for such occasional torrid passages, however, *The Rival Priests* is mechanical and dull, with pompous, literary dialogue and trite songs. The plot unfolds as a Spanish tale of
intrigue, set in Madrid, whereby Don Antonio—an old lecher—is
discomfited in his intrigue with the beautiful Aquilina and inglori-
ously cuckolded, to boot. The usual theatrical bag of tricks, including disguises and hiding in a chest, is liberally utilized.[54]

While most of the fifteen songs employ the artificial pastoral diction of the time, at least one stanza sung by Don Antonio has a
little D'Urfeyan liveliness:

> Ah! turn my dear Nacky, and see your poor Slave,
>   Mumpaty, mumpaty, mump:
> Oh! send not poor Tony so soon to the Grave,
>   Glumpaty, glumpaty, glump.
> If I look but on you, my Heart beats the Tattoo,
>   Thumpaty, thumpaty, thump.
> Then yield me thy Charms, and fly into my Arms,
>   Plumpaty, plumpaty, plump.[55]

The Rival Priests proves fairly readable, but no such damning
with faint praise can be accorded to Joseph Peterson's *The Raree
Show, or The Fox Trap't*, acted at York in 1739 and published at
York and at Chester in 1740. Banal, incoherent, illogical, it is obvi-

ously, as called in the preface, "the first Effort of an unexperienc'd Undertaker," whose chief boast is that the play contains nothing offensive to morality or good manners. The author, interestingly enough, was reputed an elegant and versatile actor and was long attached to the Norwich company of players. He made his debut at Goodman's Fields in November, 1740, as Lord Foppington and played Buckingham in Garrick's original performance of *Richard III*.[56] We must therefore consider the possibility that the play may have been more acceptable in actual representation, where excellent acting may have helped "put over" the parts of the cowardly coxcomb Sir Fopling Conceit and of the servant Smart, who impersonates a Raree-show-man with his box of wonders. The piece belongs to the straight intrigue school with a stratagem, the discomfiture of a fop, and a triple wedding. Reference to foreign singers and actors is made in the Raree-show-man's ballyhoo, sung by Smart:

Here you see Signior Farinello, *the famous Singer from* Italy!—*Here you see de Ladies of* England *kneel to him, and beg of him not to leave 'em; which is a vera prette Fance, a brave gallante Show,* &c.— *Here you see de* French *Comedians in de* Hay-Market, *who come over and get noting; but go back vid dere Labour for dere Pains* ....[57]

The same mediocrity characterizes most of the intrigue farces of the decade of the 1740s. *The False Guardians Outwitted* by William Goodall, apprentice to a clothier and apparently to the muses as well, was published in 1740 in *The True Englishman's Miscellany* but never reached the stage. It, too, offers the customary deceptions, leading to a pair of matches, and the conventional characters of the obdurate uncle, the ridiculous fop, the cowardly captain, etc. The dull plot is matched only by the literary, artificial language. Equally wretched is *The Sharpers* by Matthew Gardiner, played at Dublin in 1740 and printed the same year.[58] Here we have an intrigue that fails with the exposure of the highwayman villain, and thus Freelove is free to marry Loveit. The plot is ill-motivated and the coherence poor. Some slight measure of promise, however, may be accorded to a one-act ballad opera, *The Whim, or The Merry Cheats,* which appears in the Larpent Collection of the Huntington Library with the date March 30, 1741. It is an inconsequential, but not badly written, farce of intrigue with a stratagem and a match according to the usual pattern. No author or cast is indicated.

Two ballad farces of 1742 afford a momentary relief in this stretch of banality. Not that Joseph Yarrow's *Love at First Sight, or The Wit of a Woman* has anything particularly original about it other than a feminine slant in that the heroine dominates the action and proves the superiority of woman's wit. The center of the plot is the ancient device of having the heroine make an assignation with her lover—under pretense of denouncing it—through the medium of her unsuspecting father. But in spite of the conventional elements, Yarrow has written a pleasant little opera of two acts with a particularly engaging heroine in Aurelia. No players are listed in the York edition of 1742. The *Biographia Dramatica* states that the opera was acted at York by the company of comedians, of whom the author was one. Yarrow, it may be remarked, was father of the actress Mrs. Davies, whose beauty earned commendation by Churchill in the *Rosciad*.

The vivid episodes of *Don Quixote* and the boundless admiration of the seventeenth and eighteenth centuries for that work proved a temptation to many dramatists. D'Urfey, it may be remembered, attempted a dramatization in three parts of five acts each, with incidental songs. In a satirical opera of 1734 Fielding transported Sancho and Don Quixote to the English countryside. Far less original but quite good in its own way is a three-act opera of 1742 by a Gentleman, late of Trinity College, Dublin. Baker and others identify the Gentleman as James Ayres, who—according to the entry on the Library of Congress card[59]—may have been James Eyre Weeks. The play, *Sancho at Court, or The Mock Governor* (1742), was offered by Torbuck, the publisher, to the manager of Drury Lane with very unsatisfactory results in the way of delay and alteration, of which he complains bitterly in a preface. Chetwood, who was employed to abbreviate the play, professed considerable admiration for it, asserting of his own revision that "tho' lame, 'twill walk with the best of the One-Act Gentlemen."[60] Nevertheless it failed to appear at Drury Lane, and Torbuck, in disgust and desperation, offered it to the public in print.

Sancho at Court faithfully and amusingly presents the sententious Sancho as Governor of Barataria until the mock battle at the end which induces him to relinquish his high office. Love interest is provided in the courtship—abetted by Sancho—of the coquette Lucinda by her lover Antonio. Despite the tricks played upon him Sancho emerges as a sympathetic, if humorous, figure. Mary, his daughter, is portrayed with some gusto as a "romp," fully determined not to lead apes in hell. She is not quite as bawdy, however, as in the D'Urfey plays. The dining-room scene and the judicial decisions of Sancho provide two of the high spots of play.

The twenty songs betray no weakness other than lack of originality. The usual types are present—the songs about the power of gold, about the villainy of lawyers, about the beggary of mankind. The "simile song" and the "old maid" lyric are combined in Antonio's advice to Lucinda in Air V.

Sancho at Court is almost the last of the intrigue operas. In 1745 James Miller adapted a farce of Molière as *The Picture, or The Cuckold in Conceit,* but the presence of five songs, all of them set by Mr. Arne, would not suffice to qualify it as a ballad opera. A belated arrival, however, made its appearance at Drury Lane on March 18, 1746—*The Double Disappointment* by Moses Mendez, the wealthy Jew whose musical pastorals were greatly admired by his contemporaries and capably sung by Mrs. Clive, Miss Norris, Beard, Vernon, and others. *The Double Disappointment* has only six songs, three of them to specified ballad airs and the others, if we may judge from the refrains, probably also of popular origin. In romantic and highly artificial treatment, we have here again the villainous guardian, the forfeited "papers," the heroine who contrives to marry the man of her choice. The conversation, while generally pleasing, remains stilted throughout. "I am undone!" exclaims miserly Gripe. "She will unravel my secret Correspondence with the Lawyer, to defraud young *Spendall* of his Estate. I must retire, and think what's most for my Advantage."[61] And the Irishman Phelim O'Blunder depends for the humor of his characterization merely upon the idiocy of his statements, as in the line, "I wish I had a Lantern, to see whether the Moon be up or no."

Phelim's Irish songs provide, perhaps, the greatest interest of the play. The chorus of one air runs as follows:

> Laring go lee, I for radleum, bobum a rue,
> Sing a Woradleum, sing a boare, smorus for Moggame,
> S'derth maran dogad, sing burn my Wig.[62]

The last stanza of another may deserve quotation for its breezy swing:

> On that happy Day when I call you my Bride,
> With a swinging long Sword, how I'll strut and I'll stride,
> With Coach and six Horses, with Honey I'll ride,
> As before you I walk, to the Church, on your Side.
> Sing Balinamone o-ra, Balinamone o-ra,
> Balinamone o-ra,
> A Kiss of your sweet Lips for me.[63]

As one glances over *The Double Disappointment,* one feels that even though the songs are few the emphasis has shifted from the play proper to the music. The spirit and mood of the writing have suffered a subtle metamorphosis. Even the cast forms a complete break with the performers of the old ballad opera. Phelim O'Blunder was played by Barrington, the villain Gripe by Collins, the hero by Lowe, and the heroine by Miss Young.

The plays considered in this chapter reveal the essential barrenness of ballad opera. Unable to compete with the brilliancies of Gay, the professional writers were satisfied to resurrect the old successes with only the addition of songs and no regard to logic. Even in the lyrics they showed a minimum of originality, remaining content to imitate the types and words of the *Beggar's Opera* songs. It must be granted, on the other hand, that the continued repetition of ballad tunes did not allow much room for experimentation or expansion. With the popularity of ballad opera as afterpiece, the tendency became even greater to do journeyman work, to boil down the old comedy of intrigue to a residuum of stale plot and type characterization. It remained for the amateur authors and the provincial playwrights to plumb the depths of triteness and triviality. The post-Gay ballad opera had its interest and its value, but not in farce or intrigue. Rather were its best contributions to be found in satire, in the *pièces de circonstance,* and in political pamphleteering.

CHAPTER EIGHT

Satire and Burlesque

DURING its brief existence ballad opera remained at best a mongrel form, particularly sensitive to the winds and currents of theatrical fashion, uncertain in purpose, unified only by the fact of its being comedy—if not always comic—interspersed with what were presumably—but not always—popular airs. The plays mentioned so far—the low-life operas, the village operas, the pastorals, the farces of intrigue—do not offer us types that are mutually exclusive, nor can we readily pick out a dozen pieces here or there and group them neatly under the heading of satirical operas. If by satire we mean merely ridicule or derision it would be difficult to find any ballad operas untinged by it, at least in isolated lines or passages. A more formal literary satire appears regularly in the songs. Much of this is purely conventional, reducing itself to mild and rather general reflections on the villainies of the professions, the injustice of statesmen, the follies of mankind, the susceptibility of women to the power of gold. Such Lilliputian thrusts are directly traceable to the *Beggar's Opera* songs, where Gay set the fashion—in excellent verse. The present chapter will not deal with incidental or isolated ridicule, or with satirical songs, but with examples of more sustained satire showing greater attention to literary form. In a number of operas the use of caricature and distortion, with the aid of extravaganza effects and "broad" farce, turned the ridicule into the form of burlesque, as in some of Fielding's pieces and in the numerous "rehearsals." These will come under discussion here also. Two other more or less satirical types—the political plays and the *pièces de circonstance*—will, however, be reserved for unified treatment in the next chapter.

The subjects of ridicule show no surprising variety. As in *The Beggar's Opera,* the satire might be social, ethical, political, literary, or personal. Among the individuals most frequently held up to scorn were, beside Walpole, the Cibbers and Orator Henley. The literary satire or burlesque was directed primarily at some of the fashionable or popular forms—Italian opera, pantomime, and farce. For a more complete account of these various topics, it will be advisable to turn to the ballad operas themselves.

The manners and cynicism of high life—especially of the court —laid it open, as in all ages, to satirical representation. In the attempt to vilify and degrade, a favorite device was the liberal introduction of low-life elements in order to reveal and emphasize the vices of the noble lords and ladies. We find this, of course, in *The Beggar's Opera* and likewise in one of the earliest of the high-life satirical pieces, Thomas Odell's *The Patron, or The Statesman's Opera,* played once at the little theatre in the Haymarket on May 7, 1729. The two acts and nineteen songs give us a profoundly disillusioned and cynical view of society and humanity. Just who—if any particular person—was designated by Lord Falcon, the patron in the play, remains obscure. Odell, who had handsomely supported the Court interest, complains of lack of patronage since the death of the Earl of Sunderland, who had provided him with a pension of two hundred pounds, paid only two years and then discontinued. The dedication to the new Earl of Sunderland, in relating the loss of the pension, bemoans the death of the Earl's father. Regarding the play and its subject, the author explains hastily "that the Sham-Patron, its chief Character, and from which it takes its Name, is drawn corrupt, vicious, and unsincere; and serves only as a Foil, to illustrate the Virtues of the real Patron ..."

The opera illustrates merely how Merit, denied a lucrative place in the patent office, finally secures this preferment with the assistance of Peggy Lure, a woman of the town, who poses as his wife and in this capacity makes an assignation with Lord Falcon. After a bedroom scene which leaves little to the imagination, the "patron" admits frankly that Merit has been useful to him heretofore only in elections but that since he is now serviceable to his pleasures he will get considerably more in return. The play ends with the discomfiture of several personages who have all been "bit" by Peggy —Lord Falcon, Sir Jolly Glee, and Pointer, pimp *par excellence.* Merit and Peggy then part as the best of friends.

The characters in this spirited picture of human vices are clearly
and distinctly drawn. Sir Falcon shines most vividly at his levee,
where he dispenses promises and flattery with casual abandon; he
is effective also in his scenes with Peggy Lure, in which he reveals,
with genial and outspoken cynicism, his utilitarian attitude toward
pleasures and politics. His later behavior is thoroughly vicious.
Merit and his misanthropic friend, Stout, remain minor characters,
as do Sir Jolly and Pointer, but all are delineated sharply. Peggy
Lure is a really interesting character, steadfast as a friend to Merit
but a true libertine at heart, who knows the ways of men and is
perfectly able to cope with them. The epilogue, spoken by her,
shows her as a fully emancipated woman, insistent upon her freedom to range and unburdened with morals. Even for one day, when
she pretended to be Merit's wife, her neck was "gall'd with the
nuptial Yoke." So she returns upon the town, with incidental reflections upon her recent experience:

> To me, 'tis true, when Merit's Wife in jest,
> 'Twas some Relief to seem to Horn his Crest;
> And such Intrigues who wou'dn't be pursuing,
> When 'twas to save one's own Good Man from Ruin?

Later in the same year Odell erected the theatre in Goodman's
Fields, which he subsequently was obliged to dispose of to Giffard,
the Sir Jolly Glee of his play. Eventually he became Deputy Master
of the Revels under the Duke of Grafton and William Chetwynd,
from which we may assume that Odell had the good fortune of finding another patron.

Another satirical portrait of high life came in 1732 under the title
of *The Footman: An Opera*. It appeared at Goodman's Fields,
where it attained half a dozen performances. The author remains
anonymous, but he was a writer of no mean ability. Genest praises
the dialogue of the play but rightly asserts that two acts would have
sufficed instead of three. The mock-heroic dedication "To the Society of Footmen in Great-Britain" and the *dramatis personae*
would suggest low life rather than high, but it soon becomes evident that the satire is double-edged, that the foibles and vices of the
fashionable world are ridiculed as they filter down below stairs. The

maids and footmen affect the manners as well as the names and titles of their masters—as in Townley's comedy later,[1] which may have been inspired by the present piece. They speak with decorum, draw swords, have their amours, show a passion for gaming, and even hold a fashionable assembly—at the home of the bawd, Mrs. Jessamy. While they display the airs of the *beau monde,* they show little respect for it. Concerning the Gentlemen, Harry says, "Nay, as to that, a Footman has generally the advantage in point of Education; and I believe there is not much difference in the Blood."[2] Or consider the exclamation of the jealous Betty: "O the Villain! he hadn't the Assurance—Then there's no such thing as Honesty, and Footmen are as great Rogues as their Masters."[3]

Most amusing of all are the love passages between Charles and Jenny, Mrs. Jessamy's daughter, carried out in the most delicate sentimental strain. Poor Jenny's virtue baffles and exasperates her mother, who wishes to prostitute her to Lord Gaylove. The girl hasn't the least spark of ambition, thinks Mrs. Jessamy, to whom Jenny replies bitterly, "I am glad, Madam, you've so much Tenderness for me, as not to let any one have the debauching of me but your self." No wonder Jenny reflects how difficult it is for women, especially the necessitous, to preserve their virtue. But in Charles she has a worthy lover, who, though loath to relinquish the single state, finally capitulates to love. When their lottery ticket proves worthless, Charles adheres to his resolution to marry her—"I'll retrench my Superfluities," he says elegantly, "and as you affect nothing of Gaudiness, you shall make a decent, tho' not as glaring a Figure, as any Lady about Town."[4] He adds, however, that a girl should never inquire into her lover's or husband's amours. The jealousy of Charles's erstwhile mistress, the maid Betty, leads to his dismissal from service, but when it appears that it was Lord Gaylove the footman, and not Lord Gaylove the master, who won ten thousand pounds in the lottery, the play ends happily.

One must resist the strong temptation to quote other good lines and to speculate on the identity of the author. The play has many little resemblances to *The Beggar's Opera*—in wording, in the introduction leading to the overture, in the jealousy between Betty and Jenny, in the sentimental love scenes, in the character of Mrs. Jessamy, and for that matter in the entire topsy-turvy treatment of the theme. In other ways the diction, the lines, the songs, and the love passages are not so far from the style of Fielding; perhaps they come even closer to the manner and treatment of James Ralph, Fielding's associate, who had a tendency toward wordiness in style.[5] On the basis of internal evidence alone *The Footman* can scarcely be laid at the door either of Gay or of Fielding, but it is not by any means unworthy of them, or of such writers as Ralph and Odell.

Whoever the author was, he has too many songs—sixty-eight in all—but they deserve praise for being lively and witty. An amusing musical denunciation appears in Betty's short apostrophe to Charles as she leaves in a passion:

> Villain away to the Rose,
>   There try your raking Rallery,
> Or your vile Manners disclose
>   To some kind Nymph of the Gallery:
>
> A Pint with your Kisses then mix,
>   And they'll not fail to give to ye,
> She, Sir, may shew you her Tricks
>   Fit for your Front and Livery.[6]

Only mildly satirical is a ballad opera of 1736, *The Female Rake, or Modern Fine Lady,* which was played at the Haymarket by Fielding's company and was printed the same year. In 1739 it appeared again in print in a collection, *The Curiosity,* attributed to Joseph Dorman, under the new title of *The Woman of Taste, or The Yorkshire Lady.* The earlier edition has an elegant frontispiece representing one of the scenes—set in St. James's Park—and bears on the title-page the well-known couplet by Pope:

> Men, some to Business, some to Pleasure take;
> But ev'ry Woman is at Heart a Rake.

Graceful and pleasing in general treatment, *The Female Rake* suffers merely from being dull. The satire, which remains perfectly well-bred and genteel, seems directed primarily at two foppish coxcombs, Lord Fashion and Beau Dapper, who prove equally boastful and cowardly, and at a lady of fashion, Libertina, who stays out until dawn at such iniquitous affairs as balls, operas, and masquerades. But the female rake promises to reform her ways after her marriage to Clerimont, whose erstwhile fiancée has married another in his absence from England. A relief from the sentimentalism and gentility of the main characters is provided in the two servants, Phillis and Tim—the latter played by the versatile Mrs. Charke—whose lines are not always marked by delicacy. The prose dialogue of the play is interrupted occasionally by rhymed couplets, usually tags at the close of scenes—a convention which is not usual in ballad opera. Allusions are made to Pontack's, to Farinelli, and to Dr. Pill and Drop; all of these aiding to give an effect of pleasant realism to the picture of high life in 1736. The two acts of the play have sixteen airs and a "medley overture" at the start.

Several of Fielding's plays have been considered among the ballad farces of the last chapter. His most mordant satire among the operatic pieces, *The Grub-Street Opera*, will be reserved for discussion with the political plays. At this point, however, it will be convenient to glance at some of his other satirical operas, which range from a mild ridicule of society to a broad and farcical burlesque. Fielding was no meticulous artist in the theatre, no purist in form—he was too robust and original for that; hence some of his work is difficult to classify. Not the best but probably the most interesting of the lot is *The Author's Farce; and The Pleasures of the Town*, which may be considered a ballad opera only by courtesy. The first two acts have each one ballad song, but the third act introduces a puppet-show (played on the stage, however, by real actors) with a total of fifteen airs in the *Beggar's Opera* manner. This odd medley appeared at the Haymarket on March 30, 1730, where it enjoyed over forty performances. It was revived in later years at the various theatres and went through several printings. The third edition, in 1750, based upon the acting version of 1734, was enlarged and thoroughly revised and will be used as the basis for the present discussion. For this revision Fielding amplified and improved the satire, added Theophilus Cibber to the list of his victims, and increased the number of songs in the puppet show to twenty-five.

It would require an impressive catalogue to record all the satirical shafts showered by Fielding upon contemporary life and personages. The first two acts of *The Author's Farce* are perhaps better than the last act because the satire is handled in a more realistic way. In the penurious author, Luckless, who is dunned by his landlady, abused by his bookseller, and treated cavalierly by the managers, we find a convincing picture of Grub-Street life which is only slightly exaggerated. The milder exposure of Wilks and Colley Cibber in the 1730 play was sharply accentuated in the revised delineation of the Marplays, Senior and Junior, evidently representing Colley and Theophilus Cibber, with whom Fielding waged an extended literary warfare. Their stupid comments on Luckless's play, their nonsensical revisions, their utter ignorance, their failure to bring new plays on the stage, all are mercilessly ridiculed. When the younger Marplay complains that his own writings so far have fared ill, his father offers a sympathetic explanation. "That is, because thou hast a little mistaken the Method of Writing. The Art of Writing, Boy, is the Art of stealing old Plays, by changing the Name of the Play, and new ones by changing the Name of the Author."' The last statement finds remarkable verification in the plays discussed in the preceding three chapters. Elsewhere in *The Author's Farce* Colley is satirized as Mr. Keyber and as the Goddess of Nonsense's agent—"Mr. What-d'ye-call-him, the Gentleman that writes Odes—So finely!"[8]

Equally acid is the representation of Bookweight's establishment, comparable to Edmund Curll's or to the one described in *Humphrey Clinker*, where scribbling hacks—Scarecrow, Dash, Quibble, and Blotpage—are hired to plagiarize and "translate." A prospective addition to the literary factory admits that he knows no language but his own and that he translated Virgil out of Dryden. "Lay by your Hat, Sir," exclaims Bookweight, "lay by your Hat, and take your Seat immediately. Not qualified! Thou art as well vers'd in thy Trade as if thou hadst labour'd in my Garret these ten Years."[9]

In *The Pleasures of the Town*—the play within the play—the satire becomes wholesale. Nothing escapes, nor is anyone spared: the professions, especially the law; the popular dramatic forms—Italian opera, pantomime; and various and sundry individuals—Cibber, Orator Henley, "Count" Heidegger (as Count Ugly), Sir John Gonson (as Sir John Bindover), Mrs. Haywood (as Mrs. Novel), etc. Even the ending presents ridicule of the idiotic "discoveries" of contemporary drama, as Luckless is found eventually to be King of Bantam and his fiancée to be Henrietta, Princess of Old Brentford. The amazing characters in the puppet-show include, in addition, the Goddess of Nonsense, Some-body, No-body, Parson Murder-text, Punch, and many others. As a unifying element throughout the play, Fielding presents a sincere love affair between the indigent poet and Harriot, his landlady's daughter, who would sooner starve with a man she loves than ride in a coach and six with him she hates. Add to this incomparable mélange of realism and extravaganza the ballad airs in Fielding's vigorous satirical verse, several dances, and an epilogue spoken by four poets and a woman representing a cat—and you have *The Author's Farce*.

To achieve the proper comic and satirical effects *The Author's Farce* needed an excellent cast; this it was fortunate enough to secure in the enlarged version of 1734, which came out at Drury Lane. Genest gives the cast for the night of January 19, from which it appears that Kitty Clive played the romantic heroine, Harriot, in *The Author's Farce* and Mrs. Novel in *The Pleasures of the Town*. Macklin had first attracted notice in another of Fielding's plays, *The Coffee-House Politician*, in which he played two small parts. In *The Author's Farce* he was cast for the role of Marplay Junior, the caricature of Theophilus Cibber, whereas the elder Marplay was interpreted by Stoppelear, another capable comedian and a favorite actor in ballad opera. According to the printed play, Mr. Seedo, who composed the overture for *The Pleasures of the Town*, appeared on the stage in person at the beginning of Act III.

A realistic and satirical little farce in one act which Fielding brought out at Drury Lane in January of 1732 proved considerably more popular than the preceding piece. Baker reports in 1764 that it was then regularly presented near the time of the drawing of the state lotteries.[10] In *The Lottery,* as it was entitled, we have the exposure of an alley-broker and his fellow sharpers in London, with effective ridicule of the popular passion for gambling on numbers. We may remember that the theme recurs in *The Footman,* performed in March of the same year at Goodman's Fields, where a lottery ticket brings the plot to a satisfactory termination. In Fielding's play the situation is simple but original. Chloe, fresh and ingenuous from the country, comes to town to escape the solicitations of Lovemore. Her declared fortune of ten thousand pounds —consisting only of a lottery ticket, however, in which she has implicit faith—establishes her credit in London and leads to a marriage with the adventurer Jack Stocks. Jack is more than glad to relinquish her to Lovemore when her ticket comes out a blank and he learns the unsubstantial nature of her fortune.

Until her final disillusionment, Chloe, played by Catherine Raftor, is very much taken with the ways of the city. She learns rapidly. Milliners, mantua-makers, dancing-masters, and fiddlers emerge in procession from her door, arousing the worst fears of Lovemore about her virtue. She asks her maid Jenny about her new appearance. "Eh! does not the nasty red Colour go down out of my Face? Han't I a good deal of pale Quality in me?"[11] Fielding excels in this pleasant type of satire, arising from the naiveté of the character speaking. A more direct shaft is illustrated in Stocks's explanation of the Charitable Corporation—something of a scandal of the time: "That is, Madam, a Method, invented, by some very wise Men, by which the rich may be charitable to the Poor, and be Money in Pocket by it."[12] The Guildhall scene showing the drawing of the lottery tickets combines satire with good fun, with the ingenious device of proclaiming the winning and losing numbers in songs.

Fielding's familiarity with French drama is revealed sometimes in isolated passages. For example, Jack Stocks's remarkable speech to Chloe is a perfect illustration of the type of *fleurette* found a hundred times in Gherardi's *Théâtre-italien* and elsewhere. "I shall never forgive my self being guilty of so great an Error; and unless the Breath of my Submission can blow up the Redundancy of your Good-nature, till it raise the Wind of Compassion, I shall never be able to get into the Harbour of Quiet."[13]

As usual, Fielding's songs, as also his prologue and epilogue, have more than their share of vigorous wit. Ten of the twenty-two airs[14] were set by Mr. Seedo. The prologue, "spoke by Mr. Cibber, Jun.," defines the province of farce and offers other interesting dramatic criticism. For the original Drury Lane production a capable cast was headed by Catherine Raftor. Stoppelear took the part of Lovemore, and Theophilus Cibber that of Jack Stocks. The elder Stocks, the alley-broker, was played by Harper. The Mrs. Stocks of Mrs. Wetherilt and the Jenny of Miss Williams complete the roster of the important female characters.

In *The Grub-Street Opera* Fielding had already attempted spirited political satire. Politics enter also, in part, in *Don Quixote in England,* a three-act ballad opera played at the Haymarket in April, 1734. This was an operatization of a comedy begun by Fielding at Leyden in 1728 for his private amusement, as he tells us in the preface, and now revised for Drury Lane. After the mutinous players under Theophilus Cibber had deserted Drury Lane in 1733, Fielding attempted to assist the loyal actors by providing them with plays. *Don Quixote in England,* one of the pieces designed for them, was put in rehearsal at Drury Lane. When the new manager, Fleetwood, ended the theatrical mutiny, however, Fielding's opera was put aside in favor of the pantomimic *Cupid and Psyche. Don Quixote in England* eventually came out at the Haymarket, in April, with the assistance of some of the actors from Drury Lane. For the occasion Fielding added three satirical political scenes and dedicated the printed play to the Earl of Chesterfield, whom he calls "the most favourite Offspring of the *British* Muses." This interesting dedication includes a plea for the freedom of the stage and of the press, as well as a denunciation of political corruption. As Wilbur L. Cross points out, the author was here offering his services to the Opposition, or the Country Party, as it preferred to be called.[15]

The famous Knight de la Mancha is skilfully presented with

Sancho at a country inn, which he mistakes as usual for a castle and from which he sets out on several wild adventures, including the overturning of a stage-coach. The bewilderment of the country people at his strange actions and his talk of kings and queens lead them to surmise he represents the Court interest and to nominate him for Parliament. For all of his delusions the Don, as in Cervantes, has flashes of lucid sanity in which he proves the world to be much madder than himself. A few farcical scenes result from the impersonation of Dulcinea by the maid Jezebel and a particularly hilarious episode occurs when Don Quixote, about to fight a duel with Squire Badger, peremptorily refuses when he learns his opponent is a mere squire—a rank he considers far beneath his notice. The unwilling Sancho is requested to fight the duel instead. Into such scenes of farce and burlesque Fielding dovetails a love plot between the runaway Dorothea and Fairlove, carried out with a good deal of engaging sentiment. The play suffers from the fact that the various episodes are rather loosely strung together, but it manages to hold the interest—at least, in the reading. *Don Quixote in England* did not prove as popular on the stage as most of Fielding's other operas, although Arne found occasion to use it in 1772 as the basis of his burletta, *Squire Badger*.[16]

In the drunken boor, Squire Badger, we have satire of the country gentry and a prototype of the more famous Squire Western. In the words of Sancho, "Sir, your true *English* Squire and his Hounds are inseparable as your *Spanish* and his *Toledo*. He eats with his Hounds, drinks with his Hounds, and lies with his Hounds; your true Errant *English* Squire is but the first Dog-Boy in his House."[17] Badger was played by Macklin, who joined the Haymarket company during the summer of 1734 and who showed particular skill in the acting of low-comedy roles. The introduction, ending with the customary request of the manager for the overture, has amusing satire of the conventional prologues of the time. The political elections with their attendant bribery are more severely ridiculed and we find likewise a denunciation of lawyers and the law. On the positive side, Fielding gives utterance to occasional patriotic and democratic sentiments.

Among the songs is one version of "The Roast Beef of Old England" to the tune of "The King's Old Courtier," an earlier wording having appeared in *The Grub-Street Opera*. It was not unusual for Fielding, by the way, to press his songs into double service, although he usually made some improvements in their second appearance. Another well known lyric was set to the air "There was a Jovial Beggar."

> The dusky Night rides down the Sky
> And ushers in the Morn;
> The Hounds all join in glorious Cry,
> The Huntsman winds his Horn:
> And a Hunting we will go.
>
> The Wife around her Husband throws
> Her Arms, and begs his Stay;
> My Dear, it rains, and hails, and snows,
> You will not hunt to-day.
> But a Hunting we will go.
>
> A brushing Fox in yonder Wood
> Secure to find we seek;
> For why, I carry'd sound and good,
> A Cartload there last Week.
> And a Hunting we will go.
>
> Away he goes, he flies the Rout,
> Their Steeds all spur and switch;
> Some are thrown in, and some thrown out,
> And some thrown in the Ditch:
> But a Hunting we will go.
>
> At length his Strength to Faintness worn,
> Poor Renard ceases Flight;
> Then hungry, homeward we return,
> To feast away the Night:
> Then a Drinking we will go.[18]

An Old Man Taught Wisdom, or The Virgin Unmask'd, usually known by its second title, appeared at Drury Lane early in 1735 and proved immediately popular, over two hundred and fifty performances being recorded by Nicoll up to 1750. It is a one-act farce with twenty ballad songs.[19] The satire reveals primarily Fielding's scorn of fools and knaves as represented by a series of types—the Oxonian pedant, the apothecary, the dancing master, etc. In Lucy— like Chloe, a sentimental variant of the Miss Prue character— female foibles are ridiculed, but in a perfectly good-humored way, as when she offers her reason for preferring Mr. Thomas, my Lord Bounce's footman: "His Head is so prettily drest, done all down upon the top with Sugar, like a frosted Cake, with three little Curls on each side, that you may see his Ears as plain!"[20] In the final analysis, however, Lucy shows much good sense in scorning her unworthy suitors and marrying Thomas, the footman. Being a woman, albeit sixteen, she is not as ingenuous as her father believes.

Goodwill, who wishes to dispose of his fortune of ten thousand pounds to his daughter's husband, has some resemblance to Squire Allworthy in *Tom Jones:* his intentions are good, but his goodness prevents him from seeing life as it really is. The other characters, the suitors, are drawn in broad caricature—a fact which leads Baker to say in 1764 that they are *outré* to the greatest degree but that the laughable portions of the play somehow have managed to this day to please the *Canaille.*[21]

After the first performance of the piece one of the characters and several passages were omitted from representation. The original cast at Drury Lane included Mrs. Clive as Lucy. The minor part of Wormwood, a lawyer, was played by Macklin.

The Virgin Unmask'd was unusual in having a sequel, which, in defiance of tradition, proved better than the original. This new play about Lucy and Mr. Thomas—now Squire Thomas—did not come out until 1742,[22] at a time when Fielding, silenced by the Licensing Act of 1737, was turning once more to the theatre. As it was, *Miss Lucy in Town* ran afoul of the Lord Chamberlain and was suppressed for a while, presumably on the objection of a lord who thought himself satirized in the unflattering character of Lord Bawble. As Cross points out, there was disapproval also of the part of Mrs. Haycock, a "take-off" on the notorious procuress Mrs. Haywood, which was acted with lifelike faithfulness by Mrs. Macklin.[23] When the play reopened the next season, Mrs. Haycock had become Mrs. Midnight. Satire of a personal nature appeared also—as

Horace Walpole tells us—in the singing of Mrs. Clive and Beard, whose interpretations of Lucy and Signior Cantileno mimicked two singers of the Italian opera, the Muscovita and Amorevoli, to the great delight of the audience.[24]

Fielding's favorite device of bringing country personages to town enabled him to indulge in the customary satire of the ways of London. Tawdry does not recommend the Tower, the Abbey, or the Lions to the young wife, but more fashionable pleasures—"O yes, Madam; there are Ridottos, Masquerades, Court, Plays, and a thousand others, so many, that a fine Lady has never time to be at home, but when she is asleep."[25] And in answer to Lucy's inquiry about what ladies do at plays, Tawdry explains, "Why, if they can, they take a Stage-Box where they let the Footman sit the two first Acts, to shew his Livery; then they come in to shew themselves, spread their Fans upon the Spikes, make Curt'sies to their Acquaintance, and then talk and laugh as loud as they are able."[26] Under such instructions Lucy's head is soon turned, and she receives willingly the addresses of Lord Bawble and of Zorobabel, a rich Jew from Exchange Alley. Her country simplicity does not prevent her from asking and accepting valuable presents. Before any permanent harm is done, however, Mrs. Haycock is exposed as a bawd and Lucy rescued by her husband, allowing Fielding to express a few noble and patriotic sentiments. "How, my Lord, resign my Wife!" exclaims the former footman. "Fortune, which made me an *Englishman,* preserved me from being a Slave. I have as good a Right to the Little I claim, as the proudest Peer hath to his great Possessions; and whilst I am able, I will defend it."[27] In one of the last speeches of the play, Goodwill subscribes to a highly democratic doctrine, quite worthy of Robert Burns: "Henceforth, I will know no Degree, no difference between Men, but what the Standards of Honour and Virtue create: The noblest Birth without these is but splendid Infamy; and a Footman with these Qualities, is a Man of Honour."[28]

There are only eight songs, including the rival airs by Mr. Ballad and Signior Cantileno for the favor of the lady. The Englishman, of course, wins, having thus apostrophized his Italian opponent:

Be gone thou Shame of human Race,
　　The noble Roman Soil's Disgrace;
Nor vainly with a Briton dare
　　Attempt to win a British Fair.

For manly Charms the British Dame
　　Shall feel a fiercer nobler Flame;
To manly Numbers lend her Ear,
　　And scorn the soft enervate Air.[20]

Lucy, as in *The Virgin Unmask'd,* was played by Mrs. Clive, with Neal as her footman-husband in the present play. In the part of Mr. Zorobabel, Macklin—the Wormwood of the earlier opera—had an opportunity of representing a more modern Jew than his customary Shylock. Perhaps this portrait too, like that of Lord Bawble, had an element of personal satire. Cross acted Lord Bawble. Beard and Lowe appeared as the rival singers, Cantileno and Ballad. As has been said, Mrs. Macklin played the pious bawd Mrs. Haycock, with Mrs. Bennet as Tawdry, one of her satellites.

In the last act of *The Author's Farce* we have already observed Fielding's tendency to fall into burlesque with farcical and extravaganza effects, a tendency shared, of course, by other writers of the period. Johnson's *Hurlothrumbo,* Carey's *Chrononhotonthologos,* and Fielding's own *Tom Thumb,* all proved exceedingly popular. The last play, while not particularly adapted to ballad-operatization, did become a temptation in that direction to some of the Grub-Streeters. Fielding had written under the name of Scriblerus Secundus. On January 1, 1731, *The Battle of the Poets, or The Contention of the Laurel,* introduced in the second act of *Tom Thumb,* came out at the Haymarket, written according to the title-page by Scriblerus Tertius, usually, but perhaps inaccurately, identified with Thomas Cooke, of *Dunciad* fame. The three songs of *The Battle of the Poets* may scarcely entitle it to the designation of ballad opera, but the form is there in embryo as the airs are set to specified tunes. The brief burlesque, roughly satirizing some of the important poets of the time, is occasionally amusing and not lacking in interest. King Arthur has ordered epithalamiums to celebrate the wedding of Tom Thumb and Huncamunca, but the death of the laureate—with reference, of course, to that of Eusden—makes it necessary to determine his successor. Colley Cibber, the new laureate in real life, was mercilessly satirized as Fopling Fribble. Another of the contestants in the farce, Coment [sic] Profound, who declares, "I write Plays and Operas with the utmost Expedition; and I can't blow my Nose, but out flies an Entertainment," was obviously intended for Lewis Theobald. Fribble and Profound were acted by Woodward and Lacy, respectively. The other aspiring laureates include Sulky Bathos, Noctifer, and Flaile, in whom the anonymous author was satirizing John Dennis, James Ralph, and Stephen Duck.[30]

Another operatic version of the same original, this time by William Hatchett and Eliza Haywood, appeared in 1733 under the title of *The Opera of Operas, or Tom Thumb the Great* with music in parody of Italian opera. The thirty-three songs were set twice the same year, by Arne for the Haymarket and by Lampe for Drury Lane. The nature of the music, naturally, rules the piece out of the ballad-opera class. It is an amusing burlesque, couched in the common form of the "rehearsal," with Sir Crit-Operatical exclaiming at the conclusion, "Wondrous, astonishing Plot! more sudden than the Reprieve in the Beggar's Opera—a Transformation exceeding all Transformation . . ."[31] With regard to staging it may be of some interest to note that the diminutive hero of the opera was played by a child, Master Kilbourn. Some of the other players are familiar to us from the ballad-opera repertoire—Stoppelear as King Arthur and Kitty Clive as Queen Dollalolla. A man, Mr. Topham, acted the giantess Glumdalca.

John Frederick Lampe, the composer of one of the versions, had a hand in later parody of Italian music, notably in the two operas by Carey, *The Dragon of Wantley* (Covent Garden, 1737) and its sequel, *Margery* (Covent Garden, 1738), the former enjoying great popularity. Such pieces deserve mention because it must be remembered that other types of musical entertainment were existing side by side with ballad opera, employing in lieu of the simpler ballad airs a music that was satirically grand, artificial, and pompous.

Before considering the "rehearsals," we return to some of the other burlesque operas, which have no connection with Fielding. Nicoll lists a piece entitled *Hudibras, or Trulla's Triumph* which came out at Lincoln's Inn Fields for a single performance in March, 1730, but which was not published. One may surmise on the basis of the names of the title that it had some relation or other to a burlesque piece, *Hudibrasso,* not a ballad opera, that was published in an obscene pamphlet having the title of *A Voyage to Lethe by Captain Samuel Cock* (1741). *Hudibrasso,* like other plays of the time, offers an involved allegory in which Italian opera with other dramatic forms of the period is personified to emphasize the degeneracy of British taste.

Distinguished by little besides its incoherence is a burlesque opera by Tony Aston, *The Fool's Opera,* apparently merely a parody of Gay's play. According to the title-page of the work, dated 1731, it was performed at Oxford. The eleven pages include some dialogue and a total of seventeen songs, the latter often repeating or paraphrasing the words of several of Gay's lyrics. The entire sketch, for it is little more than that, seems to offer a jumbled reflection of *The Beggar's Opera,* distorted and refracted almost beyond recognition. The Poet, played by Tony Aston, stirs the jealousy of the Lady (Mrs. Motteux) and of the Maid (Mrs. Smith). Later the Poet, like Macheath, is arrested but here also comes a reprieve— after he has sung a medley of songs, as did the valiant Captain in Newgate. Only one other character appears, a Fool, played by Aston's son, probably the Walter Aston who wrote a ballad opera in 1732, *The Restauration of King Charles II, or The Life and Death of Oliver Cromwell.*[32] Various allusions to Gay and his opera appear in Tony's play. In an introductory note, the author disclaims any intention of representing particular persons although he says he has been accused of meaning by his Fool *"such a Great Person"* (perhaps a hit at Walpole), etc. "They are all mistaken—" he continues, " 'tis Fiction this; *Fools, Poets, Idle-headed Ladies,* and *Amorous Chambermaids* are NATIONAL."[33]

Tony's wit is usually as obscure as it is labored. Perhaps with the aid of his buffoonery, however, it may have been acceptable on the stage. The printed play gives the author as Mat. Medley, and the piece may very well have been one of the miscellaneous items in the noted "Medley" that Aston played throughout England. Its only real importance lies in the appended sketch of the author's life, which mentions some of his itinerary in the New World and throws some faint light upon the early American drama. The volume includes also a frontispiece representing all four actors of the opera and an appended "Ballad, Call'd, a Dissertation on the Beggar's Opera" in eight inconsequential stanzas. *The Fool's Opera*, whatever its historical importance, remains a wretched piece of work, entirely devoid of merit.[34]

The depth of dramatic incoherence has not been plumbed until one has examined an undated ballad opera called *The Ragged Uproar, or The Oxford Roratory*, "a new Dramatic Satire; in *many* Scenes, and one very long Act" with a dedication "To the Dignify'd Informer."[35] Various personages appear—a justice, a lawyer, a tailor, a thief, constables, witches, fortune-tellers—all in an incredible and ill-printed jumble. The piece may have had some basis in local history at Oxford or some political import, but whatever allusions may be present seem undecipherable and unworthy of second thought. We may call it a burlesque, but it is perhaps an unintentional one.

An interesting group of ballad operas derived their form and inspiration from that perennial favorite of the age, the Duke of Buckingham's *Rehearsal*, written in 1671 to ridicule Dryden and the heroic plays. The original work offered, in actuality, a dramatic criticism that was truly dramatic since it presented simultaneously on the stage both text and comment. Frequent revivals of Buckingham's burlesque appeared throughout the eighteenth century, sometimes with alterations and topical allusions, as in the performance by Colley Cibber that so enraged Pope. Traditionally the form employed burlesque effects with the usual admixture of personal or literary satire.

A play within the play, but with no particular satirical intent, had been employed by Gay in 1715 in his farce *The What D'ye Call It*. For that matter, *The Beggar's Opera* itself consists somewhat of a rehearsal in view of the introductory scene between the

Beggar and the Player and their brief discussion at the end, a procedure followed with modifications by many of Gay's imitators. The last act of *The Author's Farce,* as we have seen, presented a puppet-show within the framework of the main action. The first of the ballad operas, however, to adopt fully the "rehearsal" form in the manner of the Duke of Buckingham was *Bays's Opera* by Gabriel Odingsells, writer of three plays and eventually a suicide, becoming—as the *Biographia Dramatica* tersely has it—lunatic. The piece was offered three times at Drury Lane in 1730 and once in 1731, with very mediocre success, as the author himself explains in a preface. The performance, he writes, was interrupted the first night and thereafter so amputated as to break the chain of the allegory, with the inevitable result of obscurity and unintelligibility. Odingsells goes on to defend himself against various insinuations or attacks, asserting that the character of General Briton, who loves a wench and a bottle, is entirely fictitious and was given the title "General" merely to carry out the allegory. The author's explanation leads us to wonder whether some contemporary personage thought himself designated. There was apparently, also, an accusation of plagiarism (possibly by Ralph, Fielding, or the anonymous author of *Hudibras*), to which Odingsells replies that his play was written a year before the date of the alleged theft and was known to many gentlemen. Finally, the introduction disclaims any intent to expose the celebrated author of *The Beggar's Opera.*

While *Bays's Opera* has many interesting features, it was obviously far too involved in its "allegory" to prove successful on the stage. As a result, in spite of the desperate efforts of Bays to explain the design to his two female companions, Arabella and Belinda, one cannot blame the Drury Lane audience for being confused. The scene is England, a battleground for contending forms of dramatic entertainment. Cantato—by whom is meant Italian opera—has usurped the empire of wit and imprisoned Tragedo, the lawful heir, who in turn falls in love with Dulceda, Cantato's daughter. In the opposite camp are Pantomime, pretender to the throne of wit; Harlequin, his chief minister; and Crispin, a cobbler, his most devoted supporter. With the aid of the debauched General

Briton and the defection from Cantato's ranks of Bassoon and Crowdero, Cantato and his daughter—now married to Tragedo as a symbol of·the allegorical sympathy between music and dramatic poetry—are defeated and captured. It is their further disgrace to be left to the mercies of Crispin, the cobbler, who has been declared absolute Judge over all Works of Wit—so great has been the depreciation of true taste in England. So runs the main design, although the "allegory" as presented in the play is much longer and more intricate.

Obviously an action of this kind fails to enlist human interest in spite of some good scenes of drunkenness and seduction between General Briton and Farcia (i.e., farce), the daughter of Pantomime. On the other hand, Odingsells appears to be a capable writer with adequate command of prose, and the symbolism, if complicated, is at least sound and logical. For this reason the student of literature will find *Bays's Opera* rather interesting reading. The author follows the usual practice of clearing the stage at the end of his acts— a necessary procedure in the days before the curtain was dropped at the close of each act. We find, therefore, that the impecunious Bays escorts his two charming guests to the Green Room for a dish of chocolate and incidentally to conclude the first act. His device on the second occasion is more ingenious. Belinda suddenly feels faint. "My Chocolate, I think, lies too heavy on my Stomach," she exclaims, and the gallant poet, believing it may be a love qualm, hastily supports her and leads her outside.

Two pantomimes are presented on the stage by the victorious forces. In addition to such spectacular effects, Odingsells has thirty-five songs in the three acts. Some of the actors are of sufficient importance to be mentioned. The long list of *dramatis personae* records Theophilus Cibber as Bays, accompanied to the rehearsal by Mrs. Butler and Mrs. Shireburn as the two ladies. The usurper Cantato was played by Mrs. Roberts. Miss Raftor, as Cantato's daughter, marries the neglected Tragedo, played by Mr. Charke. The triple alliance of Pantomime, Harlequin, and Crispin was acted, respectively, by Berry, Miller, and Harper. Bridgwater played Lord Briton, the General who aroused the criticism of the audience by his loose behavior in the play, with Mrs. Heron—Letitia Pilkington's *bête noire*—as his mistress, Farcia.

Of greater interest and dramatic merit is a three-act ballad opera by James Ralph, friend of Benjamin Franklin and of Fielding, the Noctifer of the *Battle of the Poets* and one of the victims of Pope in the *Dunciad. Bays's Opera* appeared at Drury Lane on March 30, the same day that witnessed the opening of Fielding's *Author's Farce* at the Haymarket. Ralph's play, *The Fashionable Lady, or Harlequin's Opera,* came almost immediately after at Goodman's Fields, on April 2, and enjoyed a considerably longer run than its rival by Odingsells. With three plays appearing almost simultaneously—not to mention the unpublished *Hudibras* at Lincoln's Inn Fields—all dealing with the same general theme, no wonder there followed such charges of plagiarism as were made in Odingsells's introduction.

The Fashionable Lady renews the assault upon the polite varieties of entertainment, using also the "rehearsal" form, but Ralph did not commit the error of making his characters mere allegorical abstractions. At best, however, "rehearsals" prove disjointed and cumbersome and the present play is far from an exception—it is too long, the action drags, it is talky. Nevertheless such defects do not prevent us from enjoying excellent dialogue and a veritable dissertation on the pleasures and manners of the time. The persons at the rehearsal are four. Mr. Ballad heartily approves of ballad operas and pantomime—"There is more Wit in a fiery Dragon," he maintains, "than in all the Plays in Europe."[36] He wants particularly to laugh: "I love your loud Horse-Laugh most exceedingly. I always distinguish my self at the Play-house by my Laugh."[37] His guests, Modely and Meanwell, however, are more fashionable and prefer Italian to English opera. As for the author in the play, Mr. Drama, he has been forced against his better judgment to include much pantomime and many songs—sixty-eight in fact—within his opus.

In the rehearsal proper we find Mrs. Fashion, an arrant coquette, beleaguered by a multitude of suitors including the infatuated Merit, the fashionable Smooth, and the boisterous Captain

Hackum—a loud and picturesque tar whose language is a delight.
"Blood and Thunder!" he exclaims in a fit of jealousy. "Favours!
who dares dream of Favours? I'll Keel-haul the Dog. I'll put him
in the Bilboes for a whole Voyage. I'll hang him up at the Yard-
Arm."[38] Two of Mrs. Fashion's other admirers belabor one another
and in so doing beautifully characterize for us two of the common
types of the day, the Humorist and the Virtuoso:

TRIFLE: —But you are a downright Humorist, a Son of the Spleen, a
Regarder of Winds, a Prophesier of ill Weather, a Dealer in
Omens, the very Image of Caprice, and almost a Lunatick.

. . . . .

WHIM: Why, what a Devil! do I live to be insulted by a Dealer in
Counters, a Warehouse-keeper of Fragments, a Destroyer of
Insects, a Worshipper of Graven Images, a meer Book-worm.
The Caterpillar of Science—[39]

The main characters are all taken on a visit to Harlequin, the
Dumb Conjurer, where they are regaled with silly and spectacular
antics. It is here, finally, that Merit is disillusioned about Mrs.
Fashion. After a long struggle between passion and reason he falls
into the willing arms of the witty and sensible Mrs. Sprightly. Mrs.
Fashion's other suitors desert her one by one until she is reduced
to marry Harlequin—but only after the author has indulged in
lively burlesque of pantomime.

In an ironical essay in the *Grub-street Journal* poor Ralph is
much ridiculed for his predilection for similes, in which the play
abounds. In her description of Mrs. Fashion, for example, Sprightly
says: "Besides, her Brain is as empty as a Harpsichord, and her
Heart as various as its Musick; her Conversation is trifling as an
Opera, and her Passions a Medley like an Entertainment."[40] The
overuse of such sentences would naturally leave the author vulner-
able to literary attack. But Ralph's style is nevertheless vivid and
picturesque, in the songs as well as in the prose. Kipling was obviously not the first to make certain observations about the Colonel's
lady and Judy O'Grady:

The Lady, with Diamonds and Laces,
By Day may heighten her Charms;

> But Joan, without any such Graces,
>   At Night lies as warm in your Arms.
> The Night, when her Sables o'ershade ye,
>   Will veil all the Pomp of the Day;
> Then Joan is as good as my Lady,
>   And Cats are all equally grey.[41]

Air XXXIII is interesting for its mockery and its opportunities for action and mimicry on the stage. Mrs. Sprightly sings it at the entrance of Smooth, the man of fashion:

> For Wit, the fawning Coxcomb cries,
>   Look you, fair Lady, beautiful Lady!
> Dancing Step, and courtly Air,
>   Look you, my Lady fair!
>
> How sweet my Voice! genteel my Bow!
>   How soft my Ogle now!
> He speaks, he bows, he rolls his Eyes,
>   In Sighs the Lady dies.[42]

The companionship at this time between Fielding and Ralph seems to have had results in the similarity of their themes and spirit. Both authors were satirizing the same things, often in the same way. Both for their pains were ridiculed in the *Grub-street Journal*. Fielding's wit was sharper and less wordy. Ralph's contributions, however, must not be considered negligible. Indebtedness of other writers to him seems evident from a review of *The Touchstone, or ... Essays on the Reigning Diversions of the Town* (1728), which was reissued in 1731 as *The Taste of the Town, or A Guide to All Publick Diversions*, attributed to Ralph through the pseudonym A: Primcock. The similarity in subject to the ballad operas we have just been considering should, of course, be noted. In one chapter of the book, written in mockery of Italian opera, the author suggests a number of native themes that might deserve operatic treatment. One is the "noted combat betwixt Moor of Moor-hall, and the Dragon of Wantcliff,"[43] upon which he expatiates considerably and which may have given Carey the hint for his *Dragon of Wantley*. Another suggestion, that *"Tom Thumb* would be a beautiful Foundation to build a pretty little Pastoral on,"[44] seems to have been seized upon by Fielding himself. For that matter, a line from *The Fashionable Lady*[45] may possibly have proved an inspiration to the anonymous author of *The Footman*, if indeed this opera did not come from the pen of Ralph himself, whose style and wit it resembles. While such literary influences are difficult to prove, they are not for that reason non-existent.[46]

Fielding's *Author's Farce* has already been mentioned as employing the device of the play within the play. A better example of the "rehearsal" form by the same author appears in *Tumble-Down Dick, or Phaeton in the Suds*, produced in 1736 by Fielding's own Great Mogul Company of Comedians at the Haymarket. The full title of the piece, consisting of no less than seventy-seven words, offers in itslf a satirical onslaught upon pantomimes and "entertainments." It ends as follows: "Being ('tis hop'd) the last Entertainment that will ever be exhibited on any Stage. Invented by the Ingenious MONSIEUR *SANS ESPRIT*. The Musick compos'd by the Harmonious SIGNIOR *WARBLERINI*. And the Scenes painted by the Prodigious MYNHEER *VAN BOTTOM-FLAT*." This is a perfect parody of the title-page of the current entertainment, *The Fall of Phaeton*, which was "Invented by Mr. Pritchard. Musick compos'd by Mr. Arne. And the Scenes painted by Mr. Hayman." Fielding's remarkable title is followed by an ironical dedication to Rich as "Mr. John Lun, Vulgarly call'd Esquire," with pointed satirical reference to Rich's popularization of the entertainment form.

Wilbur L. Cross in *The History of Henry Fielding* indicates the genesis of *Tumble-Down Dick*.[47] John Rich, attacked in *Pasquin* and aggrieved at the success of that piece, produced a satire upon it at Covent Garden on March 10, *Marforio*, which, however, lasted only one night. In *Tumble-Down Dick*, presented on April 29 as afterpiece to *Pasquin*—likewise a "rehearsal"—Fielding effectively killed two theatrical birds with one stone, revenging himself on Rich and at the same time burlesquing *The Fall of Phaeton*, the entertainment at Drury Lane, in which Rich is said to have had a hand.[48]

Not to be outdone by his model, Fielding begins his piece with a delightful parodied "Argument." There follow, at intervals, amusing scenes between Prompter, Fustian, Sneerwell, and Machine—the author—in satire of the nonsensical rehearsal displayed before them. When Fustian, for instance, protests that he would have thought it "more natural for the Gods to have talk'd in Heroicks, and the Cobler and his Wife in Prose," Machine explains, "You think it would have been more natural, so do I, and for that very Reason have avoided it; for the chief Beauty of an Entertainment, Sir, is to be unnatural."⁴⁹ The entertainment proper has the usual division into "Serious" and "Comick," with the wholesale degradation—common on the French stage— of heroes and gods into low-life characters, so that Clymene becomes an Oyster-Wench and Apollo the leader of the watchmen in the Roundhouse. The settings include, among others, a cobbler's stall, King's Coffee House, and the "open country," where the Goddess of the Earth and a dancing-master join in dancing the White Joke. A supreme touch of extravaganza is offered in the character of the Genius of Gin, who is pictured rising out of a tub. Various satirical allusions that might escape the casual reader are carefully noted by Wilbur L. Cross.⁵⁰ Phaeton's mother—played by none other than Mrs. Charke—is called Clymĕne in contradistinction to the inaccurate Clymēne of Drury Lane, where Kitty Clive was interpreting the corresponding part. In the passages dealing with Harlequin we find allusion to Rich's reputation for plagiarism and to his inability to read. Thus, while *Tumble-Down Dick* cannot fail to amuse, it will entertain doubly if one reads between the lines. The final scene shows the two playhouses—Drury Lane and Covent Garden—side by side on the stage with the actors and managers closing the play by singing in praise of Harlequin.

Only five ballad songs appear in the play, some of them illustrating general satire in the manner of Gay, as when Mrs. Charke sings:

> Great Courtiers Palaces contain,
>   Poor Courtiers fear a Gaol;
> Great Parsons riot in Champaign,
>   Poor Parsons sot in Ale;
> Great Whores in Coaches gang,

> Smaller Misses,
> For their Kisses,
> Are in Bridewell bang'd;
> Whilst in Vogue
> Lives the Great Rogue,
> Small Rogues are by Dozens hang'd.[51]

The printed copy of Pritchard's *Fall of Phaeton*—the victim of Fielding's burlesque—is immediately followed, with no break in pagination, by *The Songs in Harlequin Restor'd, or Taste Alamode*, a series of eight ballad songs with incidental stage directions. The scene shows Harlequin's tomb with several players representing Comedy and Tragedy ranged on each side in mournful posture, the curtain rising to the tune of "Margaret's Ghost." Before long, a conjurer resurrects Harlequin, to the great joy of the actors. Then follow the songs, the last one being an address to Men of Taste. The final stanza runs as follows:

> Here with Wit and Spirits flowing,
> Only Guineas five bestowing,
> You with Ortolans in Plenty,
> Have a Dinner may content ye;
> Cares removing,
> Joy improving,
> Don't delay, Sir,
> I can't stay, Sir,
> Shew your self a Man of Taste,
> Shew your self, &c.[52]

This strange piece in praise of Harlequin, a mixture of pantomime and ballad opera, may have been one of Rich's answers to Fielding's attacks.

Before dismissing entirely the English warfare of the Phaetons, it is worth noting that a similar contest had long occupied the stage in France with numerous burlesques of Quinault's serious opera, *Phaéton*. Gherardi's *Arlequin Phaéton* begins the series of parodies in 1683. It was followed in 1692 by J. Palaprat's *Arlequin Phaéton*, a three-act piece with songs presented by the Théâtre-Italien.[53] Two unpublished burlesques are recorded, one in 1691 and one in 1721. After a revival of Quinault's opera in 1730 two more parodies appeared, including one by Carolet under the title of *Le Cocher maladroit* (1731), set in the "halles" with Phaéton as the son of a Parisian coach-driver. It is not unlikely that Pritchard or Fielding may have derived some suggestions from these many plays, some of which were published.[54]

In April, 1737, another "rehearsal"—this time a "Maiden-Farce" —reached the London stage. Written by a Gentleman of the Inner Temple, identified as Robert Baker, the piece has the rather cumbersome title of *A Rehearsal of a New Ballad-Opera Burlesqu'd, Call'd The Mad-House: After the Manner of Pasquin*. Its dedication to Lady Elibank expresses an ingratiating and sanguine hope of patronage:

> Extend thy Hand, fair Lady; be to me
> A Queensborough [*sic*], for I'll be a *Gay* to thee.

The opera that follows combines oddly a variety of themes—attacks on Harlequin and entertainments, a plot of intrigue, and an exposure of conditions in "Mad-Houses." The last, declares the writer, is a subject of satire never touched upon before in the dramatic way. Scenes in a madhouse, of course, had appeared much earlier in Middleton's *The Changeling*, but with a different intent. Baker explains his interest in the subject as follows:

The only Ideas that are to be collected from visiting Houses of Confinement, are the Wretchedness of the Wards merely, or perhaps the Severity of the Keepers; but the manifold Injuries and Impositions that have crowded themselves in, are only to be learnt by conversing with miserable Wretches under Confinement, who are not to be credited truly, because they are reputed Lunaticks.[55]

In the rehearsal, Lucy—as the result of her intrigue with a lieutenant—is placed by her father in the establishment of Hyppo, a fortune-teller now turned mad-doctor, who promises to restore her with bleeding, a proper regimen, and the discipline of his house. Later the madhouse itself is represented on the stage with the patients chained down in their respective cells. Baker's indignation, however, is mainly directed at improper incarceration of patients by greedy relatives. In a scene in the manner of Peachum, Hyppo is shown in a nightcap going over his papers. He calls to his servant, Whipcord.

Here, *Tom,* bring me the list of Lunaticks for the Year—36 (Whipcord *gives him the list.* Hyppo *reads.)—Peter Longitude* the Mathematician, the 26th Day of *January* last.—*Cent. per Cent.* the Pawnbroker's Wife, ditto.—*February* the 28th, *Tobias Feesimple,* of *Feesimple-Hall;* Esq;— ay he's in for Life, his Heirs are the punctuallest Men in the World, and pay every Quarter-day precisely;—*Jeremiah Rag,* of *Rag-Fair,* put in at the Suit of his Wife, *April* the third; he goes out To-night; that Whore of a Wife of his is so backward in her Payments, that 'tis impossible he can be mad any longer! why, the Slut pays me worse than her Stallion;— therefore, d'ye hear, *Whipcord, Rag* is come to his Senses, for his Wife has lost all Sense of Payment;—therefore enlarge *Jeremiah Rag.*[56]

The love-plot, naturally, runs to a satisfactory conclusion with the customary help of the chambermaid. Of greater interest, how-ever, are the scenes between the spectators of the rehearsal— Friendly, Satyre, and Crambo—where we find some discussion of contemporary drama. Theophilus Cibber is soundly ridiculed as the strutting Pistol, with an allusion in passing to the Cibber-Clive controversy over the acting of Polly. Baker has no kind words for the entertainments and flying machines at Covent Garden. Nor is he at all well disposed toward Farinelli, whom he ridicules by in-troducing a ballad-singer on the stage with a basket of songs, crying,

A Ballad, a Ballad, a new Playhouse Ballad—call'd *Farinelli pos'd;* or *the Bagpiper Triumphant.* Set to the Tune of, *He pull'd out his Farra-diddle.*

The interesting stage direction, "Curtain draws up again, and discovers a Mad-house,"[57] suggests what was no doubt the usual practice of lowering the curtain after certain scenes of the rehearsal to permit the other actors—the critics or the spectators—to in-dulge in comments or discussion regarding what they have wit-nessed. While the performance of *The Mad-House* at Lincoln's Inn Fields on April 22, 1737, is duly mentioned by Genest, neither he nor the printed play gives the members of the cast. The eighteen songs include one lyric set by the author and one of rather classical hue when placed in the company of "The Twitcher" or "Lumps of Pudding," the air being "Ille prae Amore demens."

It is regrettable that the Gentleman from the Inner Temple was not a more expert playwright. He obviously tried to combine too many conflicting elements. The play suffers further from being too long and overly confused, with startling lack of motivation. But Baker should be remembered for having employed the more or less original topic of insane asylums with unusual social consciousness for an eighteenth-century individual, and a lawyer at that.

Little satire but much patriotism pervades the next operatic "rehearsal," Edward Phillips's *Britons, Strike Home, or The Sailor's Rehearsal*, played at Drury Lane on December 31, 1739, and the next year at Bartholomew Fair. As Genest says, it is "full of claptraps."[58] Lieutenant Meanwell, acted by Macklin, offers for the benefit of his friends a "little piece of Drollery" rehearsed on board the St. Joseph, a ship captured from the Spaniards. The Drollery proper shows a group of British tars taken prisoner in the West Indies, although the captain protests that Spain has no authority to board, search, and plunder ships carrying no contraband. The "true Hearts of Oak"—as they are called in a song—are released by the Spaniards, but the ship is confiscated. Later, the conquerors are themselves captured on board the *St. Joseph* but treated far more generously. The "fable," thus, is slight but developed rather agreeably. The entire piece serves as a protest against Robert Walpole's pacific foreign policy regarding Spain, and as such is not without interest. The martial title *Britons, Strike Home* is itself the name of a ballad air. While no tunes are indicated for the other seven songs, Mr. William Barclay Squire has identified most of them as ballad airs.[59] Kitty Clive appeared in the lieutenant's entertainment as Donna Americana, probably the very first of the Miss Americas!

A final "rehearsal," although not a ballad opera, deserves mention for its authorship. In 1750 the Drury Lane company performed *The Rehearsal, or Bays in Petticoats*, a play by none other than the esteemed Mrs. Clive, the vivacious high priestess of ballad opera. Her acting career covers the entire span of the genre—with an extra decade or so for good measure—from her first important role as Phillida in Cibber's play to her last appearance, in 1769, as

Winifred in *The School for Rakes*. Scarcely a ballad opera could appear at Drury Lane during this long and interesting period without the inevitable presence of Kitty—acting, dancing, and singing with her customary *élan*. Nell, Polly, Rosinda, Chloe, Lucy, she played them all and many others to the universal applause of her contemporaries. Her original roles in ballad opera amount to almost thirty, and of course she played in numerous revivals as well, and in musical pieces other than ballad operas. It seems perfectly reasonable to assume that many ballad plays were written with Kitty in mind for the leading musical character. We have some small evidence for this. The parts assigned to her were sometimes given the significant name of "Miss Kitty," and in *The Intriguing Chambermaid*, as we have seen, Fielding altered an originally masculine role in order to present Catherine as the chambermaid.

Her play, *The Rehearsal, or Bays in Petticoats*, may not rank as a masterpiece of dramatic art but it does manage to be witty, airy, and attractive. A few songs, "written by a Gentleman," were set by Dr. Boyce and sung by Beard, Miss Thomas, and Kitty herself. The treatment is chatty and personal, with Mrs. Hazard—played by the author—represented as writing a play and rehearsing it under difficulties with the aid of Cross, prompter at Drury Lane, and others. Mild satire is directed at Covent Garden, at actors and actresses, and at Italian song. Nor is malice entirely lacking, as when Mrs. Hazard is asked to define the meaning of "burletta": ". . . Why then, let me die if I can tell you, but I believe it's a kind of poor Relation to an Opera." Best of all, Mrs. Clive does not take herself too seriously. What other "Virgin-Authoress"[60] would have shown Witling, one of the spectators, falling asleep at the end of a duet in the rehearsal of her supposed play? Of course, Witling has good reason for his slumber, as he has been witnessing a pastoral with recitative and song. Despite its slightness, *Bays in Petticoats* supports Henry Carey's excellent characterization of the authoress in his poem, *The Beau's Lamentation for the Loss of Farinelli:*

> There's Beard, and there's Salway, and smart Kitty Clive,
> The pleasantest, merriest mortal alive.[61]

And with this brief tribute to Kitty we may end the chapter.

CHAPTER NINE

Topical Operas: Social Scandal and Politics

THE SATIRICAL and realistic tendencies of ballad opera naturally could not fail to bring it in close *rapport* with the life and events of the reign of George II. It is this very contemporaneousness, in fact, which acounts largely for the evanescent and transitory character of the form. Often the ballad pieces were hastily composed to capitalize on topics of current interest, to dramatize—so to speak —the pages of the *Daily Courant* or the *Grub-street Journal,* to add their shrill voices to the political clamor against Walpole or to shriek out the discomfiture of the latest prude. Not only are they comparable in this way to the multitudinous pamphlets of the century, but often they are themselves pamphlets, couched in dramatic form it is true, but with no intent whatever of appearing on the stage. As soon as interest in any given news began to cool, the entire mushroom growth of pamphlets and operas alike perished, to be resurrected only by the inquisitive antiquarian.

Many of the plays considered so far have had topical interest— the satires of Fielding, for example, or the *Harlot's Progress* operas. It remains for us to review a small number of *pièces de circonstance* on various topics, and then to examine other operas, acted or unacted, which deal more specifically with social scandal or with politics.

A lurid story from France, the trial in 1731 of Father Girard, Rector of the college of Jesuits at Toulon, for the seduction of a Miss Cadière, whose confessor he had been for several years, formed the basis of two ballad operas and a non-musical play by Fielding. The Jesuit father was brought to justice on serious charges, "for seducing her by the abominable Doctrine of Quietism, into the most criminal Excesses of Lewdness"; the process against him—according to the *Gentleman's Magazine*—"charging him with Inchantment, Rape, Spiritual Incest, Abortion and Subornation of Witnesses; and with seducing of six other Penitents.'" Since the end of the trial found the judges equally divided, twelve in favor of burning at the stake and twelve for acquittal, the defendant was freed in accordance with French law, but not without tremendous expense on the part of the Jesuits and considerable loss of prestige for their order.

It is obvious that, apart from the sensational aspects of the case, Father Girard's amatory adventures would appeal in England to the strong popular feeling against Catholicism and at the same time would carry on the tradition of such plays as Dryden's *Spanish Friar* and Cibber's *Non-Juror*. A ballad opera, the anonymous *The Wanton Jesuit, or Innocence Seduced* was published under the date of 1731, purporting to be a translation of a French play which had enjoyed—so claims the preface—a run of thirty nights at a private theatre in France. The title-page indicates performance of the English play at the Haymarket, but the only representation recorded by Nicoll came on March 17, 1732. Since publication of *The Wanton Jesuit* is not announced in the *Grub-street Journal* until March 23, 1732, the date of 1731 on the title-page is perhaps inaccurate. The opera, in any event, gives a literal and sometimes incoherent account of the entire Cadière episode, with an understandable attempt to blacken almost beyond reality the already dark character of Father Girard. The doctrine of Quietism with its implications of passivity earns much ridicule in connection with Miss Cadière's seduction. The subject allows, in addition, plenty of opportunity for bawdy songs, whose effect was no doubt accentuated by their having been set appropriately to the same tunes as some of the more indecent songs in D'Urfey's *Pills,* such as "A Lovely Lass to a Friar Came" and "The Old Woman Sent to the Miller her Daughter." Association between the present songs and the originals would be likely to occur in the mind of the reader or listener. With unexpected flippancy, in view of the supposedly serious attack on the Jesuits, the epilogue inquires of the audience whether they would not willingly supply Father Girard's place.

The other ballad play, unpublished but dealing obviously with the same circumstances, has the unusual title of *Father Girard the Sorcerer, or The Amours of Harlequin and Miss Cadiere.* While

Nicoll lists the play as a ballad opera, the title suggests that it may have included some pantomime. It came out at Goodman's Fields in February, 1732, for a dozen performances. Fielding's play, *The Old Debauchees,* appeared likewise in 1732, with much freer handling of the material than we find in *The Wanton Jesuit* but without benefit of song.

W. J. Lawrence mentions an Irish topical piece, *Johnny Bow-wow, or The Wicked Gravedigger,* played at Smock Alley in 1732 for Layfield's benefit.[2] It seems to have been concerned with a ghoul of the graveyards who had stolen corpses for the use of medical students and had been put in jail for his pains. He was subsequently transported—to America presumably, though Lawrence does not specify. While it may have proved amusing, it was obviously a slight and ephemeral ballad farce.

A considerably more interesting opera, *The Oxford Act,* was published in 1733 "As it was Perform'd by a Company of Students at Oxford." Whether actually played there or not, it made bold to represent on the stage the Vice-Chancellor of the University, the Proctor, the Terræ-Filius, several fellows and scholars, and four Oxford-Toasts, of whom more anon. The university was supposed by statute to hold a "Publick Act" every year, but the practice had fallen into disuse, becoming reserved for special occasions at intervals usually of ten or twelve years. In the spring of 1733 a Public Act was decided upon and held at Oxford in July to celebrate the approaching nuptials of the Princess Royal and the Prince of Orange, and incidentally to show the loyalty of Oxford to the royal family—perhaps a political gesture, because Oxford had been notoriously addicted to treason and Jacobitism. According to custom, a Terræ-Filius was appointed to make a formal address satirizing the university authorities but apparently was not permitted to deliver his attack.[3] From the *Grub-street Journal* we learn that two oratorios and one serenata by Handel were to be performed as part of the ceremonies of the Public Act—"Athalia," "Deborah," and "Acis and Galatea"—and that the music eventually proved so popular that it brought away two thousand guineas.[4] In the meantime, the alleged speech of Terræ-Filius came out in London and was followed immediately by the Oxford-Toast's answer to it, an amusing if indecent pamphlet.

To return to the opera, we find in *The Oxford Act* a spirited attack on the entire affair on the ground that it has brought financial disaster to all concerned—the students, the fellows, and the Oxford-Toasts—with the sad result that Flippant, one of the Toasts, offers to sell her old pair of stays so that she and Thoughtless may proceed to London. The anonymous writer shows particular bitterness toward Handel and "his crew," the only ones to gain anything by the Act. "In the next Place," complains Thoughtless, "there's the Furniture of my Room procur'd for me some Tickets to hear that bewitching Musick, that cursed *Handel*, with his confounded *Oratorio's*."[5] Even the fellows voice similar complaints. Nevertheless the students and the Toasts raise enough money to enjoy a rousing drinking scene at New Inn and then decide to apply for free passage to the new colony of Georgia, which was at this time being formed, where they may increase and multiply, and teach the Indian ladies how to dress and patch "Alamode de Paris."

For an answer to the justifiable query of just what was an Oxford-Toast, one must turn to an entertaining satirical book, *Terræ-Filius, or The Secret History of the University of Oxford* (1726), by Nicholas Amhurst, who was himself expelled from the university. Amhurst, it should be remembered, became one of the guiding spirits of the *Craftsman*, the violent Opposition paper. Here is how Nicholas defines the Oxford-Toast, an eighteenth-century version of the fraternity lass of the present day:

She is born, as the *King* says, of *mean estate*, being the daughter of some insolent *mechanick*, who fancies himself a *gentleman;* and resolves to keep up his *family* by marrying his girl to a *parson* or a *schoolmaster:* to which end, *he* and his *wife* call her *pretty Miss*, as soon as she knows what it means, and send her to the *dancing-school* to learn to hold up her head, and turn out her toes: she is taught, from a child, not to play with any of the dirty boys and girls in the neighbourhood; but to mind her own *dancing*, and have a great respect for the *gown*. This foundation being laid, she goes on fast enough of herself, without any farther assistance, except a *hoop*, a *gay suit of cloaths*, and *two* or *three* new *holland smocks*. Thus equipt, she frequents all the *balls* and *publick walks* in *Oxford;* where it is a great chance if she does not, in *time*, meet with some raw coxcomb or other, who is her *humble servant;* waits upon her home; calls upon her again the next day; dangles after her from place to place; and is at last, with some art and management, drawn in to *marry* her.[6]

While the Public Act and the literature about it were diverting the town, a series of events much nearer home focussed popular interest on the purlieus of Drury Lane, where a theatrical mutiny had taken place under the leadership of Theophilus Cibber. The players had become dissatisfied with the management of John Highmore, who had secured control of Drury Lane with the retirement of the elder Cibber, leaving the aggrieved Theophilus shorn of much of his former power as acting manager. The disaffected players proceeded to give performances at the Haymarket in spite of the efforts of the patentees, Rich and Highmore, to stop them by legal means. It will be remembered that Mrs. Clive had remained faithful to the interests of Highmore, for which she received high praise from Fielding in the dedication to *The Intriguing Chambermaid.*

A topical skit on the players' revolt was not long in appearing. *The Stage-Mutineers, or A Play-House to Be Lett* came out at Covent Garden in August, 1733, written "by a Gentleman late of Trinity-College, Cambridge," who may safely be identified with Edward Phillips.[7] This clever ballad piece was blessed with a witty prologue, a few lines of which run as follows:

> *He sings no* Fable, *but Domestick Jars,*
> *Heroic Dudgeons, and Theatric* Wars:
> *Wars without* Armies, Battles *without* Blood,
> *For* Seas *of* Pasteboard, *and for* Realms *of* Wood.

Two managers appear on the stage. The mutinous actors and actresses, led by Pistol, as usual representing Theophilus Cibber, engage in much ranting and fustian verse with a superb display of theatrical jealousy and temperament. The managers eventually win an empty victory and the players are reduced to consider the formation of a strolling company. The Gentleman from Cambridge maintains the mock-heroic tone sucessfully throughout. In a scene with Mrs. Haughty, Truncheon—the "heavy" actor—finds that he has played parts of Honour so long that he feels bound by habit to observe it. Truncheon is later appointed general of the rebellious forces only to discover that Pistol expects to be general over him. In costume and "make-up" the various characters were no doubt intended to mimic individual players of the revolting faction. The songs are amusing, particularly the one by the Prompter, who expresses his uncertainty concerning which side to take. He decides to "close with them that win." All things considered, *The Stage-Mutineers* must have proved an entertaining and spirited piece.

Another theatrical war reached the stage in 1736 on the occasion of the quarrel between Kitty Clive and Mrs. Cibber—the former Miss Arne and Theophilus' second wife—over the part of Polly in *The Beggar's Opera*. *The Beggar's Pantomime, or The Contending Columbines*, as the piece was called, is briefer and less coherent than *The Stage-Mutineers*, with no dialogue except in the songs and long stretches of pantomime. Here again the treatment is mock-heroic, though it tends to fall into burlesque. Theophilus Cibber earns ridicule once more as Pistol, both for his bombastic acting and for his championship of his wife's claims to Polly by writing letters to the newspapers. To settle the dispute the Ghost of Gay is made to rise and give a judgment in favor of Kitty Clive, the "Fierce Amazonian Dame." There are satirical thrusts at Rich and others, but in a preface the author—presumably Woodward[8]—cautiously denies any attempt to affront the two ladies involved in the quarrel.

The play made its appearance at Lincoln's Inn Fields with a total of thirteen songs.[9] The rivals were interpreted by Mrs. Roberts as Polly (Kitty Clive) and Mrs. Hamilton as the Pretender to the part (Mrs. Cibber). Mrs. Charke took one of the male parts, that of the Deputy-Manager. Lun Junior played Harlequin Macheath, with Lyon rising and sinking as the Ghost of Gay.

All was fish that came to the Grub-Streeters' net, including subjects of topical interest quite remote from theatrical quarrels or politics. The knowledge of medicine and surgery in the eighteenth century remained still too rudimentary to prevent the rise and success of various quacks whose skill or ignorance could not be determined by any positive methods. James's famous powders have left their traces in the literature as well as in the graveyards of the period. Much noise began to make itself heard in the 1730s concerning a certain Dr. Joshua Ward whose single medicine in the form of a pill or a drop was dispensed impartially to all comers, regardless of age, sex, or condition, as a specific for all maladies. The pages of the *Grub-street Journal*—which disapproved of Dr. Pill and Drop, as he was often called—are strewn with the records of death and destruction caused by this infallible cure-all. Some witnesses, on the other hand, sing only the praises of Dr. Ward and attest to marvelous recoveries. The records agree in only one particular, namely the violence of the pill or the drop, as the case might be. Dr. Ward himself managed to survive many of his patients, dying in 1761 with liberal bequests to his appreciative family. Contemporary analysis of his medicine showed that it was largely composed of antimony.

In January, 1735, John Kelly, a member of the Middle Temple and translator of French comedies, wrote a short ballad opera called *The Plot,* which deals in part with the learned doctor. While the piece seems a little obscure in purpose, it appears to be mainly a puff of Dr. Pill and Drop, which leads us to assume either that Kelly was remunerated for his services or that he had managed to survive the pill. Briefly, the opera shows a group of disappointed doctors and undertakers who, in desperation at the loss of their business, make an unsuccessful attempt on Dr. Ward's life. One of their professional objections to the doctor is that he cures like a poacher without sufficient attention to the niceties of the game. Coupled strangely with this sinister topic is an attack on visiting French players, who are roundly denounced for taking money out of English pockets. Very properly the author himself, in an epilogue, calls the play a "Hodge-Podge." A large cast, including such well-known players as Macklin, Harper, and Mrs. Charke, interpreted Kelly's piece at Drury Lane.

If the *Grub-street Journal* waged merciless warfare on Dr. Ward, it made some slight compensation by printing favorable notices of Dr. Taylor, an oculist, whose "progresses" throughout England and Wales are reported (ironically perhaps) at frequent intervals. A far

from roseate opinion of the famous oculist, however, was brought
out in *The Operator: A Ballad Opera,* an unacted piece published
in 1740. Whether the portrait is accurate or not, the play is rather
well written with a certain passionate vindictiveness, inspired it
would seem by hatred rather than mere satire. Dr. Hurry is exposed
as an ignorant and unscrupulous scoundrel, robbing both patients
and tradespeople of their money, performing operations that
lead to the blindness of his victims, seducing girls on his various
"progresses," and consorting with prostitutes, whom he insults by
offering a mere ten pence each. The remarkable thing about the
whole performance is that it should seem at all convincing. Yet the
hall where the patients are waiting with cloths over their eyes, for
example, gives an impression of actual observation. The "progresses" so highly puffed in the newspapers are here presented in a
different light. In the words of one of the characters to Dr.
Fallopius:

Why, *Hurry* first set out to cure bad Eyes, equipp'd with the Science of
a Farrier, and, I believe, no more; so that Woe was to them, that first fell
under his Operations. His Way was to sound his own Fame in Paragraphs
in the Home-News; juggle at one Town, and pass on to another, and another, before News of his Pranks could reach that he was at.[10]

From this and other passages far less flattering, one is left to conjecture whether the play arose from professional jealousy or personal grudge. While it is definitely called a ballad opera, no tunes
for the ten songs are indicated in the text.

Several years earlier a more pleasant occasion for topical writing
had presented itself—the nuptials, in 1736, of Frederick, Prince of
Wales, with Princess Augusta of Saxe-Gotha. One panegyric ballad
opera, published but never performed, was written by a gentleman
of the university of Oxford to commemorate the event. Unlike most
performances of this nature, *The Royal Marriage* is attractively
and capably written. The three acts follow the procedure—so common with Fielding, Vanbrugh, and other writers of the century—
of bringing a country squire to town with his naive daughter. They
come, of course, to attend the royal wedding. Sir Joseph Wronghead, the Devonshire rustic, does not relinquish his country man-

ners. At the banquet held at Lord Clincher's, he insists upon putting on his hat as he is accustomed to do in his own parlor, and, not satisfied with the size of the glass of brandy tendered him, he calls for a larger one. Confronted with a choice of delicacies at the inn, he finally decides upon Devonshire beer and cheese. Viewing the Prince and Princess in state proves an expensive experience to Sir Joseph, for after the ceremonies he is "bubbled" out of a vast sum of money by a prostitute posing as the Duchess Dowager of Dive-in. He escapes from this amorous interlude to find his hoydenish daughter in a bagnio with Lord Clincher's son, and under threat of death forces the unwilling gallant to marry the girl. Whereupon a group of shepherds and shepherdesses enter the room for a dance and a two-page epithalamium!

It will be admitted that the anonymous author from Oxford has ingeniously combined the genteel and the realistic. The title-page says the piece was performed by a private company of gentlemen near St. James's, but we cannot give too much credence to this assertion. Except for one, the tunes for the twenty songs are not specified in the play.

For a topical opera of 1740 it is necessary to refer again to W. J. Lawrence, who records the performance at Aungier Street, Dublin, of *The Queen of Spain, or Farinelli at Madrid,* with James Worsdale playing the part of the Queen of Spain.[11] The opera was attributed to Worsdale, but in view of Mrs. Pilkington's charges of "ghosting" perhaps some reservations should be made concerning his authorship. The great Farinelli had been invited to Madrid by the Queen of Spain in an effort to cure the King's melancholia, an unusual undertaking in which the singer proved successful. This episode in Farinelli's life seems to have provoked Jemmy's farcical opera.

The interpretation of the topical operas so far has not been difficult because of the open references to the personages and events in the newspapers. A more intricate problem arises in connection with the numerous plays that deal with politics or with scandal in high places. The cautious journalists tread softly over the frailties of lords and ladies on the rare occasions when they do not completely ignore the scandal. Often they were not themselves possessed of the necessary information. Rather must we turn for enlightenment to the secret histories and the verse or prose pamphlets that came out in such profusion. But in these as well as in the ballad operas the names are highly fictitious and the allusions veiled almost beyond recognition. Sometimes reference to Hervey's *Memoirs* or to Horace Walpole's *Letters* and *Reminiscences* will throw a sudden light on an obscure episode, but only occasionally, and the sudden inferences that the scholar is tempted to make may as readily prove wrong as right. Perhaps a more charitable point of view is that expressed by Baker in his brief notice of *The Wanton Countess, or Ten Thousand Pounds for a Pregnancy,* when he states that it was

written for the Propagation of some Tale of Private Scandal in the Court Annals of that Time; but what that was, is neither my Business to enquire, nor my Inclination to perpetuate.[12]

Where the allusions are at all possible of explanation, the present chapter will succumb to a morbid curiosity so nobly scorned by Baker, but frequently the inquiry will prove fruitless. Since it is difficult to disentangle the scandal from the politics, the two types of operas will be considered together.

Undoubtedly many of the following pieces were motivated by a bitter partisanship or by a mere love for indecency. Except for Fielding's *Grub-Street Opera,* which has been included here because of its political angle, and a play ascribed, with more irony than truth, to Mrs. Manley, the operas were all anonymous. They are marked generally by a prurient cynicism and a disillusioned bitterness. Most were never intended for the stage—they are pamphlets pure and simple, strangely garbed in dramatic form with songs not designed to be sung in the theatres though they may have figured as street ballads. In technique the plays consist usually of a series of brief scenes developing half a dozen intrigues at the same time but with the situations only suggested or half expressed. Often the ending is inconclusive and the purpose veiled. The excellence of some of the writing, however, leads us to wonder who the anonymous writers were. Along with the hacks and the Grub-Streeters, is it not possible that some of the noble authors—the Herveys, the Pulteneys, and the Chesterfields—tried their hand at the *Beggar's*

Opera form? Since Hervey included two dramatic sketches in his *Memoirs,* Chesterfield composed biting epigrams, and all the political figures wrote pamphlets, the supposition is more than half plausible. The Prince of Wales himself is said to have written a play with the aid of Hervey and to have had it submitted anonymously to the theatres.[13] Such noble authors at least would know the inside stories of politics and intrigue, but they are, unfortunately, safe from identification behind their masks of anonymity.

From whosever pen it was, *Calista,* an opera of 1731, capitalizes on a scandal of the time, the criminal conversation between Lady Catherine Abergavenny and Richard Lyddel, Esq., which was discovered and brought into the law courts by the lady's husband. What particularly amused the town was that Lady Abergavenny gave birth to a child less than one month after the detection of the affair, but had the discretion or good fortune to die in so doing. Immediately she became the subject of various satirical poems and pamphlets under the name of Calista, with allusion to the heroine of Nicholas Rowe's tragedy. Our ballad opera retails her plight and her demise, and includes in addition the amours of the Countess de Ulto with Count Hermio and Melanthus successively, entered upon with the casual knowledge of her mother, the Princess del Carmel, who tells the aggrieved husband that until a woman has run through a score of intrigues she isn't worth the attention of a lackey. More easily identifiable than the last few characters are the Scotch Colonel Francisco, obviously our old friend Colonel Francis Charteris, and the sly Beau Nation, possibly Beau Nash, who brawl through a series of bawdy and riotous adventures. Despite some vivid characterization, the play remains confused and mediocre. In a dedication to the Duchess of Queensberry, perhaps an ironical one, the author says:

But tho' the Beauty of this *Opera* has been faded for want of a Representation, yet it will soon recover its Colour, if your Grace shall please to countenance it.

The three acts have thirty-nine songs, many of them indecent.

In coming to Fielding's *The Welsh Opera, or The Grey Mare the Better Horse,* also of 1731, we tread upon firmer ground. The title, as noted by Schultz,[14] shows indebtedness to an ironical comment in the *Grub-street Journal* on the news of the performance of *The Highland Fair*, a Sotch opera: "*A Welsh Opera may be proper to succeed this.*" The resulting *Welsh Opera* in two acts came out at the little theatre in the Haymarket for occasional performances in April, May, and June. Fielding then revised and lengthened the play into three acts and in satirical answer to the *Grub-street Journal*, which had been attacking him, renamed it *The Grub-Street Opera*, though it was not allowed to go on the stage by the authorities—as he relates in the preface to the printed edition of *The Welsh Opera*. In its full-length version it seems to have appeared eventually in July. *The Grub-Street Opera*, rather than its shorter predecessor, will be considered for the present discussion.

To those uninitiated in the ways of eighteenth-century satire the political interpretation of plays may seem a trifle fanciful, and in details it may be—as a matter of fact—inaccurate, but to anyone who has traversed the history, pamphlets, and memoirs of the period the general pattern remains unmistakable. As Professor Cross effectively brings out in his biography of Fielding, a perfectly innocent exterior may conceal a well organized satirical thesis, perfectly patent to a contemporary audience. With the aid of Cross, Hervey, and others we may trace many of the allusions and innuendos in Fielding's play. A hit at Bavius and Maevius of the *Grub-street Journal* occurs in the acted introduction, where the entire wit of Grub Street is said to consist of the two words, "You lie." Scriblerus, the author, goes on to explain that a plot has been omitted in the piece that follows but that the design is very deep. "It is a sort of family Opera, the husband's *vade-mecum;* and is very necessary for all married men to have in their houses." The Welsh family of Squire ap Shinken represents clearly the royal ménage of Great Britain, whose serio-comic adventures are best revealed in Hervey's *Memoirs*. The henpecked Squire himself, whose only pleasure lies in smoking his pipe undisturbed, represents George II. It was well known at the time that Robert Walpole owed his real power in the government to the support and influence of Queen Caroline, who is here delightfully ridiculed as Madam ap

Shinken. Frequent allusions are made to her governing the household, to her dabbling in Latin and divinity, to her parsimony (which
leads Susan, the cook, to sing "The Roast Beef of Old England" as
a tribute to the departed English hospitality), to her entente with
Walpole. Sir Robert receives the brunt of the satire as the dishonest
butler, Robin—"There's cheating in his very name. — Robin, is as
much as to say, robbing."[15] William, the coachman, accuses the
butler of stealing spoons, of "making master brew more beer than
he needed, and then giving it away to your own family; especially
to feed the great swoln belly of that fat-gutted brother of yours—
who gets drunk twice a-day at master's expence"[16]—an obvious
thrust at Walpole's much-ridiculed brother, Horace. The waiting-
woman Sweetissa, with whom Robin is in love and who has "kept
her virtue so scrupulously," clearly represents Maria Skerrett, Walpole's mistress since 1728, whom he married ten years later on the
death of his wife. One of Sweetissa's songs, barbed with satire, begins as follows:

> Why should not I love Robin?
> And why should not Bob love me?
> While ev'ry one else he is fobbing,
> He still may be honest to me.[17]

Regarding her, William later declares, "Your mistress—any man
may have your mistress that can out-bid you; for it is very well
known, you never had a mistress without paying for her."[18] This
accusation comes notwithstanding the dialogue where the lovers
declare their passion in mock-romantic vein:

> ROB. Mine is as deep as the knowledge of physicians.
> SWEET. Mine as the projects of statesmen.
> ROB. Mine as the virtue of whores.
> SWEET. Mine as the honesty of lawyers.
> ROB. Mine as the piety of priests.
> SWEET. Mine as—I know not what.
> ROB. Mine as—as—as—I'gad I don't know what.[19]

William, the coachman, who wishes to displace Robin and become butler himself, is evidently meant for William Pulteney, and
the quarrel between the two men refers to the political break

between them. Pulteney—with the aid of Carteret, Bolingbroke, Wyndham, and others—soon became the mainstay of the Opposition. In the booby son, Master Owen ap Shinken, who is chasing the maids of the household—as he was doing in real life—we have reference to Frederick, Prince of Wales. "The Griff" was soon to break with his parents and add his considerable strength to the Opposition. In John, the groom and Robin's friend, we have probably a portrait of John Hervey, and it is not unlikely that his delivery of the challenge to William makes allusion to the duel between the two statesmen. To follow the parallel in the given names, Thomas may well represent the Duke of Newcastle. Near the end of the play Robin delivers a kind of "theme-song" for the entire performance, not calculated to please the censors:

> In this little family plainly we find
> A little epitome of human-kind,
> Where down from the beggar, up to the great man,
> Each gentleman cheats you no more than he can.
> Sing tantarara, rogues all.[20]

This interesting play, which Genest rather maligns as "a moderate opera," has sixty-five songs,[21] including a few that Fielding employed in other pieces as well. The earlier *Welsh Opera* included only thirty airs.[22]

We now turn again to affairs of the heart, scandalous tales of gallantry and adultery written large in the amorous annals of the time. Not that the spirit of romance hovers over the pages of three unacted ballad operas of 1732. On the contrary, the treatment is cynical, prurient, and ribald, motivated by derisive laughter—with an added suspicion of political coloring. It would be vain to attempt untangling all the threads in this amorous history, but a few main strands are clearly indicated in the journals and memoirs and may not fall below the dignity of our present study. The main story of scandal had reference to Frederick, who had been recalled from Hanover to become Prince of Wales. In 1730 he formed an intimacy with John, Lord Hervey, writer of the *Memoirs*, which lasted for a year or two until they became bitterly estranged. Among the maids

of honor to Queen Caroline—young ladies who proved readily sus-
ceptible to amorous intrigues—was a Miss Vane, who had been
mistress of Hervey and (it was said) of Harrington as well. She
subsequently fell into the arms of Frederick, who maintained her
handsomely after she was obliged to resign her place at court. In
1732 she gave birth to a son, Fitz-Frederick Vane, who lived only
to 1736, a few months before Miss Vane herself died. The boy was
openly accepted as son of Frederick, in spite of the private suggestion of the Prince of Orange to Hervey that it was probably the
child of a triumvirate. In view of the prominence of the personages
it is not surprising to find the Prince's amour forming the *pièce de
résistance* of numerous poems, pamphlets, and plays.

The best of the ballad operas under discussion was entitled *The
Humours of the Court, or Modern Gallantry*. An amusing preface
declares that a preface is so much the fashion "that a Book looks
as much in a Dishabille without it, as a Lady without Stays." We
must not take the author too seriously when he goes on to deny
satire of particular persons, "Love and a Bottle being the only
Subjects handled in this Piece." The opera presents half a dozen
intrigues—most of them concerned with the court and the maids
of honor—which are run concurrently in a large number of brief
but well-written scenes, scarcely characterized by delicacy. Not all
of the persons are now clearly identifiable. Frederick appears as
Adonis, an amorous young prince, and Miss Vane as Vanessa, a gay
young lady with child by him. Aldemar, a young rover of quality
who was formerly favorite of Vanessa, must indicate either Hervey
or Harrington. The Prince is shown in dalliance with other maids
of honor, who are jealous of his favor to Vanessa. To this and other
intrigues the anonymous author joins the episodes of a law case—
then diverting the town—in which Catherine Weld, a lord's daughter, sued for divorce on the grounds of her husband's insufficiency.
After Mrs. Weld and her husband had been examined by midwives
and surgeons respectively, and after lengthy debate, the learned
judge enjoined the unhappy couple to live together and be happy—
a decision which aroused the mirth of the *Grub-street Journal*. The
characters of the law case, even to the surgeons and midwives, are

brought on the stage in short scenes woven into those of court intrigues. It may thus be gathered that *The Humours of the Court* at least succeeds in revealing an abundance of scandalous history, which in its presentation is frank and forceful, if ribald.

Equally disillusioned concerning the vices of mankind, but not so well written as the preceding, is a play on similar themes— *Vanelia, or The Amours of the Great.* The *Dictionary of National Biography* ascribes the piece to the Reverend James Miller, who almost starved to death on Grub Street for several years and, ironically enough, did die in 1744 just at the time that he received clerical perferment. The opera, whether by Miller or not, tells again the story of Miss Vane, with Vanelia as the heroine and Prince Alexis as her lover. Lord Almirus, the Prince's predecessor in the affections of Vanelia, corresponds to Aldemar in *The Humours of the Court.* A jealous rival of Miss Vane is likewise shown—Flirtilla —who attempts unsuccessfully to destroy Vanelia's credit with the Prince. The play has probably a political slant, for Lord Haughty seems to represent Robert Walpole, with his mistress, Maria Sker- rett—Fielding's Sweetissa—appearing here as Skirressa. The play offers as climax the exposure in bed of Lord Haughty and the prud- ish Skirressa to the merriment of the other characters until all decide that they are in the same boat, so to speak:

> Then since alike in Sin,
>   Let one ne'er gibe another,
> But live like Folks a—kin,
>   As Sister and as Brother,
>   Neighbours all.[23]

Except for its dispensation of scandal *Vanelia* appears rather un- certain in purpose. If any attack was designed, it was probably directed more at the morality of St. James's than specifically at Sir Robert or the Prince of Wales.

The last of the three plays for 1732 is only in part a ballad opera. Inserted within the five-act comedy, *The Intriguing Courtiers, or The Modish Gallants,* is found an interlude, ostensibly by one of the characters, called *The Promis'd Marriage, or The Disappointed*

Lady. This short piece includes nine ballad songs. The play taken as a whole suffers from being tedious and incoherent. Frederick and Miss Vane are inevitably present as Learchus and Vanetta. Among the other characters we find the Count del Ponto and his mistress, Fentonia. The name of the latter and some of the circumstances certainly suggest Lavinia Fenton, the creator of Polly in *The Beggar's Opera*, who had been taken off the stage by the Duke of Bolton. In Lord Whistler, delineated as a coward, a poet, and a former intimate of Vanetta, we have apparently a portrait of Hervey. While here again no definite proof can be adduced for these identifications, they are perfectly in accord with the custom of the times and are reasonably accurate.

The anonymous operas of 1733 turn also to other matters, primarily to a barrage of vitriolic attacks on Walpole and the Excise. One opera, however, that disregards political pamphleteering for the usual dissemination of scandalous history may as well be considered first. *The Wanton Countess, or Ten Thousand Pounds for a Pregnancy* sufficiently outlines in its title the main thesis of the play. Just who is designated by the Countess Woodmore, who is uneasy for want of an heir and does her best to remedy this deficiency, remains obscure. The scene of the opera is laid "abroad," apparently in France. The incidents include the exposure of a lecherous priest and the marriage of a certain Clara, Van Dunder's niece, to Count Wriggle. Without a "key," the opera seems obscure and confused, but like the other plays it was no doubt founded on "true history," recorded with eighteenth-century literalness. The same opera, with some slight changes, reappeared in the same year as *The Fox Unças'd, or Robin's Art of Money-catching*.

Composing his memoirs in the 1730s Lord Hervey declared:

Nor was writing ever in England at a higher pitch, either for learning, strength of diction, or elegance of style, than in this reign. All the good writing, too, was confined to political topics, either of civil, military, or ecclesiastical government, and all the tracts on these subjects printed in pamphlets.[24]

The capable writing described by Hervey had a vital share in the most serious bid for power yet made by the Opposition, the onslaught in 1733 upon Walpole's plan for an excise tax on tobacco and wine. Many of the ablest pens of the kingdom were occupied in writing a multitude of pamphlets, tracts, articles in the *Craftsman*, and what not, to denounce and vilify the "Project" and the "Grand Projector." History has rather vindicated Sir Robert, for the Excise would have lightened the land tax and made of England one vast free port, benefiting many of the classes most clamorous in opposition. But the very word *excise* had been in the past anathema to English ears, and, distorting the facts beyond all recognition, the party writers succeeded in inflaming public indignation to such extraordinary heights that in the midst of shouting mobs, rioting, bonfires, and the burning of Walpole and the Queen in effigy, the Excise had to be postponed and eventually laid to rest.

Numerous ballad operas of 1733 wage political warfare against Excise in a variety of ways. Most of the plays rely upon scurrility and personal abuse, falling readily into indecency. The clearest and fairest attack appears perhaps in *The Honest Electors, or The Courtiers Sent Back With Their Bribes,* published after the defeat of the Excise.[25] The antagonists appear as the noble William Worthy (Pulteney) and the villainous Sir Positive Screenall (Robert Walpole). Bolingbroke is represented as Lord Exile. In view of Bolingbroke's political ambitions and machinations, the song given to Lord Exile in Act I concerning the joys of retirement bears much unintentional humor:

> I in this sweet Retirement find
>   A Joy unknown to Kings,
> For Scepters to a virtuous Mind,
>   Seem vain and empty Things.[26]

Lord Hervey is ridiculed as Lord Challenge, friend to the Prime Minister. The name and one of his lines allude to his duel with Pulteney, while a more personal innuendo occurs in the description of him "at *Hampton-Court* amongst the Ladies, and sometimes with the People of Quality's Children, who all admire my Gold Key." In a scene between several ladies at the tea table, we find another one of the attacks on the administration—the match of the Princess Royal with the deformed Prince of Orange.

I was told . . . by a certain Dutchess [says one of the ladies on the subject of the Princess] that she can't see an *Orange* without changing Colour.[27]

As might be expected under the circumstances, the play totally lacks action. It presents a series of short, disconnected scenes, ending with the celebration of the victory against Excise at the Swan Tavern, with special praise for the Lord Mayor of London and the pious hope that Walpole will be beheaded.

The gist of the attacks on the Prime Minister that occur in the opera may be given here, for they recur in the other plays. It must be admitted in passing that some of the charges had a large portion of truth in them. Robert Walpole is accused: (1) of being conceited and blundering; (2) of defeating an Opposition inquiry into the affairs of the South-Sea Company; (3) of relying upon wholesale bribery and charging the costs to the secret-service funds; (4) of owing his protection to the army and discharging any officers opposed to him; (5) of being cuckolded by his wife and of keeping numerous mistresses; (6) of having a blockhead of a brother; (7) of sacrificing the Princess Royal to a repugnant match. As in several other political operas, a ballad singer is brought on the stage to deliver one of the street songs against Excise while the mobs outside shout the battlecries of "No Excise," "No Standing Army," "Liberty and Property." Adopting a legal phrase from a statute of Queen Elizabeth's reign, the opponents of Excise called themselves *Sturdy Beggars,* a term employed triumphantly in this and other plays of 1733. How far afield the political writers wandered for inflammatory arguments may be found in the dedication of *The Honest Electors* to the city of London with the statement "that your opulent City could never submit to be Frenchified, nor its Inhabitants to wear wooden Shoes."

Other operas do not treat Sir Robert with equal charity. *Rome Excis'd* is interesting in its use of a Roman setting and its presentation of George II on the stage as Augustus Caesar. The King, as in many pamphlets, is characterized as having the welfare of his people at heart but as being misled by Cyrenius, the Prime Minister, the intent of the Opposition being in part to arouse George against the influence of Caroline and Walpole. Sir Robert's brother, Horace Walpole, is ridiculed as Doodle. The usual charge of bribery makes its appearance, particularly in connection with Walpole's private life. Lucinda, obviously a portrait of Molly Skerrett, is shown as enduring the Prime Minister's embraces merely in return for liberal sums of gold. She shows perfect willingness to deceive him with a Roman citizen who is seeking "Petticoat-Int'rest." The play is not badly written, with the usual short scenes in the form of tableaux, and, unlike most of the political operas, it has excellent songs.

Lord Blunder's Confession, or Guilt Makes a Coward, if we may believe the statement on the title-page that it was written by the author of *Vanelia,* came perhaps from the pen of James Miller. Mediocre in style, it unfolds a bitter attack on Walpole with a liberal infusion of what modern psychology calls wish-fulfillment. Poor Sir Robert, as Lord Blunder, not only has been robbed of valuable documents regarding the Spanish affairs but he is later confronted with the supposed ghost of Phillippo, said to have been murdered at the orders of Walpole for knowing too much. At the apparition the Prime Minister grovels, begs for mercy, and swoons! The wives of the Court party are shown properly unfaithful to their husbands, with particularly acid satire of Horace Walpole's wife as "descended from the Dregs of the People, of Foreign Extraction, excessive silly, and ridiculously proud."[28] The author derives great pleasure from mentioning the red paint on her face, running down in streaks. Horace himself is described as the most honest of the Blunders but as an ignorant and ill-bred buffoon. "He grin'd like a Dog in a Halter, and shew'd his depopulated Gums, to the great Diversion of the Company."[29] Maria Skerrett again appears as Skittilla, a professed prude, mistress to Lord Blunder but unfaithful to him. One must admire the endurance of the members of the Opposition, who, not satisfied with the labors of politics, seem to have spent most of their spare time in dalliance with the wives and mistresses of the ministers. Not only are they ardently solicited by the good ladies, but they are frequently rewarded in gold for their services—certainly an inducement for joining the ranks of the Country party.

Among the opponents of Walpole we discover Chesterfield as Lord Sparkle with allusion in the play to his recent dismissal from his employments. Lady Meanwell, a lady of great beauty, represents Anna Maria Gumley, the wife of Pulteney. To the usual charges against Walpole are added his demanding rebates on the large fees paid to his porter for admission and the liberal subsidizing of Dick Dash and James Trimwell, party writers, who spend money profusely on wenches and champagne. The two writers, Osborne of the *London Journal* and Walsingham of the *Free-Briton*, suffered much vilification at the time for their approval of the Excise.

Some of the scenic effects of Shakespearean tragedy appear in *The Sturdy Beggars*, a similar attack on the ministry, dedicated to the Lord Mayor, the aldermen, and the merchants and citizens of London. Walpole, as Sir Simon Wronghead, quails before omens, visions, and portents. The stolen papers about Spain, the easy virtue of the womenfolk, the arguments against Excise, the paid scribblers (Thickhead and Numscull), the burlesque characterization of Horace Walpole and his lady, all are present. While the opera is well written in parts, it is salacious and vituperative at the same time. Included in it is a then-popular street ballad, printed and sold on the streets as a broadside, "The London Merchants Triumphant: Or, Sturdy Beggars Are Brave Fellows"—an attack on the Excise consisting of no less than twenty-three stanzas.

A milder denunciation of the "Grand Project" is amusingly combined with a genteel love affair between Worthy and Celinda in *The Commodity Excis'd, or The Women in an Uproar*, a ballad opera by the fictitious "Timothy Smoke." The piece develops a favorite argument that the Excise would soon be extended to all commodities, thus restricting two of the cherished English liberties —"Tryal by Juries, and the Freedom of their own Houses." Furthermore, the admittance of the thousands of required excisemen to the houses of the citizens—claims the author—would take a heavy toll of seduction and rape on the wives and daughters. Another pseudonymous play, this one by "Mark Freeman," appeared late in 1733 in connection with a Somersetshire election. It was called *The Downfall of Bribery, or The Honest Men of Taunton,* and derived its inspiration from a news item in the *Craftsman.* Resuming the charge of bribery, it reveals in an exciting last scene at the town-hall how the vote stands forty-eight for Trimmer to forty-six for Steadfast until four heroes—impervious to gold— swing the election to the Opposition. What was apparently another hit at the ministers reached the stage of Goodman's Fields on December 31 but never secured publication. The title, *A King and No King, or The Polish Squabble,* indicates another favorite line of attack against Walpole—his foreign policy—with reference to the delicate situation in Poland. On the other hand, the piece—which Nicoll lists among the ballad operas—may have been merely a farce. Of *Wat Tyler, or The State Menders,* also unpublished, which was acted once at Drury Lane in January, we can only guess that it probably had some political coloring.

Several scandal and political operas of 1733 remain yet to be considered, albeit briefly. *The Court Legacy* came out in print as written by the author of *The New Atlantis.* As Mrs. Manley died in 1724, however, her part in the opera may have been spiritual or inspirational rather than actual. *The Court Legacy* incoherently combines four themes: opposition to the Excise; court scandal involving the Prince of Wales and other figures; charges of rape against a man-midwife, Dr. Gregorius; and criticism of the delay in the marriage of the Princess Royal. We find the usual bribery of the party writers, here called Arnold Wronghead and Osborn Blunder. The Princess, called Huncamunca in the present play, forms the main subject of another ballad opera, *The Court Medley, or Marriage by Proxy,* which appeared with small alterations in 1734 under the new title of *The Fortunate Prince, or Marriage at Last.* The impossibility of finding a more favorable consort for Anne impelled the King and the Ministry to enter into negotiations with the Prince of Orange, a deformed homunculus of very little fortune and—if we may believe Hervey—of unspeakably foul breath. The delay of the phlegmatic Dutch authorities, the suggestion that the marriage be held by proxy, and the grave illness of the Prince on his arrival in England, all served to delay the nuptials until March, 1734, to the impatience and criticism of the general public. *The Court Medley* refers ironically to this delay. As Prince Flavius, the prospective bridegroom fares relatively well in the play except for a charge of indolence and parsimony—much better certainly than he did in a poem entitled attractively, *The Disappointed Marriage, or an Hue and Cry after an Outlandish Monster*. Other characters include the Princess as Seraphina, Walpole as Sejanus, and Miss Skerrett as Belinda, the work ending mildly enough in a panegyric of the royal wedding.

A final opera for 1733, *The State Juggler, or Sir Politick Ribband*, seems rather puzzling in its point of view. Its treatment of the political situation is profoundly cynical. Walpole, as Sir Politick Ribband, is attacked, but not too severely. More antipathy falls upon Sir Robert's brother, Chevaliere [*sic*] Wou'd-be, who is exposed as a coward and who is cuckolded by his wife. The strongest picture of villainy, however, occurs in connection with Monsieur San Jean, meant for Bolingbroke, who betrays his professed friend Don Gulimo (Pulteney) by carrying on an intrigue with the latter's wife, Pulcheria. Don Gulimo—if anyone—is the hero of the play. After denouncing the treacherous San Jean, he nobly forgives the errant but repentant Pulcheria. His political motives, on the other hand, appear far from lofty, as he is pictured desirous of displacing Walpole for the mere purpose of securing power himself. In the character Sarina, jealous of the Prime Minister's ascendancy and greedy for gold, we have seemingly a portrait of Sarah, the old Duchess of Marlborough. *The State Juggler* has three acts and a number of ballad songs of varying degree of decency. The author may have been one of the disaffected Whigs, but of one thing at least we may be sure—he was no friend of Bolingbroke.

A clever ballad opera of the next year carries, like *The Grub-Street Opera*, a perfectly innocent mien. Its pastoral name, *The Wedding, or The Country House-Wife*, suggests merely another of the village or country operas, but the date along with the title appears more significant when it is remembered that 1734 saw the long-delayed nuptials of the Princess Royal and the Prince of Orange. The innocuous lines of verse on the title-page which indicate the theme of the opera—

> The various Turns of Matrimonial Strife,
> The Hen-peck'd Husband, and obstrap'lous Wife—

further lead us to the conclusion that the writer is offering another burlesque of the royal household, whose tribulations form the main theme of Hervey's maliciously entertaining *Memoirs*. Nor are we disappointed on examination of the text, for the sly allusions and references are too clear in their general intent to be disregarded. Squeesall, a peevish and wealthy country justice, henpecked by his wife, corresponds clearly to the picture of George II presented in the *Grub-Street Opera*, although it is even less flattering:

Why, his Worship moves like a Figure made in Wax; his Eyes resemble those of a dead Calf, as it hangs dangling over a Butcher's Shoulder. As to his Sense, I am no Judge; I did not hear him speak a single Word; I fancy, he takes Formality and Silence, for the certain Marks of Wisdom.[30]

Even greater satire enters into the portrait of Madam Squeesall, a dominant and miserly lady who is interested in religion but has no use for men of letters. She gives her daughter, Blouzella, about to marry Sir Harry, her own formula for governing her husband—a formula whose cardinal points were to make friends with Squeesall's mistresses and to secure control of the purse strings:

As soon as I heard he had a new female Favourite, I made it my Business, to get acquainted with her, and treated her with the greatest Civility; this singular Behaviour of mine gave your Father very favourable Ideas of me, and never failed to ruin my Rivals; yet, for some Years, the Love of Variety overcame all the Resolutions he had made, to reward my Patience with Fidelity, each new Face prevail'd. 'Tis true, by my prudent Management, their Reign was very short, 'till this Widow with matchless Cunning found the Way to fix him. Thus, Child, you have the true Reason of my pretended Friendship for her; she is rich, and past having Children, so, of Consequence, can do no great Damage to my Family.[31]

Not only does this represent with startling accuracy Queen Caroline's behavior toward George II's mistresses, but the widow of matchless cunning must certainly refer to Mrs. Howard—Lady Suffolk in 1731—whom the King visited with such methodical punctuality each day that Horace Walpole reports his pacing the room, watch in hand, waiting for the exact hour to come, yet unwilling to arrive a moment ahead of schedule. Mrs. Howard's age and deafness, joined to the extreme respectability of her demeanor, bely any passionate attachment on either side, the King merely desiring the prestige of a recognized mistress. When Mrs. Howard eventually married George Berkeley, a close friend of Pulteney, the King wrote to his wife from Hanover: "Je ne voudrois pas faire de tels présens à mes amis; et quand mes ennemis me volent, plut à Dieu que ce soit toujours de cette façon."[32]

In the play, when Blouzella protests that the widow is old and ugly, Madam Squeesall explains, "An ugly Woman, my Dear, is more dangerous than a Beauty,"[33] a suggestion which is amplified in Air XVIII:

> 'Tis not the Bloom of Beauty bright,
>   A Brow, a Cheek, an Eye,
> Can give a Lover long Delight,
>   Or make him ever sigh.
>
> With nameless Power, with secret Art,
>   Do studied Wantons lure;
> Tho' slow, yet deep, they strike the Heart,
>   Beyond the Reach of Cure.[34]

With regard to Blouzella, also, the facts and references in the opera correspond to the situation in real life. She shows no particular enthusiasm about her approaching marriage, objecting mildly to the lack of fervor shown by her suitor and to her not having been allowed to choose for herself. The villagers are shown in considerable doubt as to whether the young man will come at all. We have seen that similar wonder and criticism were voiced in 1733 at the delay in the Prince's arrival. When Sir Harry Heartfree, "the Bridegroom, a young Gentleman of a Family but of small Fortune," does arrive, Blouzella maliciously suggests that he remain a month at the house, for if her parents are forced to keep open house a month, they'll certainly die of grief before the end of it! As in the *Grub-Street Opera,* the parsimony is emphasized further by the orders and directions to the cook.

Some danger lies in any attempt to identify the other characters specifically, but in the rich old scoundrel Cantwell, Clerk to the Justice, who "has made Beggars of half the Parish," we have a fairly patent allusion to Sir Robert Walpole. Despite the excellence of the play, both in dialogue and song, it never reached the stage—another fact supporting the view that it offered a clever and biting parody of the royal family. The author, whoever he was, must have possessed accurate knowledge of the private life at court, some of the characterizations reminding us strongly of those in Hervey's *Memoirs*.

For several years after *The Wedding* no political ballad operas made their appearance, although contemporary events afforded ample opportunity for topical treatment. The tremendous effort of 1733 found the Opposition foiled but not totally defeated. Walpole seemed to bear a charmed political life. Even after the death of his main supporter, Queen Caroline, he retained his favor with the King, until the rising tide of patriotic fervor forced him into war with Spain and eventually displaced him in 1742. But the intervening years were crowded with events. In 1735 Bolingbroke, Walpole's inveterate enemy, found it advisable to retire to France. Frederick, long estranged from his parents, was banished from St. James's on account of his erratic and mysterious behavior at the birth of his first legitimate child, the Princess Augusta. He fell into the welcoming arms of the Opposition and set up his own court at Kew. In 1737, the Queen died. When his first wife died, in 1738, Robert Walpole was free to marry the faithful Maria Skerrett, in spite of the derisive sneers of the anonymous pamphleteers. Queen Caroline, with the usual candor of the time, had felt a certain admiration for the Prime Minister's mistress, thinking her a clever gentlewoman for hoodwinking the aged Walpole "avec ce gros corps, ces jambes enflées, et ce vilain ventre"—as the Queen describes him. All these varied happenings found commemoration in plays and pamphlets, but not in the ballad-opera form. One opera concerned with social scandal did appear in 1735, *The Ladies of the Palace, or The New Court Legacy*, but this was merely *The Court Legacy* (1733), under a new name.

The eventual downfall of Walpole and the rise to power of the
Country party, however, inspired one bitter anonymous opera in
1743—a poorly written but interesting piece in three acts and
forty-two songs. Sadly enough, the national hero of 1733 and his
Pulcheria have become the knaves and renegades of 1743 and the
awaited triumph of the Opposition has brought only disillusionment to many of its followers. Not only had Walpole been created
Earl of Orford and his daughter by Maria Skerrett legitimated, but
in a clever political stroke the King had elevated Pulteney to the
peerage as the Earl of Bath, thus removing him from the Commons.
The rage of the Country party was boundless, and poor Pulteney
found himself assailed on all sides with particularly cruel jibes at
his wife as "Bath's ennobled doxy."

Court and Country, or The Changelings, written from the point
of view of the citizens of London, represents this animosity. A sinister entente is shown between Rob-Roy (Walpole) and Will Vizard
(Pulteney), with the former still in control of political affairs—a
situation which had some slight element of truth in it if we consider
the new regard for the dismissed Prime Minister as revealed in
Horace Walpole's letters. One can scarcely credit, however, the
charge in the play that the Earl of Orford was able to promise ap-
pointments as sea-captains to a person who had seen the ocean only
once in his life—in anticipation of *Pinafore!*—and to a four-year-
old child. Walpole's enemies did their best to commit him to the
Tower by means of a Secret Committee, but without success, and
the anonymous writer of the opera is particularly caustic about
this failure. Pulteney's turncoat behavior is blamed primarily upon
his wife—now Lady Vizard—who appears exceedingly foolish and
vain over her new title. Walpole's natural daughter, legitimated
and given the rank of an earl's daughter, also finds a place in the
opera under the name of Molly Preference. She is described as a
mere pawn to the ambition of her father, who has even considered
making her mistress of "the old squire"—no doubt the King. While
Walpole's policy had been to keep George II well supplied with
mistresses after the death of Caroline, no evidence appears for this
particular accusation. Mary did, as a matter of fact, marry General

Churchill's natural son by Mrs. Oldfield. But in spite of the occasional sallies in court scandal, the main brunt of the attack falls upon the unfortunate Pulteney:

> Nor trust any Guide for a fair seeming Port,
> Since now Country Billy's grown Billy at Court.[35]

Gay's brilliant enlivening of *The Beggar's Opera* by the use of veiled satire on Walpole, then, started a tradition that outlived the poet himself and lasted appropriately until the end of the Prime Minister's reign. The topical operas that ensued became in effect pamphlets and diatribes, early examples of the modern propaganda play, usually anonymous in authorship and with little pretense of securing stage production. Most are poor in style and workmanship; a few are excellent and at least journalistically effective. They keep us in touch with the pulse of the century, and in their command of the inner scandal and politics of the court make us wonder what hired scribblers, or what noble lords and ladies, were responsible for their existence. It is a question, unfortunately, that we cannot answer.

CHAPTER TEN

Other Ballad Operas: 1728-1800

WITH some violence to the principle of coherence it will be necessary to tumble pell-mell into a final chapter a number of miscellaneous operas from 1728 to the end of the century that do not conform entirely to the classifications suggested thus far. Most of these remaining plays are capable of segregation under smaller headings according to some main characteristic or other, but in its lack of unity as a whole the present chapter must be considered in the nature of a literary grab-bag, from which almost anything may emerge.

Perhaps the largest of the minor groups may be christened by the name of "mythological" or "classical" operas. A favorite comic device in France, as we have noted earlier, was the burlesque and degradation of the characters of tragedy—the gods and goddesses, the heroes of antiquity, the kings and queens—into low-life figures in an ignoble setting. Satire, parody, or mere horseplay would be the purpose and guiding spirit of this non-heroic drama. Later, with the advent of the sentimental *drame* in France, the Roman gods and heroes were again resurrected to provide a mild and allegorical satire of mankind, full of commiseration and philosophical reflections on the foibles of human nature and frequently inspired by a moral purpose. Both types appear in England, with or without French originals. Of the realistic burlesques James Ralph—as we might expect—has something to say in *The Fashionable Lady, or Harlequin's Opera,* that curious dramatic disquisition on the pleasures of the day. Mr. Ballad believes that all the characters in an English opera should be the heroes and heroines of tragedy—

Othello should be a Serjeant in the Guards, and keep an Ale-house at *Charing-Cross; Desdemona* should be a Bar-keeper; and *Cato* make him a Cuckold; Hah! *Tamerlane* should be one of the *Quorum; Brutus,* a fat, cheating, miserly Alderman; and *Phocyas* a Stock-Jobber, turn'd Jew.[1]

Tumble-Down Dick, as we have seen, employed Mr. Ballad's formula, but Fielding was not the first to introduce it to English opera. The rather dubious honor of doing so fell to Mottley and Cooke, to the great detriment of the latter, for their opera *Penelope* appeared shortly after the publication of Pope's *Odyssey* and the vindictive poet, believing that ridicule of his work was intended, subsequently pilloried the second collaborator in the *Dunciad*. John Mottley, a typical Grub-Streeter, had a hand in numerous plays, including the popular *Devil to Pay*. Thomas Cooke, called "Hesiod" Cooke because of his excellent translation of the works of Hesiod, entered late into the collaboration of *Penelope,* the first of the three short acts having been written by Mottley about a year before.

Starting under the unfavorable auspices of "a miserable Set of Players,"² *Penelope* had a brief, inglorious career at the Haymarket in April, 1728. No prose was employed, the dialogue being wholly in heroic—or mock-heroic—verse, written with considerable rhythmic grace. The play nevertheless remains negligible. Ulysses, degraded to the lowly station of a "Serjeant of the Granadiers," returns to the faithful Penelope, here the landlady of an alehouse. As in Homer, he is recognized first by his dog, Tray. He proceeds forthwith to drive out three suitors—a butcher, a tailor, and a parish clerk. The goddess Minerva "descends" amid thunder and lightning to visit her Telemachus and drink with him a "double Dabber of Beer" at the Royal Oak—the like of which cannot be found in heaven. Eventually, after such scenes of burlesque humor, the main characters join in dancing the hay, and the play ends. Pope must be considered unduly sensitive to have been upset by so slight a performance.

A better and somewhat more successful opera came out at Lincoln's Inn Fields in 1729 with the title of *Momus Turn'd Fabulist, or Vulcan's Wedding*. It is attributed by some writers to Ebenezer Forrest,³ one of Hogarth's fellow-pilgrims in the five-day peregrination around the isle of Sheppey. Originally the piece came from France, as the English author merely adapted and ballad-operatized the extremely popular *Momus fabuliste, ou Les Noces de Vulcain* (1719) by Fuzelier and Le Grand, a gentle philosophical play on contemporary manners. The gods of Olympus again appear as the main personages, but the author cautions against taking them too literally, since "those Ancient Fictions and Characters are so accommodated, as to Expose and Ridicule the Vices and Follies of the present Age."⁴ Thus do we find Jupiter presented as a rake, somewhat henpecked; Juno as a prude; the spruce Apollo as a coxcomb, "powder'd down to the very Rump; the tip of the Mode"; and Venus as a coquette, "a pretty Piece of Household-Stuff." All these and others are subjected to the railing of Momus—a common character in satire since the Renaissance—who appears as a "Plain-dealer" but is reduced to moralizing in fables since Jupiter has forbidden him the use of satirical speeches. The fables of the original play have been set to ballad tunes by the English author, offering an apt and effective innovation. A mere suggestion of plot has been devised for the piece in the amusing gathering of the gods to hear the decree of Destiny on where the newly arrived Venus is to reside and on what husband she is to select. When the choice of both is granted by Destiny to Venus herself, she decides to remain in heaven and to marry Vulcan—the most discreet of the gods—for if she were to accept an agreeable husband she would immediately lose the services of all her other suitors.

Such a play obviously presupposes a genteel and polite audience, not the boisterous rowdies that would applaud Hob in *Flora* or Nell in *The Devil to Pay*. Excellent in dialogue and mildly amusing in satire as it is, *Momus Turn'd Fabulist* totally lacks action. Its popular success in France merely reveals the advent in that country of an emasculated comedy, sentimental and philosophical, delicate and temperate, undisturbed by loud plaudits and vulgar laughter, a type which was later to cross the Channel and take possession of English comedy through the influence of the *drame* and the *comédie larmoyante*.

Many of the stalwarts of *The Beggar's Opera* appeared in the assemblage of the gods and goddesses, with Thomas Walker as Mars, Milward as Jupiter, Salway as Apollo, Mrs. Egleton as Juno, and Mrs. Cantrell as Venus. Hall and Hippisley, of Lockit and

Peachum fame, were translated into Vulcan and Plutus. To Hulett
as Momus fell all the satirical fables ridiculing the other gods. The
three acts of the opera contain a total of forty-two songs.

Achilles, the last of Gay's three ballad plays, belongs clearly to
the category of "classical" operas. It appeared at Covent Garden
in February, 1733, about two months after the death of the author,
with a contemporary report—unsubstantiated otherwise—that a
number of the songs were supplied by Pope and Arbuthnot and even
Pulteney.[5] In spite of this alleged assistance the opera is much
inferior in dialogue and song to its two predecessors by Gay, although the situations manage to provide a few amusing moments.
Based on the classical story, the piece shows Achilles disguised as a
girl—Pyrrha—and subjected to the violent love-making of several
members of the court, including King Lycomedes himself. The jealous Queen Theaspe orders Pyrrha to share sleeping quarters with
one of her daughters, Deidamia, with the perfectly natural result
that the latter finds herself with child. Achilles is finally revealed
in his proper identity by the wiles of Ulysses and Diomedes, who
disguise themselves as merchants and take note of his loving and
unfeminine attention to a suit of armor. Credit must be allowed the
hero for his perfect willingness to marry the girl.

Despite its weaknesses, *Achilles* enjoyed the relatively long run
of twenty performances the first season, largely through the efforts
of Gay's prominent friends. At one performance—according to the
Daily Courant—Pope, Pulteney, and Sir William Wyndham were
all present.[6] The play was revived for several occasions in 1734 and
1735, then remained unacted until its unsuccessful alteration by
George Colman in 1744, when it appeared as *Achilles in Petticoats,*
with new music by Arne.

Gay's contemporaries found political significance even in the innocuous *Achilles.* The *Daily Courant,* for example, accused the
opera of including much obscenity and scurrility. In the pamphlet
*Achilles Dissected: Being a Compleat Key of the Political Char-
acters in that New Ballad Opera, Written by the Late Mr. Gay*
(1733), Alexander Burnet attempts to identify Robert Walpole
with the Prime Minister Diphilus in the play, who acts as procurer

for the king. The jealous Theaspe would then represent Queen Caroline, blessed in real life, as in the play, with several daughters. In the duel between Ajax and Periphas, Burnet see a "Representation of what lately happened between a *Little* Lord and a *Great* Commoner'"—with probable reference to the duel between Hervey and Pulteney. Whether Gay really intended such allusions, of course, is another matter, but Burnet aptly illustrates the tendency of the time to read secret references into almost any given text. From the standpoint of dramatic effectiveness the author of the pamphlet justly criticizes the overabundance of songs—there being fifty-four in all—and adds the gratuitous comment that "some of them are very *low*, and others very *luscious*."⁸ All things considered, the failure of the entire opera—as well as the songs—to approximate remotely the excellence of *The Beggar's Opera* must surprise the reader; the epigrammatic quality of Gay's style is almost entirely absent, to the great dearth of any really quotable lines or verses.

Achilles nevertheless had the advantage of an excellent cast. Quin, who had refused the part of Macheath five years before, played Lycomedes with Mrs. Cantrell as his Queen and Miss Norsa as his oddly seduced daughter, Deidamia. A minor part was assigned to the aged Leveridge, the most celebrated bass singer of his time, who survived beyond the middle of the century and died at the ripe age of eighty-eight years. Charles Burney remembered

his singing 'Ghosts of every occupation,' and several of Purcell's base [*sic*] songs, occasionally, in a style which forty years ago seemed antediluvian; but as he generally was the representative of Pluto, Neptune, or some ancient divinity, it corresponded perfectly with his figure and character.⁹

Another importation from France reached Drury Lane in 1733, John Kelly's *Timon in Love, or The Innocent Theft*, an adaptation of de Lisle's *Timon misanthrope*. Like *Momus Turn'd Fabulist* it is a good example of the philosophical *drame*. According to the words of the prologue—

'Tis no gay Opera: But there's much that's smart in 't,
The God of Wit vouchsafes to act a Part in 't!

One must admit, indeed, that *Timon in Love* is no gay opera, but it remains a pleasant and readable piece, with plenty of aphorisms and didacticism but no plot to speak of. Timon, having squandered a fortune on unworthy friends, has retired in disgust to solitude with an ass as his sole companion. Now a cynic, he spends most of his time railing at humanity. At this juncture Jupiter decides to reconcile him to the world with the aid of Mercury and the ass, who is conveniently metamorphosed into Pierot. Timon eventually reforms his opinion and marries Aspasia, whereupon Mercury voices the moral of the play:

> Follow then the Voice of Reason!
> Use the Moment as it flies!
> Calm, in ev'ry cloudy Season;
> Gay, beneath serener Skies.[10]

As for Timon, he is forced to admit:

I am confounded; instead of hating the World, I hate my self. I see my Resentment was the dangerous Effect of Self-love; I only condemn'd the Passions I my self was not guilty of.[11]

The most attractive character in this grave comedy is the ass, who retains his naiveté after he has been changed into Pierot and is even induced to steal Timon's fortune in the belief that he will relieve his master of worry. His metamorphosis is particularly amusing:

What the Devil is come across me? I am alter'd, I know not how! Such a Change as this I never felt before! What's become of that reverend Length of Face, and those venerable Ears which us'd to adorn it? My Body too has lost its charming Form, and the Warmth of its convenient Hide—I had once a loud, sonorous Voice, clear, and musical; now 'tis faint, and so unequal, that it frightens me! What in the Devil's Name am I chang'd to? O ho! my Reason, forsooth, explains it. I am a Man—Alas! a Man; my whole Form resembles my Master's, and I fear too is become almost as ridiculous.[12]

The ways of the world remain a constant wonder to him:

. . . Already I have found fine young delicate Girls that wou'd love for Money, Friends that offer'd their Service for Money, and Flatterers that wou'd praise me for Money—O, this Money can do any thing; ev'ry thing, all things, ev'n in spite of the Gods, Nature or Common Sense.[13]

There is little occasion for genuine comic laughter, except perhaps in Pierot's encounter with Socrates, where the sage of Athens, incidentally, offers an excellent definition of the *drame*. Comedies, he says, are "Performances of Wit, in which the Authors publickly ridicule the Vices of Men, and make 'em laugh at their own Follies."[14] In order to please, an author

must say reasonable things, with Wit and Spirit; and give a Comick Turn to Nature and Truth, that the Wise and Good mayn't be asham'd of being pleas'd. You must avoid all low and trivial things, observe the most delicate Decorum, and reject ev'ry Thought and Expression that might offend Modesty and Virtue: On these Terms, you may be sure to have all Persons of Reason and Taste on your Side, and I hope *Athens* has still many such to boast of.[15]

Unfortunately, one must surmise that in 1733 England was not yet entirely ready for the "delicate Decorum" of Kelly's play, for *Timon in Love* lasted only three nights. Genest suggests that *The Innocent Theft*, played in 1736 at Covent Garden, was probably the same play reduced to an afterpiece. The original cast has Mrs. Clive in the combined roles of Mercury and Aspasia. The opera—fifty-five pages in length—has only seventeen songs.

The next of the "mythological" plays reveals little of the decorum or philosophical contemplation that we have just witnessed, but it succeeds in arousing far more laughter. It was a "mock-Opera," *The Rape of Helen* by name, written by John Breval—author of one of the long poems on the *Harlot's Progress* mentioned earlier—who often hid under the pseudonym of Joseph Gay. The piece was acted at Covent Garden in 1733 but not published till 1737. Here we find the customary degradation of the Roman gods in a burlesque version of the escape of Helen and Paris from Troy. Juno and Minerva become "a couple of town-bites" and the twins—Castor and Pollux—a very amusing pair of "swaggering Bravoes." Menelaus and Helen quarrel in good eighteenth-century domestic fashion over late hours and pin-money. No wonder the lady is taken in by the dapper beau, Paris. "What a side Ogle was there!" says Paris to himself. "Let me practise the new-fashioned Stile of Courtship a little, and play my fine Shapes in her Eye.—Wit and

Eloquence might ha' done in the last Age;—now they are as much out of Doors as the Ruff and the Farthingale."[16] Whereupon he struts elaborately before "this Pink-stern'd Vessel," the fair and admiring Helen. Nor has he much respect for the goddesses— "*Minerva* at the Tavern! that Prude of Prudes cracking a Bottle with a sober Midwife and a Couple of Cudgel-Players, to the eternal Scandal of Arts and Sciences!"[17] Though necessarily slight, the play is clever and pleasantly spicy, with tripping rhythms and excellent parody of contemporary manners. To Breval, in short, credit must be given for writing one of the best of the burlesque operas. Of his twenty-five lively songs, only about half are to specified airs. One example of the verse follows:

> As cold as the Ice
> And of Vertue so nice,
> Can you think that Minerva the chaste,
> Would, before an idle Knave,
> Shew the Charms that Nature gave,
> Or indulge her in so lewd a Taste?
> As a Hum, Hum, etc.

> As for the two others,
> Who've been Wives and Mothers,
> They perhaps no such Measures need keep:
> By the by tho', 'tis my Mind,
> That the Sight was too refin'd,
> For a Boy that was tending his Sheep,
> With a Hum, Hum, etc.[18]

An unpublished two-act farce of 1735, *Macheath in the Shades, or Bayes at Parnassus,* combines such oddly assorted characters as Roman gods, Horace, Cleopatra, Ben Jonson, and Cardinal Wolsey, with various personages from *The Beggar's Opera.* The anonymous author calls the piece a "serio-comico-farcical-Elysian Ballad Opera"—a designation which must necessarily offer some slight difficulties in classification! The cast is given in Genest, but beyond the names of the players no information is available.

Except for some of the village or country pieces, ballad opera made few incursions into the romantic and spectacular, preferring modest stage effects and realistic or satirical themes. A half dozen

operas now to be considered, however, did essay subjects of a historical or quasi-historical nature and were driven of necessity into
more colorful and romantic channels. These few plays came in the
thirties, two of them—Chetwood's *The Generous Free-Mason, or
The Constant Lady* and the anonymous *Robin Hood*—both appearing in 1730 at Bartholomew Fair.

William Rufus Chetwood's piece, which he calls a tragi-comi-
farcical ballad opera, came out at the booth of Oates and Fielding
in August and then moved to Southwark Fair in September. It was
played with additions at the Haymarket in December of the same
year and was occasionally revived in other seasons. In its use of
blank verse for the serious scenes and in its melodramatically
romantic episodes it was perhaps a reflection at second hand of the
numerous plays which the author must have witnessed as prompter
of Drury Lane. Few plays, in any event, exhibit as much naiveté
and unconscious humor, Chetwood's main purpose apparently being to sing the praises of the Masonic order, of which he was
obviously a member. The main characters, Maria and Sebastian,
flee from the shores of England for love, the hero's only regret being
to leave the Masons:

> But yet one Pang I feel, thro' all my Joy
> That from my noble Brethren I must part,
> Those Men, whose Lustre spreads from Pole to Pole,
> Possessing every Virtue of the Soul.
> But yet all Climes the Brotherhood adorn.[19]

His profound love for Maria is expressed succinctly in the line,
"I'll be thy Lover, Father, Brother, All."[20] Many vicissitudes follow,
including capture by Mirza the Moor, who conducts them as prisoners to his master, the King of Tunis. The King forthwith falls in
love with Maria while the Queen, not to be outdone, feels the same
tender passion for Sebastian. The lovers thus appear doomed to
separation and worse, until Mirza the Moor reveals himself as no
Moor at all but an erstwhile Englishman, and more surprisingly
still, as a Mason initiated "in most perfect Form." The three escape
amid a welter of noble sentiments and the play ends with a scene

indicating "the Sea," graced for this special occasion with the presence of Neptune and Tritons, who sing a panegyric ditty in praise of the Masons!

Interpolated at regular intervals amid these dramatic episodes, with no attention to unity of place, are the prose "Humours of Squire Noodle, and his Man Doodle"—scenes of broad farce in which Noodle is made a Mason, as he believes, in a rowdy slapstick ceremony. In poor Squire Noodle's belief that he is with child we have a comic device which Dryden employed in *The Wild Gallant*. The same conceit appeared in our day in the popular novel *Turnabout* by the late Thorne Smith, in which the hero suffers a similar blessing—a situation considered at the time of publication extremely original and daring—all of which serves to prove that there is nothing new under the literary sun. With such extremes of romance, low comedy, heroism, and indelicacy proceeds Chetwood's *Generous Free-Mason* in three spectacular acts with dances by Moors and Tritons, prison scenes, and other such theatrical effects. There are twenty-five songs in all, three of them set by Carey, two by J. Sheeles, and one by Charke. The comic scenes of the opera—involving Noodle, Doodle, Lettice, and others—were offered separately in 1733 as *The Mock Mason*.

Robin Hood, an anonymous opera, made its debut at Lee's and Harper's Great Theatrical Booth at Bartholomew Fair, with no record of the players. Using Chetwood's device of verse for the serious passages, it combines its romantic and farcical elements with far less crudeness. On the whole, it is nicely written. The Earl of Huntington and his friend Darnel are represented as banished from court through the treachery of the Earl of Pembrook. They join a band of outlaws, assume the names of Robin Hood and Little John, and pledge themselves to plunder the rich, to feed the poor, and not to molest women. Into Sherwood Forest the two men have been followed by Princess Matilda and her friend Marina, disguised as shepherdesses, and eventually the lovers are all united. A battle takes place at the end, in the course of which Huntington kills the villainous Pembrook and earns vindication from the King.

This simple and familiar romantic theme is handled with much

freshness and humor. Perhaps the fact of its having been calculated
for the meridian of the fairs has tended to preserve some of the
robust popular quality of the old Robin Hood ballads. The prose
scenes in and about the forest deserve special praise for their farcical gusto. Certainly little decorum of the French variety graces the
assignation between Little John and Peter Pindar's wife, which is
thrice interrupted by the unsuspecting husband, each time with
the wife giving a more fantastic explanation than before. A Puritan
—inevitably called Prim—is introduced into the play for the mere
purpose of having his money stolen. All such popular material is
deftly woven into the opera, offering the motley populace of Bartholomew Fair a variegated assortment of romance, chivalry, love,
horseplay, innuendo, and social justice—truly a dish to its own
liking. The piece is not overburdened with songs, having only nineteen for the three acts, but they are attractive in their own right.
That numerous other plays and operas on the subject of Robin
Hood appeared after 1740 may be worthy of note.[21]

The next year, 1731, saw one of the early plays to exploit "local
color"—*The Highland Fair, or Union of the Clans,* an opera by
Joseph Mitchell, a convivial and improvident Scotchman who remained always in financial distress although he had the great distinction—not shared by any other writer of the period—of being
known as "Sir Robert Walpole's Poet." The author's friend, Aaron
Hill, weary of offering him direct financial assistance, wrote a play
under Mitchell's name, *The Fatal Extravagance,* "a Piece which
seemed in its very Title to convey a gentle Reproof to *Mr. Mitchell*
on the Occasion of his own Distresses."[22] *The Highland Fair* came
out at Drury Lane for several performances in March and April,
but had the unfortunate effect of bewildering the citified London
audiences, who had little understanding of Scottish customs. In a
semi-historical spectacle set in a fair on the braes between the
Highlands and Lowlands of Scotland, Mitchell designed to show
the ancient temper, spirit, customs, manners, and costumes of his
countrymen (without their dialect, however) and at the same time
to expose the evils of feuds. This last didactic purpose is expressed
by the Poet in the introduction:

Your critical Judgment must be more Prejudic'd than Impartial, if it refuses to own that the Madness and Misery of Family Feuds and Divisions
among Neighbours are expos'd—the Charms of Peace, Unity, and all the
social Virtues display'd—sullen Pride, and imaginary State, Romantic
Bravery and blind Superstition, starck Gravity and persecuting Bigotry
are ridicul'd throughout my Piece; and their Contraries recommended for
their Loveliness, in contrast to such Deformities of Nature.[23]

To illustrate his thesis the author presents a tense meeting at the
fair between the hostile forces of a highland chief, Euen, and a
"braes laird," Colin. Following the general formula later used by
Scott, he weaves into this martial subject several love stories which
hinge upon the satisfactory settlement of the feud. Despite all the
ingredients of good drama, the action has a tendency to lag and
certain portions are downright boring. But the characterization is
effective and the pageantry historically interesting, as in the stage
directions for the meeting of the two chiefs before a spacious tent:

Enter Colin, on one side; his Piper before him, playing the March peculiar
to his Clan. Behind him, his Vassals and Servants in good Order. As he
stops before the Tent, his Musick ceases. Then, Enter Euen, on the other
side, as before, &c. The Chiefs bow thrice as they meet, Colin making the
first Steps and Reverences, according to the Ceremonial agreed upon.
During the Ceremonial (which is all in Dumb Show) a Bard rehearses the
Genealogy of their Families. Then, placing themselves in the Tent (Euen
on the right Hand) they lay their Pistols and Durks on a Table before
them. They drink to one another.[24]

After these elaborate preliminaries the three couples are presented
and the play ends with a Highland dance.

One of the beautiful heroines, Jeany, was played at Drury Lane
by Miss Vaughan; the other, Nanny, by Catherine Raftor. The
part of the romantic Davy was given to an actress, Mrs. Roberts.
One wonders why it was so often necessary for Mrs. Charke, Mrs.
Roberts, and others to play masculine roles. Perhaps the ability to
sing had something to with the practice. The fifty-one songs, most
of them to old Scotch tunes, are adequate. The printed play was
dedicated to the Duke of Argyll, "the acknowledged CHIEF of our
Scotian CHIEFS." An interesting frontispiece by Hogarth represents
the final scene.

With Walter Aston's *The Restauration of King Charles II, or The Life and Death of Oliver Cromwell* (1732) we come to another historical and spectacular opera. The title, however, proved too much for the censors, for performance was prohibited. As the author points out in a preface asserting his loyalty, the play seems harmless enough, but in troublous political times a work on the restoration of a Stuart and on the death of the tyrannical Cromwell —with whom Walpole might conceivably be associated—would scarcely prove welcome. The prohibition, in any event, came suddenly and peremptorily after the parts had been distributed and the piece rehearsed, the only given official objection being to the "treasonable title." In denying the charge the author, who may possibly have been the son of Tony Aston,[25] maintains that he only wanted his friends to enjoy the pleasure of seeing history on the stage and to get a little money thereby to support himself.

Like so many of the contemporary pieces, *The Restauration of King Charles II* succeeds in being ridiculous in its serious parts, written in blank verse, although successful enough in its comic scenes. With vague recollections of the tragic drama Aston shows Cromwell as having sealed a pact with the devil, represented in the play by Grimbald, "foulest Spirit of the Deep." Charles II, on the other hand, enjoys the conscientious protection of Brittania [*sic*]— not unlike the Attendant Spirit in *Comus*—who on one occasion, when the King is beset by the Roundheads, "descends" and takes him away in her chariot. Later, when Charles has sought refuge in a large oak tree, she prays to the gods for his safety, and in the midst of thunder, lightning, and a shower of fire the enemies are dispersed. The play abounds in similar supernatural manifestations —until finally Charles, who has managed to escape in Act II, returns triumphantly to England in Act III, Cromwell having perished in the meantime in the throes of his own iniquity. Even the Protector's daughter, Lady Claypool, has cursed him and died of grief. The best of the accompanying comic scenes show Charles in a "Country Habit" taking refuge at a humble cottage where Dame Sarah cuffs him and even throws a three-legged stool at him for his stupidity. She upbraids the monarch in no uncertain terms:

Why you Black, Tawny-face, Lanthorne-jaw'd, Charcoal-brow'd, Wide-mouth'd, Long-nos'd, Lath-back, Spindle-shank'd, Awkward-Ninny, did'st thou never see a Jack before! Stand' out o' my Way, you Booby.[26]

A slight love theme is added to the play for good measure—between Colonel Carlos and Jane Lane, "a Loyal Girl" who helps to conceal the King in his escape. For such scenes of romance and humor the author provides twenty-three songs, some of them witty and attractive.

A spectacular, if not historical, opera of 1739—*Don Sancho, or The Student's Whim*—is difficult to classify because of its incoherence. Elizabeth Boyd, the author, calls it a "Medley-Whim." Clarence, Nicoll, and others list the work as a ballad opera, and there is some slight internal evidence for this classification, but the airs to the twelve songs are not indicated in the text. According to the prologue and an "advertisement," Chetwood introduced the play to the Green Room of Drury Lane, where it met a favorable reception, but the lateness of the season and the large number of benefits prevented its actual presentation. We can only surmise that Chetwood's gallantry forbade him from telling the good lady the truth, for *Don Sancho* seems entirely unsuited for performance on the stage.

The scene is Oxford. Lord Lovewit, Jack Taste, and Joe Curious —three students—prevail on Don Sancho, "a reduc'd Nobleman," to initiate them into the mysteries of the infernal regions. Despite the admonitions of his "Evil Genii" he accedes to their request and with the aid of a stolen book raises—among others—the ghosts of Shakespeare and Dryden, who fail, however, to seize upon this opportunity to say anything of particular note. The final advice of Shakespeare to mankind would seem to be the following, sung in mediocre verse by the Bard of Avon's own ghost:

> Would you merit lasting Bays,
> Goodness practise more than Praise,
> The happy Bard no more disturb,
> Least thy Follies Thunder curb.[27]

If Elizabeth Boyd may thus claim some credit for writing an early play on occultism, she certainly deserves equal mention as an

eighteenth-century impresario with a yearning for the spectacular.
Stage effects and machines abound, with the result that much of
the action would be likely to take place in mid-air. Consider only
one modest sample of the author's stage directions:

Here a bright Cloud descends half-way, in which little Boys like Angels
are seen to hover, who swiftly waft the Ghosts upward, singing the following Chorus to soft Musick, at the Close of which the Cloud and Spirits
disappear.[28]

Such scenic effects remind us of Restoration dramatic opera.
Whether Elizabeth intended to write a farce or a fantasy, however,
is not at all clear.

In November, 1739, a short two-act ballad opera by William
Hammond—*The Preceptor, or The Loves of Abelard and Heloise*
—was acted at Smock Alley, Dublin. This extraordinary subject
for a ballad opera was attributed to "a young Gentleman in the
Army."[29] The piece, of a decidedly unmilitary cast, shows the growing love between Heloise and her tutor, which unfortunately is
reported to the lady's uncle by the jealous Agaton. A debate among
the principals follows regarding the advisability of marriage, but
nevertheless the uncle, Fulbert, vows to separate the lovers "by all
the avenging Powers of holy Rome."[30] Heloise sees the Ghost of
Virginity in a Vision and rises to grasp it, but it disappears. The
distracted and remorseful Agaton, in the meantime, reports that
"the Tutor lives—but oh! the Lover dies,"[31] the upshot of the entire
situation being that Abelard repairs to a monastery and Heloise
resolves upon a nunnery. A chorus ends the piece:

> Let this, our sad Example, prove
> The dire Effects of lawless Love.[32]

The slightness of the opera, with its obscure motivation and undistinguished blank verse, allows it no very high rating, but it has
some interest for its historical theme and its use of romantic tragedy
rather than comedy. It is graced by eleven ballad songs with a
strange assortment of tunes from "Geminiani's Minuet" to the
"Irish Howl."

The grave tone of Hammond's *Preceptor* offers a suitable introduction to a small group of ballad operas, not mentioned previously, that turn from the usual frivolous gayety of the form and concern themselves mainly with morality and sentiment. We have encountered didacticism before in such pieces as Lillo's *Silvia* or, in a more philosophical form, in the French *drames*. Sentimentality, too, has figured increasingly in our rapid consideration of ballad opera, revealing itself in the sudden reform of villains, in the emphasis on woman's virtue, in Fielding's charming lovers, in lofty speeches, in the nobility of the common man. In the few following plays, however, morality or sentimentality appear as the dominant rather than as the subsidiary theme.

Of *The Keepers*, written in 1734 by a "student at the University," little is known beyond the prologue and epilogue of the opera, which were published in the *Grub-street Journal* with the comment of the editor that he admired rather than understood them. Part of the prologue at least gives the intent of the author:

> Simple his plot, and moral his design,
> As custom sacred, and as law divine:
> Each scene's a sermon, and each verse a text,
> This world may damn him, but he'd save the next.
> Tho' dull his Farce, no dullness it affords
> Of things disjointed, or mishapen words:
> No buskin'd scene, or garter'd dress he brings,
> Statira'd queens, or Alexander'd kings:
> No frisking gods, or cap'ring devils rise,
> To please the foolish, and displease the wise:
> No Drury whore, or Temple rake you'll see,
> *Solus cum sola,* or with *rem in re:*
> Whose noisy tongues, and empty heads are such,
> They think too little, and they talk too much.
>   Attend each keeper, and amend his life,
> Th' unwholesome harlot, for the wholesome wife:
> Blameless yourself, then you may blame the whore,
> Who when infected most, infects the more . . .[33]

In this vein, with continued dependence on the cæsura, of which he seemed to be inordinately fond, the student at the University proceeds with his earnest plea against keeping.

The successful but staid career of Robert Dodsley, eminent bookseller, erstwhile footman, author of *The Muse in Livery*, patronized by Pope and friend to the Johnson-Richardson circle, has nothing in it to show affinity to the bawdy and boisterous tendencies of Grub Street. It is not surprising, therefore, to find his dramatic work properly moral and sententious, with what the century called delicacy of satire. For his particular gifts he was born at exactly the right time, for the middle-class reading public of Addison and Steele was steadily growing in strength and importance and the sentimental French drama was increasingly making its influence felt. In *The King and the Miller of Mansfield*—a non-musical play that proved popular also in French translation—Dodsley had produced a graceful and agreeable comedy in which an honest, plain-spoken, and democratic miller was knighted by the king. A sequel to this piece appeared at Drury Lane in 1738 with the title of *Sir John Cockle at Court*. As only four songs were present, none to specified old airs, it is with more than dubious propriety that Nicoll lists the piece as a ballad opera. *Sir John Cockle at Court* holds considerable interest, however, for its presentation of sentimental themes that were soon to be exploited more fully by Richardson. The play reveals a second time the honesty and sincerity of the miller (now Sir John Cockle), a subject which is enlivened by an attempted but foiled seduction of the miller's daughter Kitty, a part taken appropriately by Kitty Clive. Even stronger objection to Nicoll's classification can be made with regard to Dodsley's later musical play, *The Blind Beggar of Bethnal Green*, for the nine songs in it were set by Arne. Based on an old play by John Daye, this trifling drama offers a simple tale in a humble setting, the story proceeding through the vicissitudes of an attempted rape, a rescue, and an abundance of moral maxims. It will be observed that rape and seduction are topics of perpetual fascination to the moralist, no doubt as a form of suppression.

If such pieces as the two preceding are not ballad operas, what may they properly be called? Carey's farces, even though he composed his own music, at least looked like ballad operas. Both the songs and the dialogue adhered to the general formula of the type, and Carey's airs were themselves frequently borrowed for other ballad plays. Dodsley's musical pieces and others—coming in the late 1730s when ballad opera was no longer the fashion—mark rather a degeneration of the form. They are grave rather than comic, they are slight, they employ a mere handful of songs which appear in a purely incidental and perfunctory fashion. It is observable that the eighteenth century made no pretense of calling them either ballad operas or ballad farces, but ordinarily gave them instead the sensible title of "dramatic tales" or "dramatic fables." A variant of the preceding designations was given to James Miller's *Coffee-House* (1738), the play that ruined the unfortunate author's dramatic career. On its appearance the Templars, believing its intent was to ridicule Mrs. Yarrow and her daughter, who kept Dick's Coffee-House near Temple Bar, damned the play as well as all subsequent productions by Miller, notwithstanding the author's declaration that he had merely written an adaptation of Jean Baptiste Rousseau's *Le Caffé*. Color was given to the Templars' suspicion by the fact that the engraver inadvertently selected that very coffee-house as model for the frontispiece. The printed play indicates six songs—three by Carey, two by Henry Burgess, Jr., and one of unspecified origin. *The Coffee-House* belongs, therefore, on the outer fringe of ballad opera. It is a pleasantly realistic and mildly satirical piece, with Theophilus Cibber appearing as himself and Kitty Clive as Kitty, daughter to the mistress of the coffee-house. Cibber's interpretation of himself was an innovation by the English author, the corresponding part in Rousseau's play calling for a valet. *The Coffee-House* came out at Drury Lane, as did the two pieces by Dodsley.

Miller's "dramatic piece" has led us away from the immediate subject at hand, but we hasten promptly to the most powerful of the moral operas and one remarkably free from sentimentality—*Little John and the Giants*, a five-act play by Henry Brooke, the original and eccentric author of *The Fool of Quality*. Under its first title of *Jack the Gyant Queller* it was acted at Dublin in 1749 but suppressed by the Lord Justices of Ireland. It reappeared at Dublin in 1754 with alterations and the new title of *Little John and the*

Giants. Galligantus, acted at Drury Lane and the Haymarket and published in 1758, is said to have been taken from Brooke's play. It should be noted that a one-act piece of the same general design came out at the Haymarket as early as 1730 under the title of *Jack the Gyant-Killer.* Brooke may have been indebted to this earlier non-musical piece for his general plan.

Little John and the Giants, called a "Dramatic Opera," is in fact an allegorical sermon in rapid-moving heroic couplets and ballad songs. It represents the diminutive John Good of the family of the Goods—a sort of evangelical Tom Thumb—sallying forth from his humble and idyllic cottage to rescue Jillian Justice, Queen of the May, from the powerful family of the Giants. The latter includes Plutus (Wealth) and his three sons—Galigantus (Power), Rumbo (Violence), and Blunderbore (Wrong). It is little wonder that the play displeased the censors, for it vigorously attacks injustice in high places.

An interesting prologue asserts the author's devotion to "the high road where Truth and Nature lead." To the audience he explains:

> What antique whim, what out of fashion'd taste,
> Tempts modern meetings to a moral feast?
> No clamorous drum is here, no wanton dance,
> Nor songs from Italy, nor cooks from France:
> Your table is with mental dishes spread,
> And cates on which immortal souls are fed;
>
> .   .   .
>
> Such is the feast that's relish'd by the few;
> The Food of Angels!—[*To the Ladies.*]
> And of men, like you![34]

The intricate allegorical scheme—which lack of space prohibits giving here in full—is obviously as out of place as it is astonishing in a ballad opera, but the play has various remarkable features. One is that the ideas and sentiments are frequently the same as those that appeared in *The Beggar's Opera*—about the power of gold, the injustice of the law, and so forth—but that the mood and treatment are diametrically opposite. Instead of the flippant and disillusioned satire of the indolent Gay, we encounter here the Miltonic denunciations of the moralist—uttered nevertheless with an effectiveness which is enhanced by the virile and sardonic doggerel of the verse. A fine indignation runs in the ballad songs as well:

> The Laws they were made for the Little,
> The Laws they were made for the Little:
> In the hands of the Strong,
> All the ties, that belong
> To Justice and Honour, are brittle.[35]

Or again:

> Gold is every woman's lust!
>   Gold is every man's desire!
> Gold the covert patriot's gust!—
>   Kneel my sons, and own your sire![36]

The fact that one of the songs, by the way, was set to the air "Our Polly Is a Sad Slut" shows at least some slight connection between this play and *The Beggar's Opera*, which Brooke must certainly have read or seen.

Another remarkable point is that the man was no conventional moralist, preacher though he might be. Here is none of the stuffy morality of Richardson or Lillo or Dodsley, with their pure and perfect (and not uncalculating) heroines. Jillian Justice, held captive in the enchanted Tower, bemoans being shut up from every son of Father Adam:

> All my virgin sweets consuming,
> Far from every sense—O fye![37]

When she first beholds John Good and falls in love with him at sight, she explains that she is, in spite of Heaven and her own free will, a nun:

> Fair youth, by you I'd have it understood,
> That I am form'd of kindly flesh and blood.[38]

In a similar situation, Silvia—or Pamela for that matter—would have called for the hartshorn and spouted some moral apothegms. It is astonishing how Brooke succeeds in giving life to his abstract and allegorical figures, and, although he erred somewhat in fixing upon the ballad-opera form, we must recognize him here, as in his other work, as a vigorous and original writer, as much a non-conformist in drama as he was in religion. The last of the five acts is perhaps the weakest because of the overabundance of allegory, but the conclusion, where Jack and Jill overcome the giants and change all Wrongs to Rights, gives the reader a sense of eminent satisfaction not always produced by even the best of sermons.

A few more thrusts into the grab-bag reveal a scattering of ill-assorted operas, most of them unpublished. As a result, they are difficult to classify. The two or three that did appear in print deserve little commendation. We find, for example, *Cupid and Psyche, or Columbine-Courtezan: A Dramatic Pantomime Entertainment, Interspers'd with Ballad Tunes,* played at Drury Lane in 1734 with Monsieur Le Brun as Harlequin and Kitty Clive as Columbine. It is a hybrid production made up of "entertainment" plus pantomime plus ballad songs, the tunes for which, however, are not listed in the text. The "Serious" relates the story of Cupid and Psyche; the "Comic" shows Harlequin in a series of thefts, tricks, and miraculous escapes. Forty-seven characters appear in the cast and the spectacular effects are numerous. Several curious attempts to combine ballad opera and pantomime have already been mentioned— Theophilus Cibber's *Harlot's Progress,* for instance, and the anonymous *Harlequin Restor'd.*

Farewell and Return, or The Fortune of War (1739?) seems to have been a patriotic opera on the general style of Carey's *Nancy.* Baker believes it represented a sailor's farewell to his lass and his return after a successful cruise, the plan apparently having been borrowed from a pair of prints entitled "The Sailor's Farewell" and "The Sailor's Return." It is tentatively dated at the beginning of the Spanish war.

Another nautical piece and a candidate for the nomination as world's worst ballad opera secured publication in 1745 as *The Sailor's Opera, or A Trip to Jamaica.* Five short acts, dull and incoherent beyond measure, show "some Humours that do pass while on the Sea," including mainly various flirtations by passengers on

the way to Jamaica. It is no wonder that the title-page bears the
short statement, "London: Printed for the Author." Needless to
add, it was not acted. Nor was stage performance accorded to a
close rival of the preceding, *The Conspirators* (1749), written by a
"much-injured Person in the Drama," a brief and jumbled piece in
three acts and a handful of songs. Its main object, it seems, was to
expose a plot to cheat a certain Creolia out of her West Indies
estate.

Few excursions have so far been made beyond the year 1750.[39]
Ballad opera, as a matter of fact, reached its apogee in 1733, although it managed to linger for a number of years thereafter. The
closing of the smaller theatres in 1737, although the Licensing Act
did not prohibit musical entertainment, seemed to expedite the
demise of the ballad pieces. Meanwhile Drury Lane and Covent
Garden, too busy with their regular repertoires to countenance new
plays and showing a predilection rather for non-operatic entertainment, did not encourage a perpetuation of the genre. So far as the
metropolitan audiences and authors were concerned, ballad opera
was decidedly passé, to be revived only in the sixties in different
shape with the comic operas of Bickerstaffe and others. In the preface to *Love in a Village* Bickerstaffe denies the use of common ballad
airs, although in several of his comic operas as in much of the work
of his contemporaries we find the inclusion of tunes not specially
composed for the occasion. Such songs, however, usually borrowed
their music from the work of known composers—Boyce, Arne, Ven-
to, Cocchi, Piccini, Monsigny, Bach, Bertoni, Guétry, and numerous
others—providing as a result an intermediate form between ballad
and comic opera which has sometimes been given the name of
pasticcio. From the sixties on, the French influence—in plot, models, and music—became more pronounced, and the work of Favart,
Sedaine, Marmontel, and Vadé, to mention only a few, proved popular in England. As suggested earlier, by 1760 the term *ballad opera*
itself had become outmoded and we find the authors designating
their pieces as comic operas, even at times when popular ballad
tunes were employed. Without pretending to navigate unerringly
the vast and uncharted seas of comic opera in the second half of the

century, we may try to indicate briefly a few survivals—usually corrupt and degraded ones—of the ballad-opera form in later years.

Gasconado the Great, a "Tragi-Comi, Political, Whimsical Opera" in one act, attributed to the familiar James Worsdale, failed to reach the stage but did secure publication in 1759. In his dedication Jemmy speaks of his struggles "in endeavouring to strike out a new *Plan* of *Dramatic Burlesque,* which has never been attempted by any but himself." He might well have spared himself the exertion, for *Gasconado the Great* is a dull, worthless piece. Written entirely in verse and characterized by rabid patriotism, it attacks France—with which England was then at war—in a satirical burlesque of Louis XV as Gasconado and Mme. de Pompadour as Pampaline. The King is shown as unmoved by reports of defeat and disaster as long as he may enjoy the love of his mistress. France is specifically accused of treachery, under its ruler's direction, in its war against Prussia. Only eight of the sixteen songs were set to ballad tunes.

The decade of the 1760s shows only slight improvement in ballad-opera material. There is, to be sure, an engaging farce of intrigue by the actor Thomas King, *Love at First Sight* (1763), a two-act piece which came out at Drury Lane. It is one of those trifles where the valet impersonates the hero, the hero impersonates a language teacher, and the friend impersonates the hero's father, causing a vast amount of rather pointless confusion which is satisfactorily cleared up by the marriage of the principals, but in its own way it succeeds in being entertaining enough. Vernon and Baddely appear in the cast. The author, the original Sir Peter Teazle and one of the best-known comic actors of his age, played the clever valet. The intriguing chambermaid appears in the character of Lucy, performed by Mrs. Lee. Nine of the ten songs were set to specified airs, but it is interesting to observe that the traditional ballad-opera tunes have given place to such unaccustomed airs as "Go, Happy Flower," "The New-Flown Birds," and "Daniel Cooper."

Two other pieces of the same decade, one written in London and one in America, remained unacted. The English play, *The Coach*

Drivers (1766), tried to revive in the days of Pitt and Rocking-
ham the old practice of political ridicule and allegory in the ballad-
opera form. The piece proceeds with some incoherence through
two acts of verse, recitative, and songs, the last having a number of
ballad airs. The American play, *The Disappointment, or The Force
of Credulity* (New York, 1767) by Andrew Barton (perhaps a pseudonym for Thomas Forrest) bears some interest as being the first
American ballad opera.[40] It was designed for performance by the
American Company at Philadelphia on April 20, 1767, but was
withdrawn because of its "personal reflections."[41] The author calls
it a "local piece," founded on fact and designed "to put a stop (if
possible) to the foolish and pernicious practice of searching after
supposed hidden treasures."[42] It is a pity the play was not performed, for it is decidedly readable and interesting because of its
realism and local color. Several dialects and accents—including
Scotch, Irish, and Negro—are attempted both in song and dialogue.
The situation has the virtue of simplicity. Four "Humourists"—
Hum, Parchment, Quadrant, and Rattletrap—send a party of
"Dupes" on a wild-goose chase in search of Captain Blackbeard's
buried treasure. A love plot between Lucy, niece to Washball (a
barber), and Meanwell is added for the sake of romance. That no
color line was drawn in New York at this early time seems obvious
from the interesting Negro character of Raccoon, an old debauchee
and one of the dupes, who keeps Moll Placket, a white woman of
the town, and is neatly deceived by her. His dialect includes such
familiar spellings as "brudder" and "de" for "the." He is depicted
as well to do, and no social discrimination against him occurs on
the treasure hunt. The author provides Trueshoop (a cooper) with
an Irish brogue, and Buckram (a tailor) with a Scotch one. The
fourth of the eighteen songs in the 1767 edition was set to the tune
of "Yankee Doodle."

A few old airs—five out of forty-one—appear in Joseph Reed's
comic opera, *Tom Jones,* acted at Covent Garden in 1769. The author asserts he borrowed only two suggestions from Poinsinet's
opera of the same name: the hint of legitimating Jones and the
theme of one of the songs. The piece is amusing as offering a proper

and highly bowdlerized version of Fielding's novel, with the hero stripped of his libertinism and Western's character purged of its coarseness. Scriblerus the Second must certainly have turned violently in his grave when the opera was performed at Covent Garden.

The next decade has no ballad opera of importance. One unacted piece was printed in 1773, the anonymous *Bow-Street Opera*—a wretched and incoherent satire of Wilkes as Cock-Eyed Jack and Justice Fielding as Justice Blindman, preceded by an ironical dedication to Garrick. It is a short three-act parody of the text and many of the songs of *The Beggar's Opera* with Cock-Eyed Jack substituted for Macheath but unreprieved at the end. The thirty-two songs are set to airs used by Gay. Another piece, Charles Dibdin's immensely popular *Waterman* (1774), is called by the author a ballad opera. No tunes are indicated in the text, however, and Dibdin tells us that he primarily used ballads he had himself composed for Ranelagh and the theatre. The play—whether ballad opera or not—is a slight farce of low life.

The end of the century seems to have brought a minor revival of the ballad play. In 1784, for example, we find Archibald Maclaren's *The Coup de Main, or The American Adventurers*, played at the new theatre in Dundee. The piece is extremely amusing from an American viewpoint, for in the medium of a romantic melodrama it shows the beautiful Phoebe almost forced against her will to marry an American captain and rescued from his clutches in the nick of time by Captain Lovewell, the brave Britisher, while the cowardly Yankee soldiers flee or refuse to fight. Poor Sambo, a Negro servant, is much abused by the rascally colonists. As melodrama, the opera is effective, if not flattering to the Americans. Various dialects are attempted—French, Irish, Scotch—one purpose of the author being to point out the motley character of the rebels. Seventeen songs appear, most of them to Scotch ballad tunes. It is interesting to note that the author had a perfect right to dramatize the American scene, since he had personally seen service in the Revolutionary War under General Howe and General Clinton. When in winter quarters he is said to have submitted poetical contributions to the Philadelphia and New York papers.

Another military play came out at Covent Garden in 1785, John O'Keeffe's *Poor Soldier*, with about half of its nineteen songs set to specified airs. It is a very slight performance based upon a theme of renunciation. When Captain Fitzroy discovers that Norah does not love him but instead loves an impecunious soldier—and that his humble rival is Pat, the man who saved his life at Johnson's Ferry in Carolina—he promptly abandons his pretensions to the girl and gives Pat a commission. The slightness of the opera did not prevent immediate popularity. The main roles were taken by Kennedy as Pat, Bannister as Captain Fitzroy, and Mrs. Bannister as Norah.

It might be noted in passing that a three-act comic opera by Joseph Atkinson, *A Match for a Widow, or The Frolics of Fancy* (1788), has a few of its songs set to specified tunes. Interest in American affairs is again revealed in the air of "Yankee Doodle" and in a reference to "bundling." Like Mrs. Inchbald's The *Widow's Vow* of the same year, Atkinson's piece was taken from Patrat's *L'Heureuse Erreur* (1783).

A ballad opera by Andrew Shirrefs, A.M., was published in 1790 at Edinburgh, two years after the time of its stage performance. This was *Jamie and Bess, or The Laird in Disguise*, a five-act pastoral comedy in imitation of *The Gentle Shepherd*. The piece, as one might expect from its author, is scholarly rather than theatrical and even out-Ramsays Ramsay in its use of Scotch dialect. The ingredients are the very same as we find in its model—humorous rustics, a love plot, differences in rank which threaten the union of the lovers, and the final revelation that both are of gentle blood. The twelve songs are set to old Scotch tunes. With Tingey and Mrs. Tingey, Sunderland and Mrs. Sunderland, Newbound and Mrs. Newbound, all listed in the cast, *Jamie and Bess* must have been a veritable family affair.

Several other ballad operas appear in the 1790s. In Peter Markoe's *The Reconciliation, or The Triumph of Nature* we have another American piece, published at Philadelphia in 1790 but apparently not acted. It derived its inspiration from a harrowing and lachrymose one-act "comedy" by Gessner, to which the adapter

added a new character and twelve ballad songs, five of which end
the play in the form of a medley. In 1792 there appeared in England a reprinting of a "dramatic medley" by Leonard McNally,
Critic upon Critic, with a printed cast. Genest, however, believes
that the play was never acted and that the alleged cast and new
title-page were merely a bookseller's device to dispose of remaining
copies of the 1788 edition.[43] The piece deals with personalities of
the stage, with references to Dibdin, Cumberland, Henderson, and
others. In 1798 another farce, Richard Sickelmore's *Quarter-Day,*
employed the ballad-opera form for a simple plot—inspired perhaps by *The Devil to Pay*—revolving about a cobbler and his wife,
victims of the amorous inclinations of their landlords, Sir Grey and
Lady Grey. Eight ballad songs find employment. Finally, in 1799,
appeared a comic opera by Thomas Dibdin with overture and airs
composed by John Moorehead and with a few old songs as well,
including Gay's ballad of "Black-ey'd Susan." A foreword to the
edition of 1800, however, states that this last remains the only song
not written for the occasion. The piece, *The Naval Pillar,* is a highly
patriotic naval opera with topical mention of Napoleon, Lord
Howe, and others. It was performed "with unbounded Applause"
at Covent Garden with Fawcett, Incledon, and Mrs. Martyr among
the players.

One nineteenth-century piece needs to be added by way of conclusion, a "Scotch ballad opera" by the same author, which made
its debut at the English Opera House as late as 1835, with eighteen
songs in the two acts, most of them to specified airs. The play, *The
Covenanters,* is a meretricious affair depending for its effects upon
"melo-dramatic music," storms, disguises, shooting, escapes down
a precipice, and spectacular tableaux—all the claptrap devices of
the romantic drama. The historical setting of the action in the
reign of King William no doubt accounts for the use at this late
date of Scotch ballad tunes, the spirit being the same that motivated the antiquarian researches of Monk Lewis, Scott, and
Hugo. The opening stage direction reveals at once the dizzy plunge
from the eighteenth century into the nineteenth—"A small Romantic Farm in a picturesque Vale, surrounded by verdant Hills

dotted with Sheep. The Farm House is nearly covered with Jasmin, Roses, and Honeysuckle. A rustic Paling and practicable Wicket in front, near which Mary sits at her Wheel, as the Curtain rises." Or consider the description of Scene III in Act II: "A Rocky Defile. High Hills on each side, connected by two romantic tree and cable Bridges, one beyond, and higher than the other. A Cataract between them, and a range of blue Mountains in the distance." What could be more remote from Gay or Chetwood or Fielding?

Certainly no more dramatic termination than this could be found for our survey of ballad opera. The chronological span of a hundred and seven years from *The Beggar's Opera* to *The Covenanters* need not be taken too literally, for we have seen that for all practical purposes ballad opera as a distinct and important genre lasted no longer than about a decade. The operas of these first ten years offer variety, interest, and occasional excellence; their hearty laughter or malicious sneers or satirical innuendos grant a clearer insight into the spirit of the century, that curiously prosaic and critical spirit which made few concessions to imagination and fancy but was always touched, nonetheless, by elegant gentility. Ballad opera has the strange and perhaps unique distinction of being the only English dramatic type in which the first representative, *The Beggar's Opera*, was never surpassed or even equalled. But in the decline and fall of "comedies interspersed with ballad tunes" many representatives of the form are interesting and worthy in their own right or in relation to other European forms, and it would be a pity to pass them by superciliously as most histories of literature are accustomed to do.

Notes

CHAPTER ONE: INTRODUCTION

1. The ballad is thus defined in Bailey's *Dictionary*, the fourth edition of which appeared in 1728.

2. Among the designations on the title-page of the published ballad operas occur the following: Opera, Comedy, Farce, Comic-Opera, Farcical Opera, Tragi-Comi-Farcical Ballad Opera, Tragi-Comi-Operatic Pastoral Farce, Tragi-Comi-Pastoral-Farcical Opera, Histori-Tragi-Comi Ballad Opera, etc. Nicoll gives a fuller list (*Early Eighteenth Century* Drama, p. 237n), but it seems to include the designations of musical plays other than ballad operas.

3. The parallel, of course, does not entirely satisfy, since there is in America today no such traditional body of "ballad tunes" as existed in eighteenth-century England.

4. Nicoll, *Late Eighteenth Century Drama*, p. 192.

5. Gay's appropriation of Handel's March in *Rinaldo* for the song of the highwaymen in Act II of *The Beggar's Opera*, for example, must certainly have been intended for ridicule and parody of the original.

6. Carey, having a special aptitude for ballad tunes, often composed his own music, as for the operatization of his farce *The Contrivances*. Therefore, Sonneck (*Catalogue of Opera Librettos Printed before 1800*) calls this not a true ballad opera, though Carey designated it as such. It is with some violence to any rigid definition of ballad opera that several of Carey's musical farces will be considered in the present study.

7. Walpole to West, February 27, 1740, in his *Letters*, I, 49.

8. A thorough and scholarly account of the dramatic jig may be found in Baskervill's *The Elizabethan Jig and Related Song Drama*.

9. By the seventeenth century, as Baskervill asserts, most references to the jig are probably to the dance alone. (*The Elizabethan Jig and Related Song Drama*, p. 147). I have found no evidence to connect *The Beggar's Opera* with this minor and obscure Elizabethan form.

10. Lawrence, "Early Irish Ballad Opera and Comic Opera," p. 398.

11. *Ibid.*, p. 399.

12. One or two relatively unimportant ballad operas, such as Brooke's *Jack the Gyant Queller* (1749), are very exceptional in having five acts.

13. Martin, *Allan Ramsay*, p. 81.

14. *Ibid.*

15. *The Beggar's Opera* migrated early to America, where it was soon followed by other ballad operas. For an account of the early performances in the colonies one may consult Sonneck's *Early Opera in America* and Odell's *Annals of the New York Stage*.

16. Schultz (*Gay's Beggar's Opera*, p. 74) records one rather obscure German version in 1770, Buschmann's *Die Strassenräuber*, published "zum Behuf des Hamburgischen Theaters."

17. For the titles of some of these translations and adaptations, see *infra,* Chapter VII, pp. 107–8, 122, and n. 20, 42.

18. Weisse and Hiller, who had collaborated so successfully in a German version of *The Devil to Pay,* likewise adapted several pieces by Favart, including *Lottchen am Hofe* (from *Ninette à la Cour*) and *Die Liebe auf dem Lande* (from *Annette et Lubin*).

19. A form, based upon Buckingham's famous *Rehearsal* (1671), which, for purposes of satire, presents on the stage a play within the play. One of the best known of the non-operatic "rehearsals" is Sheridan's *The Critic.*

CHAPTER TWO: LOW LIFE AND THE MUSICAL BACKGROUND

1. Samuel Johnson, "Gay," in *Lives of the Poets,* II, 70.
2. Spence, *Anecdotes,* p. 145.
3. Schultz, *Gay's Beggar's Opera,* p. 124.
4. Written by Gay in collaboration with Pope and Arbuthnot.
5. August 30, 1716.
6. The outcome of this suggestion was no doubt Gay's *The Espousal* (1716). Cf. Schultz, *Gay's Beggar's Opera,* p. 122.
7. Spence, *Anecdotes,* p. 120.
8. Brome, *A Jovial Crew,* p. 9.
9. *Ibid.,* p. 12.
10. *Ibid.,* p. 23.
11. Bullock, *A Woman's Revenge,* p. 3.
12. *Ibid.,* p. 4.
13. "To Pretty Miss Polly Peachum," appended with other miscellaneous pieces to *A Woman's Revenge,* p. 70.
14. Pearce, *"Polly Peachum,"* p. 22.
15. Schultz, *Gay's Beggar's Opera,* pp. 169–70.
16. *The Prison-Breaker* does include one song.
17. John Dryden, Preface to *Albion and Albanius.*
18. Odell, *Shakespeare from Betterton to Irving,* Vol. I, Bk. I, particularly Chaps. IV and V.
19. *King Arthur* was sung at New York University as recently as May 24, 1935.
20. Hervey, *Memoirs,* I, 314.
21. Duffett, *The Mock Tempest,* p. 55.
22. Settle, *The World in the Moon,* end of Act I.
23. List appended to Whincop, *Scanderbeg,* p. 225.
24. Burney, *A General History of Music,* IV, 202.
25. Tufts, "Ballad Operas; A List and Some Notes," pp. 61–86.
26. One of the other songs, "When I was a Dame of Honour," appears also in D'Urfey's *Pills* and became a favorite in ballad opera.
27. Nicoll, *Restoration Drama,* p. 194n.
28. List appended to Whincop, *Scanderbeg,* p. 228.

29. Leveridge, *The Comick Masque of Pyramus and Thisbe*, Preface.

30. Addison, *Spectator*, No. 13.

31. [Mrs. Aubert,] *Harlequin-Hydaspes*, p. 36.

32. Gay, "Wednesday," *The Shepherd's Week*, lines 9–18.

33. In a striking sentence Allardyce Nicoll (*Restoration Drama*, p. 267) summarizes the tendencies of Restoration drama: "It required only a little to send comedy careering like a mad country girl along that slightly vulgar and certainly very inartistic path of noise and spectacle which includes the ballets and pasticcios of the eighteenth century."

34. D'Urfey, *Wit and Mirth: or Pills to Purge Melancholy*, II, 185–87.

35. Pope, *Imitations of Horace*, Bk. II, Epistle I, lines 304 ff. Quoted also in Irving, *John Gay's London*, p. 343.

36. I. A. Williams suggests this point in his article, "The Author of The Beggar's Opera," pp. 166–79.

37. Pearce, *"Polly Peachum,"* p. 26.

38. I have been unable to find the article in the *New Monthly Magazine* of that year or of neighboring years.

39. Pearce, *"Polly Peachum,"* p. 26.

40. The anecdote appears in full in Horace Walpole's *Reminiscences*, pp. 136–37.

41. Irving, *John Gay's London*, p. 201. Reprinted with the permission of the Harvard University Press.

42. Schultz, *Gay's Beggar's Opera*, p. 329.

43. Usually, it must be added, this was a device introduced in the non-acted ballad operas.

44. Hervey, *Memoirs*, I, xxiv.

45. Hervey, *Some Materials toward Memoirs of the Reign of King George II*, I, xxxvi.

46. *Pasquin et Marforio*, by du F** and B** (1697), in *Le Théâtre italien de Gherardi*, VI, 644.

47. Iacuzzi, *The European Vogue of Favart*, p. 4n.

48. Lesage and Dorneval, *Théâtre de la foire*, Preface.

49. *Ibid.*, Preface.

50. It is possible that the evidence still exists in some of Gay's letters that remain unpublished.

51. Air XIII appears in this collection, according to A. E. H. Swaen, "The Airs and Tunes of John Gay's Beggar's Opera," pp. 152–90. It is included also, however, in D'Urfey's *Pills*, both in French and English.

52. Bernardin, *La Comédie italienne en France*, p. 123.

53. Burnet, *Achilles Dissected*, p. 5.

54. Goulding, "Eighteenth-Century French Taste and 'The Beggar's Opera,'" pp. 276–93.

55. *Ibid.*, 278.

56. Thorndike, *English Comedy*, p. 392.

CHAPTER THREE: THE BEGGAR'S OPERA AND POLLY

1. Among these may be mentioned A. E. H. Swaen, "The Airs and Tunes of John Gay's Beggar's Opera," *Anglia*, XLIII (1919), 152–90; I. A. Williams, "The Author of the Beggar's Opera," *London Mercury*, III (1920), 166–79; Cœuroy, "Le Beggar's Opera à Paris," *Revue Anglo-Américaine*, Oct., 1923, 62–65; Sybil Goulding, "Eighteenth-Century French Taste and 'The Beggar's Opera,'" *Modern Language Review*, XXIV (1929), 276–93; and J. Loiseau, "John Gay et le *Beggar's Opera*," *Revue Anglo-Américaine*, Oct., 1934, 3–19. An interesting article by D. H. Stevens, "Some Immediate Effects of *The Beggar's Opera*," appeared in the *Manley Anniversary Studies in Language and Literature*, 1923, pp. 180–89.

2. Quoted by John Underhill in his edition of *The Poetical Works of John Gay*, I, liii, from *The Daily Journal*, Feb. 1, 1728.

3. Benjamin, *Life and Letters of John Gay*, p. 78.

4. *Ibid.*, p. 73.

5. Cooke, *Memoirs of Macklin*, p. 60.

6. Not 63 performances, as stated in error in Pope's note in the *Dunciad*. Cf. Schultz, *Gay's Beggar's Opera*, pp. 6–10.

7. Underhill edition of *The Poetical Works of John Gay*, I, lv. See also *Notes and Queries*, first series, i, 178.

8. The estimate of £2,000, given by Baker in his *Companion to the Playhouse*, appears to be too high.

9. According to Underhill, in his edition of *The Poetical Works of John Gay*, I, lv.

10. One revision of definite authorship is recorded as by Captain Thompson in 1777. It came out at Covent Garden but was never printed. The main alteration came at the end of the play with Macheath brought to trial, sentenced to labor on the Thames, and duly brought to repentance.

11. Cooke, *Memoirs of Macklin*, p. 62.

12. *Ibid.*, p. 48.

13. Spence, *Anecdotes*, p. 159.

14. Quoted by Schultz from Oxberry, *Dramatic Biography*, IV, 177.

15. For differing accounts on this point, see Schultz, *Gay's Beggar's Opera*, pp. 3–4.

16. *Biographia Dramatica*, under *The Beggar's Opera*.

17. Loiseau, "John Gay et le *Beggar's Opera*," pp. 3–19.

18. Schultz, *Gay's Beggar's Opera*, pp. 126–27.

19. List appended to Whincop, *Scanderbeg*, pp. 239–40.

20. Loiseau, "John Gay et le *Beggar's Opera*," p. 12.

21. *Ibid.*, p. 17.

22. *Beggar's Opera*, Act III, Sc. XIV.

23. *Ibid.*, Act III, Sc. II.

24. *Ibid.*, Act II, Sc. V.

25. *Ibid.*, Act II, Sc. IV.
26. *Ibid.*, Act I, Sc. VIII.
27. *Ibid.*, Act III, Sc. XVI.
28. Schultz, *Gay's Beggar's Opera*, p. 139.
29. *Ibid.*, p. 145.
30. Loiseau's analysis is interesting enough to deserve quotation: "La parodie de l'opéra italien, elle était partout. Le titre l'annonçait, en associant deux termes aussi incongrus que celui de 'gueux' et celui 'd'opéra,' et le cadre choisi: Newgate et ses abords, était une première atteinte à la dignité du genre. L'intrigue en rappelait les péripéties inévitables: des amants séparés par des parents barbares ... le héros en butte à de ténébreuses machinations, trahi, perdu, n'échappant à la mort que par miracle ... l'héroïne menacée par la jalousie d'une rivale. ... Seulement, le héros était un bandit; ses amoureuses, des fleurs du pavé; ses exploits, ceux d'un 'gangster' du XVIIIᵉ siècle; son milieu, la pègre de Londres. Il était trahi par des filles de joie au cours d'une beuverie, et il devait finir au bout d'une corde; le poison que Lucy destinait à Polly n'était que de la mort-aux-rats. Les éléments des grandes intrigues tragiques étaient rendus grotesques par l'usage imprévu qui en était fait, et le coup de théâtre final, la libération extravagante de Macheath, en soulignait l'artifice." Loiseau, "John Gay et le *Beggar's Opera*," p. 6.
31. Hervey, *Memoirs*, I, 120–21.
32. *Beggar's Opera*, Act I, Sc. IV.
33. Cooke, *Memoirs of Macklin*, pp. 55–56.
34. Hervey, *Memoirs*, I, 117n.
35. Swaen, "The Airs and Tunes of John Gay's Beggar's Opera," p. 152.
36. We must consider the possibility, of course, that Gay was employing the romantic conventions, with his tongue in his cheek, merely to ridicule them.
37. Hervey, *Memoirs*, I, 121.
38. Cooke, *Memoirs of Macklin*, p. 60.
39. Genest, *Some Account of the English Stage*, V, 583.

CHAPTER FOUR: OTHER CONTINENTAL AND ENGLISH INFLUENCES

1. *The Cambridge History of English Literature*, IX, 287.
2. *Ulisse et Circé*, in Gherardi's *Théâtre italien*, III, 536.
3. *Les Avantures des Champs-Elisées*, in Gherardi's *Théâtre italien*, IV, 562.
4. *La Descente de Mezzetin aux enfers*, in Gherardi's *Théâtre italien*, II, 405.
5. Cotton's second volume, a travesty of the fourth book of the *Aeneid*, did not come out until 1670.
6. For a discussion of the relations of Elizabethan drama to the *commedia dell'arte*, see Winifred Smith, *The Commedia dell' Arte*, Chapter VI, and K. M. Lea, *Italian Popular Comedy*, Vol. II, Chapter VI.
7. Nicoll (*Early Eighteenth Century Drama*, Appendix C, pp. 400–407) gives a valuable list of plays given by French and Italian companies at Lincoln's Inn Fields and the little theatre in the Haymarket.

8. Nicoll, *Restoration Drama*, p. 171.

9. See particularly Chapters II and III.

10. Percival, *Political Ballads Illustrating the Administration of Sir Robert Walpole*, Introduction, xi.

11. *Ibid.*, p. xii.

12. Steele, *Tatler*, Nos. 155, 160, 178.

13. Nicoll, *Early Eighteenth Century Drama*, p. 219.

CHAPTER FIVE: LOW-LIFE OPERAS

1. *The Prison-Breaker* and *A Woman's Revenge* have already been mentioned in Chapter II as possible influences on Gay.

2. Schultz, *Gay's Beggar's Opera*, p. 287.

3. Chetwood, *A General History of the Stage*, p. 217.

4. Ap-leek is one of the first singers of dialect songs in ballad opera. Air XXI, sung by her, begins as follws: "Meibon a merched, dewch yu gheed."

5. Ryan, The *Cobler's Opera*, p. 5.

6. *Ibid.*, p. 14.

7. *Ibid.*, p. 18.

8. The same theme of pressing for the navy appears also in Carey's slight but agreeable musical interlude, *Nancy, or The Parting Lovers* (1739), which, under a variety of titles, proved extremely popular during the century. It is not, however, a ballad opera, the text being composed entirely of songs set to music by the author himself.

9. Nicoll, *Early Eighteenth Century Drama*, p. 244.

10. *Biographia Dramatica*, under the title of the play.

11. Walker, *The Quaker's Opera*, p. 7.

12. *Ibid.*, p. 7.

13. Its title, as a droll, is *The Bilker Bilk'd, or a Banquet of Wiles.*

14. *Love and Revenge*, p. 16.

15. *Ibid.*, p. 51.

16. *Ibid.*, p. 49.

17. For information about Timothy Fielding, see an article by F. Latreille in *Notes and Queries* (5th series, iii, 502) and Cross, *History of Henry Fielding*, III, 233.

18. Schultz (*Gay's Beggar's Opera*, p. 293) attributes *The Prisoner's Opera* to Edward Ward, but on what evidence I do not know.

19. *The Grub-street Journal*, No. 31, Aug. 6, 1730.

20. *Ibid.*, No. 39, Sept. 31, 1730.

21. *Ibid.*, No. 38, Sept. 24, 1730.

22. Nichols, in *Biographical Anecdotes of William Hogarth*, p. 32, quotes line 53. Pope also refers to Gonson in lines 256–57 of the same poem.

23. Nichols, *Biographical Anecdotes of William Hogarth*, p. 32n.

24. *The Grub-street Journal*, No. 16, April 23, 1730.

25. Sept. 2, 1731.

26. The topical realism of Fielding's *Covent-Garden Tragedy* is evident from

a letter by "Prosaicus" in *The Grub-street Journal,* No. 127, June 8, 1732: "My man of pleasure [a lawyer who accompanied the writer] was not only very busy in explaining the beauties of the language, but the secret history, the reality of the characters, and some personal scandal."

27. Nichols, *Biographical Anecdotes of William Hogarth,* pp. 29–32. It was this likeness of Gonson that first brought Hogarth to the notice of the great.

28. *Ibid.,* p. 31n.

29. *Ibid.,* p. 194.

30. Theophilus Cibber, *The Harlot's Progress,* p. 12.

31. *The Jew Decoy'd,* p. 6.

32. *Ibid.,* p. 9.

33. Genest (*Some Account of the English Stage,* III, 399), who apparently did not find a printed copy of the play, surmises that it was only a pantomime.

34. *The Grub-street Journal,* No. 188, Aug. 2, 1733; No. 190, Aug. 16, 1733, etc.

35. Drury, *The Rival Milliners,* p. 8.

36. On the evidence of the titles, several unpublished or unavailable pieces may be added to this chapter, although their classification is of necessity uncertain and they cannot even be clearly identified as ballad operas: *The Chimney Sweeper's Opera* (1728); *The Merry Throwster* (1731); *The Sailor's Wedding, or the Humours of Wapping* (1731); *The Sailor's Opera* (1731); *The Chimney Sweeper* (1736); *The Trooper's Opera* (1736); and *The Sailor's Opera, or An Example of Justice for Present and Future Times* (1737). Another Hogarth series may have made its bow on the stage, apparently as a puppet show, but the only evidence I have found is a clipping in the Genest collection at Harvard, dated in ink February (?) 6, 1740: "At Punch's Theatre adjoining to the Tennis-Court, in James-Street near the Hay-market, this Evening, will be presented a Ballad-Opera, call'd the RAKE'S PROGRESS. The Gaoler by the facetious Mr. Punch."

CHAPTER SIX: PASTORAL AND VILLAGE OPERAS

1. Ralph, *The Fashionable Lady,* p. 35.

2. Colley Cibber, *An Apology for The Life of Colley Cibber, Comedian,* I, 199.

3. Baker, *Companion to the Playhouse,* under *Damon and Phillida.*

4. Colley Cibber, *Damon and Phillida,* p. 13.

5. See Chapter I and also Lawrence, "Reviving 'The Gentle Shepherd,'" p. 312.

6. Burns Martin (*Allan Ramsay,* p. 83) surmises that this may have been a performance by the Haddington Boys.

7. Martin, *Ibid.,* pp. 77–78.

8. *Ibid.,* p. 82.

9. *Ibid.,* p. 81, and T. F. Henderson in the *Cambridge History of English Literature,* IX, 411.

10. Tufts, "Ballad Operas: A List and Some Notes," p. 66.

11. *The Judgment of Paris,* p. 4.

12. Dr. Boyce composed the music for these two entertainments.

13. Baker, *Companion to the Playhouse,* under Charles Johnson.

14. Pope, *Dunciad*, Bk. I, line 240. A footnote concerning Charles Johnson runs as follows: "*'Charles Johnson,* famous for writing a play every season, and for being at *Button's* every day: he had probably thriven better in his vocation, had he been a small matter leaner: he may justly be called a martyr to obesity, and to have fallen a victim to the rotundity of his parts.' CHARAC. of the Times, p. 19."

15. Johnson, *The Village Opera*, p. 51.

16. *Ibid.*, p. 64.

17. *Ibid.*, p. 2. An early example of this type of song may be found in Leveridge's *Comick Masque of Pyramus and Thisbe.*

18. Genest, *Some Account of the English Stage*, IV, 281.

19. Francis Gentleman, *The Dramatic Censor, or Critical Companion*, I, 157. The punctuation in the original passage is different.

20. Genest, *Some Account of the English Stage*, III, 234.

21. Schultz, *Gay's Beggar's Opera*, p. 290.

22. *The Grub-street Journal*, No. 92, Oct. 7, 1731. Beggars and miscellaneous rascals, it might be added in passing, get into non-dramatic poetry as well as in plays—for example, in Lady Winchelsea's *Fanscombe Barn*, a precursor of Burns's *Jolly Beggars.*

23. *Ibid.*, No. 140, Sept. 7, 1732.

24. Lawrence, "Early Irish Ballad Opera and Comic Opera," pp. 397–412.

25. Baker, *Companion to the Playhouse*, under Charles Coffey.

26. Coffey, The *Beggar's Wedding*, 2d ed., London, 1729, p. 3.

27. *Ibid.*, p. 26.

28. *Ibid.*, p. 34.

29. Sonneck, *Catalogue of Opera Librettos Published before 1800,* Vol. I, under *The Jovial Crew.*

30. Genest, *Some Account of the English Stage*, III, 291.

31. Baker, *Companion to the Playhouse*, under *The Jovial Crew.*

32. Genest, *Some Account of the English Stage*, III, 288.

33. *The Jovial Crew*, Act. III, p. 55 ff.

34. Letitia Pilkington, *Memoirs*, p. 98.

35. *The Jovial Crew*, p. 45.

36. *Ibid.*, p. 19.

37. As in Baker, *Companion to the Playhouse. Flora* appears in some of the editions of Cibber's works.

38. The locale in Doggett's play and in the *Sequel to Flora* is given as Gloucester.

39. Hippisley, *Flora*, p. 19.

40. *The Grub-street Journal*, No. 46, Nov. 19, 1730.

41. Lillo, *Dramatic Works*, I, 40.

42. Lillo, *Silvia*, p. 38.

43. *Ibid.*, p. 5.

44. *Ibid.*, p. 31.

45. Genest, *Some Account of the English Stage*, III, 303.

46. Letitia Pilkington, *Memoirs*, p. 362.

47. Quoted in Pearce, "*Polly Peachum,*" p. 121.

48. Three more pieces—two of them unpublished—may possibly be added to the operas of the present chapter. *Tho' Strange 'Tis True, or Love's Vagaries* (Lincoln's Inn Fields, 1732) is listed by Nicoll as a pastoral ballad opera. The titles of the others seem to indicate their classification: *The Farmer's Son, or The Maiden's Second Slip* (Haymarket, 1733) and *The Shepherd's Opera*, attributed to John Maxwell but published anonymously at York, 1739. In addition to these, a few of the ballad operas yet to be discussed have incidental pastoral or rustic effects.

CHAPTER SEVEN: FARCE AND INTRIGUE

1. Only two or three ballad operas were written in five acts, Henry Brooke's *Jack the Gyant Queller* being perhaps the most notable one.

2. Chetwood, *The Lover's Opera,* Preface.

3. For further reference to Mr. Pilkington as a hired scribbler, see *infra,* pp. 120–21.

4. The distinction is ably discussed in Lawrence's article, "Early Irish Ballad Opera and Comic Opera," pp. 398 ff.

5. The few unpublished pieces referred to which are apparently concerned with farce and intrigue may be listed here as follows, with the usual proviso that they may not be ballad operas: *The Clown's Stratagem, or A New Way to Get a Wife* (1730); *The Jealous Taylor, or The Intriguing Valet* (1731); *The Contract, or The Biter Bit* (1736); Thomas Phillips, *The Rival Captains, or The Imposter Unmasked* (1736); *The Comical Disappointment, or The Miser Outwitted* (1736); *The Modern Pimp, or The Doctor Deceived* (1736); *The Cheats of Scapin* (1736). For the theatres where operas first appeared, see Bibliography of Ballad Operas, Section II.

6. Despite the contemporary assertions, it is only fair to add that there exists some doubt about Carey's alleged suicide. See the *Dictionary of National Biography.*

7. Sonneck, *Catalogue of Opera Librettos Published before 1800,* Vol. I, under *The Contrivances.*

8. Carey, *The Contrivances,* Dublin, 1731, p. 11.

9. Coffey's play was published in 1745, but I have not been able to see a copy.

10. Lawrence, "Early Irish Ballad Opera and Comic Opera," p. 400.

11. Coffey, *The Female Parson,* p. 26.

12. "It is a poor piece." Genest, *Some Account of the English Stage,* III, 282.

13. See Lawrence, "The Mystery of 'The Stage Coach,'" pp. 392–97, for full particulars.

14. One bit of music, it might be mentioned, appears in the original Farquhar farce, consisting of four stanzas with chorus entitled "The Stage Coach Song."

15. List appended to Whincop, *Scanderbeg.* A. E. Richards, in an article, "A Literary Link between Thomas Shadwell and Christian Felix Weisse," offers further evidence, textual and otherwise, tending to prove that Shadwell had a hand in Jevon's play.

16. Rochester's song, of course, was written some fifty years before.

17. For earlier mention of the *Singspiel,* see *supra,* Chap. I, pp. 8–9.

18. Von Borck was the Prussian ambassador to London. See Richards, "A Literary Link between Thomas Shadwell and Christian Felix Weisse," p. 828.

19. *Ibid.*, p. 828, and Iacuzzi, *The European Vogue of Favart*, p. 126.

20. Richards, *Ibid.*, p. 829, and Iacuzzi, *Ibid.*, pp. 126–27. A more complete list of adaptations may be found in Riemann's *Opern-handbuch* under the name *Die verwandelten Weiber,* one of the titles given to Coffey's opera. We may mention here F. A. Weber's *Die verwandelten Weiber* (1775) and Anton Schweitzer's *Der gebesserte Hausteufel* (c. 1780). The French version by Sedaine and Philidor, *Le Diable à quatre,* was itself the basis of other adaptations, *Die doppelte Verwandlung* (Vienna, 1767), for example, and Portugal's *Il diavolo a quattro.*

21. Air XV in the three-act version; Air VII in the afterpiece.

22. It may be of interest to note that Johnson was inspired by Shakespeare in another play, *Love in a Forest* (1732), an alteration of *As You Like It.*

23. Lawrence, "Early Irish Ballad Opera and Comic Opera," p. 403.

24. Air IV.

25. Baker, *Companion to the Playhouse,* under *The Devil of a Duke.* The editor of *The Dramatic Works of Sir Aston Cokain,* Edinburgh and London, 1874, gives the name of the French work as the *Contes de Duville* (p. 117).

26. Seedo's name does not appear in the edition I have examined, but Sonneck identifies him as composer of some of the songs. Sonneck, *Catalogue of Opera Librettos Published before 1800,* Vol. I, under *The Devil of a Duke.*

27. *The Grub-street Journal,* No. 165, Feb. 22, 1733. The play seems to be a ballad-operatization of an earlier farce by Carey called *Hanging and Marriage* (1722).

28. According to the printed play, which also gives the cast, but no other record of any performance exists.

29. Wood ("The Disappointment," pp. 66–69) gives as evidence the failure to identify "John Randall," the fact that the list appended to Whincop's *Scanderbeg* and other writers ascribe to Carey a play *A Wife Well Manag'd,* and various bits of internal evidence in the preface and songs.

30. Air XXIII.

31. *La Fille sçavante* in Gherardi's *Théâtre italien* makes use of the same device.

32. Drury, *The Mad Captain,* p. 12.

33. Genest, *Some Account of the English Stage,* III, 395. It must be admitted that Drury altered the play considerably, if not for the better.

34. The name King of Pawpaw is an interesting contemporary allusion and helps perhaps to date the actual composition of Drury's play. A news item in *The Grub-street Journal* for May 13, 1731, gives the name of an emperor on the coast of Guinea as the Grand Trudo Audato Povesaw Dangerenio Surveveveto Ene Mottee Adde Powa Powlo Co Hullo Necresy, King of Dawhomay, and Emperor of Pawpaw.

35. Genest, *Some Account of the English Stage,* III, 372.

36. *Ibid.*, III, 372. The first performance took place at Drury Lane on May 5, 1733.

37. *Ibid.*, III, 458.

38. Letitia Pilkington, *Memoirs,* pp. 361 ff.

39. *Ibid.*, p. 301.

40 In the printed play the name appears as Mecklin, as it was frequently spelled.

41. Coffey, *The Merry Cobler*, p. 21.

42. Riemann in his *Opern-handbuch* mentions, in addition to the 1759 *Der lustige Schuster,* versions by Hiller, Friedrich August Weber, and Franz Andreas Holly.

43. Genest, *Some Account of the English Stage*, III, 452.

44. Carey, *Of Stage Tyrants,* Preface.

45. Carey, *A Wonder: or an Honest Yorkshire-Man,* London, 1736, p. 19.

46. So says Nicoll (*Early Eighteenth Century Drama,* Appendix C) but as May Fair was no longer observed in London, performance must have taken place outside of the city.

47. *Biographia Dramatica,* under *The Lover his Own Rival.*

48. Genest (*Some Account of the English Stage,* X, 171–72) does list it among the unacted plays and quotes the cast from the printed play.

49. An interesting passage in Hervey's *Memoirs* (II, 491) mentions that *The Dragon of Wantley* was a topic of discussion at Court on Queen Caroline's last formal appearance before her fatal illness.

50. Nicoll (*Early Eighteenth Century Drama,* p. 249n.) says that Arthur's play was based on Charles Johnson's *The Wife's Relief* (1711), a fact which would minimize the possibility of its exploiting local scandal. While the central situation in the two plays is the same, the circumstances and treatment are very different.

51. Arthur, *The Lucky Discovery,* p. 24.

52. I have not seen a copy of the play. *The Biographia Dramatica* says it was printed by Thomas Gent and that the author was probably "poor John Maxwell, the blind man"—author also of *The Shepherd's Opera.*

53. Baker, *Companion to the Playhouse,* under Daniel Bellamy.

54. Genest (*Some Account of the English Stage,* X, 168) asserts the plot was stolen from *Love in a Chest* (1710).

55. Bellamy, *The Rival Priests,* in *Dramatic Pieces, and Other Miscellaneous Works in Prose and Verse,* I, 12.

56. The playbill spells the name of Peterson incorrectly as Paterson. Genest, *Some Account of the English Stage,* IV, 11–12.

57. Peterson, *The Raree Show,* 2d ed., Chester, 1740, p. 24.

58. Lawrence ("Early Irish Ballad Opera and Comic Opera," p. 405) mentions that after two postponements *The Sharpers* was given at Aungier Street on February 21, 1740. The title-page of the 1740 edition, however, gives the theatre as Smock Alley.

59. As authority for this identification the Library of Congress gives O'Donoghue's *Poets of Ireland.*

60. Ayres, *Sancho at Court,* Preface.

61. Mendez, *The Double Disappointment,* p. 32.

62. *Ibid.*, p. 40.

63. *Ibid.*, p. 11.

CHAPTER EIGHT: SATIRE AND BURLESQUE

1. *High Life Below Stairs* (1759) by James Townley. Allusion to this popular play was made, in 1775, in the title of Garrick's farce, *Bon Ton, or High Life Above Stairs*.

2. *The Footman*, p. 73.

3. *Ibid.*, p. 19.

4. *Ibid.*, p. 53.

5. It is amusing to note that Benjamin Franklin, who had formed a friendship with James Ralph in Philadelphia, considered him a poor poet but an excellent conversationalist.—Benjamin Franklin, *Autobiography*, English Classic Series, N. Y., [c. 1892], pp. 41–43.

6. *The Footman*, pp. 50–51.

7. Fielding, *The Author's Farce*, 3d ed., 1750, p. 26.

8. *Ibid.*, p. 41.

9. *Ibid.*, p. 32.

10. Baker, *Companion to the Playhouse*, under *The Lottery*.

11. Fielding, *The Lottery*, p. 11.

12. *Ibid.*, p. 14.

13. *Ibid.*, p. 14. An example from the *Théâtre italien*, quite similar to Fielding's line both in style and content, may be found in Evaristo Gherardi's *Le Retour de la Foire de Bezons* (1695): "Embrassez-la donc, Madame, cette fortune; et puisque vous me voyez sous ses habits, permettez que le vent de votre courtoisie, poussant le vaisseau de mon amour sur la mer de votre complaisance, je puisse mouiller l'ancre de mes desirs au port desiré de vos bonnes graces." Gherardi, *Théâtre italien*, VI, 173.

14. The first edition lists only nineteen airs.

15. Cross, *History of Henry Fielding*, I, 159–60.

16. *Squire Badger* was later revived, with alterations, as *The Sot*. Cross, *History of Henry Fielding*, III, 154.

17. Fielding, *Don Quixote in England*, p. 4.

18. *Ibid.*, pp. 27–28.

19. Including the last song of the piece, "The Yorkshire Ballad," which is not numbered.

20. Fielding, *An Old Man Taught Wisdom*, p. 4.

21. Baker, *Companion to the Playhouse*, under *An Old Man Taught Wisdom*.

22. Cross (*History of Henry Fielding*, I, 368) asserts this production was a revision of a play written in 1735, after *An Old Man Taught Wisdom*, by Fielding and another writer.

23. Cross, *Ibid.*, I, 369–70.

24. Horace Walpole, *Letters*, I, 228. The passage is quoted also in Cross, *History of Henry Fielding*, I, 369.

25. Fielding, *Miss Lucy in Town*, 2d ed., London, 1756, p. 6.

26. *Ibid.*, p. 7.

27. *Ibid.*, p. 41.

28. *Ibid.*, p. 43.

29. *Ibid.*, p. 20.

30. The poets are identified similarly in Cross, *History of Henry Fielding*, I, 96. The allusions in most of the names, of course, are perfectly clear.

31. Hatchett and Haywood, *The Opera of Operas*, p. 30.

32. Tony Aston had a son, Walter Aston, who was married in Edinburgh in April, 1728. Thornton S. Graves ("Some Facts about Anthony Aston," p. 394) believes that this is the same Walter Aston who wrote *The Restauration of King Charles II*.

33. Tony Aston, *The Fool's Opera*, Introductory Note.

34. Since *The Fool's Opera* is considered rare, it is interesting to note that there is a copy at Harvard and one also in the Library of Congress.

35. *The Biographia Dramatica* merely mentions the piece, giving the date of publication as 1754.

36. Ralph, *The Fashionable Lady*, p. 80.

37. *Ibid.*, p. 44.

38. *Ibid.*, p. 9.

39. *Ibid.*, pp. 25–26. There are several intervening speeches.

40. *Ibid.*, p. 14.

41. *Ibid.*, p. 52. The air, Number XL, is sung by Prattle, the chambermaid.

42. *Ibid.*, p. 42.

43. Ralph, *The Taste of the Town, or A Guide to All Publick Diversions*, pp. 24–25.

44. *Ibid.*, p. 25.

45. The line mentions the custom of the footmen of adorning themselves with their masters' titles. *The Fashionable Lady*, p. 74.

46. I find that Ralph's influence on Fielding has been discussed previously in an article by Helen Sard Hughes, "Fielding's Indebtedness to James Ralph," pp. 19–34, in which the Tom Thumb suggestion is mentioned and considered. Frederick T. Wood, in his edition of Carey's poems (Appendix, p. 261), has also mentioned the probable indebtedness of *The Dragon of Wantley* to Ralph's suggestion about the Dragon of Wantcliff.

47. Cross, *History of Henry Fielding*, I, 192–95.

48. *Ibid.*, I, 192.

49. Fielding, *Tumble-Down Dick*, London, 1744, p. 15.

50. Cross, *History of Henry Fielding*, I, 193–94.

51. Fielding, *Tumble-Down Dick*, p. 4.

52. *The Songs in Harlequin Restor'd*, appended to Pritchard, *The Fall of Phaeton*, London, 1736, p. 23.

53. Palaprat's *Arlequin Phaéton* is available in the Gherardi collection.

54. Levy, *The Unpublished Plays of Carolet*, pp. 178–83.

55. Baker, *A Rehearsal of a New Ballad-Opera Burlesqu'd, Call'd The Mad-House*, Preface.

56. *Ibid.*, p. 30.

57. *Ibid.*, p. 39.

58. Genest, *Some Account of the English Stage*, III, 605.

59. William Barclay Squire, "An Index of Tunes in the Ballad Operas," p. 2n.

60. It should be mentioned that Mrs. Clive wrote several subsequent plays, all of them slight.

61. Carey, *Poems*, p. 110.

CHAPTER NINE: TOPICAL OPERAS: SOCIAL SCANDAL AND POLITICS

1. *The Gentleman's Magazine*, 1731, p. 453.

2. Lawrence, "Early Irish Ballad Opera and Comic Opera," pp. 403–4.

3. *The Grub-street Journal* (No. 176, May 5, 1733) asserts that a gentleman from Baliol College was appointed and that an annuity of a hundred pounds was to be settled upon him as a reward for being expelled, "which always follows the licence and satyr of his performance."

4. *The Grub-street Journal*, No. 183, June 28, 1733, and No. 190, Aug. 16, 1733.

5. *The Oxford Act*, p. 7.

6. Amhurst, *Terræ-Filius, or The Secret History of the University of Oxford*, p. 157.

7. While I had suspected Phillips' authorship, for definite identification I am indebted to a reference given to me by Professor George Sherburn. In a list of books printed for Charles Corbett, appended to Marivaux's *Le Paysan Parvenu, or The Fortunate Peasant* (London, 1735), Phillips is named as the author of *The Stage-Mutineers*.

8. Lun, Jr., under whose authorship the play appeared, was the stage name of the actor Henry Woodward.

9. The thirteenth and final song is not numbered in the text.

10. *The Operator*, p. 3.

11. Lawrence, "*Early Irish Ballad Opera and Comic Opera*," p. 405. Nicoll gives the date of the Aungier Street production as April 16, 1741. The play reached London in 1744.

12. Baker, *Companion to the Playhouse*, under *The Wanton Countess.*

13. According to contemporary rumor, *The Modish Couple*, acted at Drury Lane in January, 1732, was written, not by Captain Bodens, the alleged author, but by Hervey and the Prince of Wales. See Historical Manuscripts Commission, *Manuscripts of the Earl of Egmont: Diary of Viscount Percival, afterwards First Earl of Egmont*, I, 205 and 216.

14. Schultz, *Gay's Beggar's Opera*, Appendix I, p. 295. The comment in *The Grub-street Journal* may be found in No. 52, Dec. 31, 1730.

15. Fielding, *The Grub-Street Opera*, p. 53.

16. *Ibid.*, pp. 26–27.

17. *Ibid.*, p. 8.

18. *Ibid.*, p. 28.

19. *Ibid.*, p. 10.

20. *Ibid.*, p. 53.

21. Another edition of *The Grub-Street Opera* has only 57 airs.

22. Really 31 in the edition that I examined, as there is an error in the numbering, two consecutive songs appearing as Air XXVI.

23. *Vanelia*, p. 55. The air is sung by Lord Haughty.

24. Hervey, *Memoirs*, I, 305.

25. While the title-page gives no date, the play apparently came out in 1733. It was republished in 1734 with the new title *The Honest Electors, or The Free-holder's Opera*.

26. *The Honest Electors*, p. 11.

27. *Ibid.*, p. 21.

28. This description of the lady, the daughter of Peter Lombard, is given in the *dramatis personae* of *Lord Blunder's Confession*.

29. *Lord Blunder's Confession*, Act I, Scene II.

30. *The Wedding*, p. 49.

31. *Ibid.*, p. 35.

32. Hervey, *Memoirs*, II, 11.

33. *The Wedding*, p. 35.

34. *Ibid.*, p. 36.

35. *Court and Country*, p. 26.

CHAPTER TEN: OTHER BALLAD OPERAS: 1728–1800

1. Ralph, *The Fashionable Lady*, p. 61.

2. List of plays appended to Whincop, *Scanderbeg*, p. 205.

3. The authorship is so given by Tufts and by Schultz, but with no mention of their authority.

4. *Momus Turn'd Fabulist*, Introduction.

5. Burnet, *Achilles Dissected: Being a Compleat Key of the Political Characters in that New Ballad Opera*, p. 4.

6. Reported in *The Grub-street Journal*, No. 164, Feb. 15, 1733.

7. Burnet, *Achilles Dissected*, p. 5.

8. *Ibid.*, p. 5.

9. Burney, *A General History of Music*, IV, 215.

10. Kelly, *Timon in Love*, p. 53.

11. *Ibid.*, p. 51.

12. *Ibid.*, pp. 4–5.

13. *Ibid.*, p. 19.

14. *Ibid.*, p. 37.

15. *Ibid.*, p. 38.

16. Breval, *The Rape of Helen*, p. 30.

17. *Ibid.*, p. 23.

18. *Ibid.*, p. 8.

19. Chetwood, *The Generous Free-Mason*, p. 3.

20. *Ibid.*, p. 3.

21. There were also some earlier plays about Robin Hood. In 1601 was published Anthony Mundy's *Robert Earl of Huntington's Downfall*. A *Robin Hood, Part I* and a *Robin Hood, Part II* by Mundy and Chettle never reached publication.

22. Baker, *Companion to the Playhouse*, under Joseph Mitchell.

23. Mitchell, *The Highland Fair*, Introduction.

24. *Ibid.*, p. 77.

25. So identified by Graves, "Some Facts about Anthony Aston," p. 394.

26. Aston, *The Restauration of King Charles II*, p. 24.

27. Elizabeth Boyd, *Don Sancho*, p. 13.

28. *Ibid.*, p. 13.

29. Baker, in *Companion to the Playhouse*, says that this information was reported in *The British Theatre*.

30. Hammond, *The Preceptor*, p. 23.

31. *Ibid.*, p. 29.

32. *Ibid.*, p. 32.

33. *The Grub-street Journal*, No. 215, Feb. 7, 1734.

34. Brooke, *Little John and The Giants*, Prologue, in Brooke, *Collected Works*, London, 1778, Vol. IV.

35. *Ibid.*, p. 8.

36. *Ibid.*, p. 13.

37. *Ibid.*, Act 3, Sc. 3.

38. *Ibid.*, p. 54.

39. Before proceeding to the second half of the century a few additional operas, unacted or unavailable, may be listed with the usual caution that they may not be ballad operas, although tentatively so recorded by Nicoll or Lawrence: Charles Johnson, *The Ephesian Matron* (1732); Mrs. Egleton, *The Maggot* (1732); *The Barren Island, or Petticoat Government* (1734); *Politics on Both Sides* (1735); *The Medley* (1736); Samuel Davey, *Whittington and His Cat* (1739); Matthew Gardiner, *The Sharpers, or Female Matchmaker* (1740); and James Ayres, *The Kiss Accepted and Returned* (1744). Undoubtedly, also, a number of ballad operas must have escaped the records—Mrs. Pilkington's, for example, or the ballad-operatization of Gay's *What d'ye Call It* mentioned in the *Grub-street Journal* as being under rehearsal.

40. The edition of 1767 has two acts and eighteen songs. A second and enlarged edition of three acts and twenty songs came out at Philadelphia in 1796.

41. Sonneck, *Catalogue of Opera Librettos Published before 1800*, under *The Disappointment, or The Force of Credulity*.

42. Barton, *The Disappointment*, 2d. ed., Philadelphia, 1796, Preface.

43. Genest, *Some Account of the English Stage*, X, 197.

Bibliography of Ballad Operas

I: PUBLISHED BALLAD OPERAS

THE OPERAS I have not found available are marked with an asterisk. For acted pieces, the theatre where each was first acted is indicated. The Haymarket, in the present list, indicates the little theatre in the Haymarket, and not the larger playhouse of the same name.

Arthur, John. The Lucky Discovery, or The Tanner of York. York, 1737 (York, 1737; Covent Garden, 1738).

Aston, Anthony (Tony). The Fool's Opera, or The Taste of the Age, Written by Mat. Medley, and Performed by his Company in Oxford. . . . To Which Is Prefix'd, A Sketch of the Author's Life, Written by Himself. London, 1731 (Oxford, 1731).

Aston, Walter. The Restauration of King Charles II, or The Life and Death of Oliver Cromwell: An Histori-Tragi-Comi Ballad Opera. London, 1732.

[Ayres, James.] Sancho at Court, or The Mock-Governor . . . Written by a Gentleman, Late of Trinity College, Dublin. London, 1742. Attributed to James Eyre Weeks.

Baker, Robert. A Rehearsal of a New Ballad-Opera Burlesqu'd, Call'd The Mad-House . . . By a Gentleman of the Inner Temple. London, 1737 (Lincoln's Inn Fields, 1737).

Bellamy, Daniel. The Rival Priests, or The Female Politician. Published in Dramatic Pieces, and Other Miscellaneous Works in Prose and Verse, 2 vols., London, 1739.

Boyd, Elizabeth. Don Sancho, or The Student's Whim: A Ballad Opera of Two Acts. London, 1739. Titles of airs not indicated.

Breval, John. The Rape of Helen: A Mock-Opera. London, 1737 (Covent Garden, 1733).

Brooke, Henry. Little John and the Giants: A Dramatic Opera. Published in Vol. IV of Collected Works, 1778. Acted once in Dublin, 1749, as Jack the Gyant Queller. Songs published separately, 1749. Published as Little John and the Giants, n.d. [c. 1754].

Calista: An Opera. London, 1731.

Carey, Henry. Betty, or The Country Bumpkins. (Drury Lane, 1732). The opera was not published but in 1739 appeared: The Songs, As They Are Sung in Betty.

———The Contrivances. London, 1729 (Drury Lane, 1729). Ballad-operatized from Carey's farce, The Contrivances, 1715. Music, however, by the author.

———The Honest Yorkshire-Man: A Ballad-Farce. London, 1736 (No record of first performance, played at Lincoln's Inn Fields, Haymarket, and Goodman's Fields, 1735). Published also under title, A Wonder, or An Honest Yorkshire-Man.

Chetwood, William Rufus. The Generous Free-Mason, or The Constant Lady, with the Humours of Squire Noodle and his Man Doodle.   London, 1731 (Bartholomew Fair, 1730).

——The Lover's Opera.   London, 1729 (Drury Lane, 1729).

*Chuck, or The School-Boy's Opera.   London, 1736 (Smock Alley, Dublin, 1729).

Cibber, Colley.   Damon and Phillida.   London, 1729 (Haymarket, 1729).   One-act version of Love in a Riddle.

——Love in a Riddle: A Pastoral.   London, 1719 [misprint for 1729] (Drury Lane, 1729).

Cibber, Theophilus.   The Harlot's Progress, or The Ridotto al'Fresco.   London, 1733 (Drury Lane, 1733).

——Patie and Peggy, or The Fair Foundling.   London, 1730 (Drury Lane, 1730).

*Cobbler of Preston (The): An Opera, As It Is Acted at the New Booth in Dublin, with Great Applause.   1732.

Coffey, Charles.   The Beggar's Wedding.   London, 1729 (Smock Alley, Dublin, 1729; Haymarket, 1729).

——The Boarding-School, or The Sham Captain.   London, 1733 (Drury Lane, 1733, as The Boarding School Romps).

——The Devil to Pay, or The Wives Metamorphos'd: An Opera.   London, 1731 (Drury Lane, 1731).   Mottley had a hand in the three-act version. It was reduced to one act by Theophilus Cibber and published in 1732.

——*The Devil upon Two Sticks, or The Country Beau: A Ballad Farce. Published in 1729 according to Schultz; Nicoll mentions only an edition of 1745 (Drury Lane, 1729).

——The Female Parson, or Beau in the Sudds: An Opera.   London, 1730 (Haymarket, 1730).

——The Merry Cobler, or The Second Part of the Devil to Pay.   London, 1735 (Drury Lane, 1735).

——Phebe, or The Beggar's Wedding.   London, 1729 (Drury Lane, 1729). One-act version of The Beggar's Wedding.

——Southwark Fair, or The Sheep-Shearing.   London, 1729 (Southwark Fair, 1729).

Commodity Excis'd (The), or The Women in an Uproar: A New Ballad Opera . . . By Timothy Smoke.   London, 1733.   Names of airs not indicated.

Country-Wedding (The), or The Cocknies Bit.   London, 1749.

Court and Country, or The Changelings.   London, 1743.

Court Medley (The), or Marriage by Proxy.   London, 1733.

Cupid and Psyche, or Columbine-Courtezan: A Dramatic Pantomime Entertainment Interspers'd with Ballad Tunes.   London, 1734 (Drury Lane, 1734). The titles of the ballad airs not indicated.

Downfall of Bribery (The), or The Honest Men of Taunton . . . By Mark Freeman.   London, 1733.

Drury, Robert.   The Devil of a Duke, or Trapolin's Vagaries.   London, 1732 (Drury Lane, 1732).

——The Fancy'd Queen.   London, 1733 (Covent Garden, 1733).

——The Mad Captain.   London, 1733 (Goodman's Fields, 1733).

———The Rival Milliners, or The Humours of Covent-Garden. London, 1737 (Haymarket, 1736).

Fabian, R. Trick for Trick. London, 1735 (Drury Lane, 1735).

*Farewell and Return, or The Fortune of War: A Ballad Farce. 1739?

Female Rake (The), or Modern Fine Lady. London, 1736 (Haymarket, 1736). Appears as: The Woman of Taste, or The Yorkshire Lady in The Curiosity (1739). Attributed to Joseph Dorman.

Fielding, Henry. The Author's Farce, and The Pleasures of the Town. By Scriblerus Secundus. London, 1730 (Haymarket, 1730). Altered and enlarged in 3d ed., 1750, as: The Author's Farce, with a Puppet-Show, Call'd The Pleasures of the Town. In part a ballad opera.

———Don Quixote in England. London, 1734 (Haymarket, 1734).

———The Grub-Street Opera. See The Welsh Opera.

———The Intriguing Chambermaid . . . Taken from the French of Regnard. London, 1734 (Drury Lane, 1734).

———The Lottery: A Farce. London, 1732 (Drury Lane, 1732).

———Miss Lucy in Town: A Sequel to The Virgin Unmasqued. London, 1742 (Drury Lane, 1742). Titles of airs not indicated.

———The Mock Doctor, or The Dumb Lady Cur'd: A Comedy, Done from Molière. London, 1732 (Drury Lane, 1732).

———An Old Man Taught Wisdom, or The Virgin Unmask'd. London, 1735 (Drury Lane, 1735).

———Tumble-Down Dick, or Phaeton in the Suds. London, 1736 (Haymarket, 1736).

———The Welsh Opera, or The Grey Mare the Better Horse, Written by Scriblerus Secundus. London, 1731 (Haymarket, 1731). Enlarged as: The Genuine Grub-Street Opera, As It Was Intended to be Acted at the Theatre in the Hay-Market. London, 1731. Appeared also as: The Grub-Street Opera, As It Is Acted at the Theatre in the Hay-Market. London, 1731 (Haymarket, 1731).

Footman (The): An Opera. London, 1732 (Goodman's Fields, 1732).

Fortunate Prince (The), or Marriage at Last. London, 1734. Almost identical with The Court Medley.

Fox Uncas'd (The), or Robin's Art of Money-catching. London, 1733. Almost identical with The Wanton Countess.

Gardiner, Matthew. The Sharpers: A Ballad Opera. Dublin, 1740 (Aungier Street, Dublin, 1740).

Gataker, Thomas. The Jealous Clown, or The Lucky Mistake. London, 1730 (Goodman's Fields, 1730).

Gay, John. Achilles: An Opera. London, 1733 (Covent Garden, 1733).

———The Beggar's Opera. London, 1728 (Lincoln's Inn Fields, 1728).

———Polly: An Opera, Being the Second Part of The Beggar's Opera. London, 1729. Altered by Colman and acted at Haymarket, 1777.

Goodall, William. The False Guardians Outwitted. Published in The True Englishman's Miscellany, London, 1740.

Hammond, William. The Preceptor, or The Loves of Abelard and Heloise. Dublin, 1740 (Smock Alley, Dublin, 1739).

Harlequin Restor'd, or Taste Alamode. (Apparently not published except for: The Songs in Harlequin Restor'd, printed at end of Pritchard's The Fall of Phaeton, London, 1736).

Hawker, Essex. The Wedding: A Tragi-Comi-Pastoral-Farcical Opera ... With an Hudibrastick Skimmington. London, 1729 (Lincoln's Inn Fields, 1729). Published the same year as The Country-Wedding and Skimmington—as acted at Drury Lane.

Hippisley, John. Flora: An Opera. London, 1729 (Lincoln's Inn Fields, 1729). Printed also as: Flora, or Hob in the Well.

———A Sequel to the Opera of Flora ... Written by the Author of Flora. London, 1732 (Lincoln's Inn Fields, 1732).

Honest Electors (The), or The Courtiers Sent Back with Their Bribes. London, n.d. [1733].

Humours of the Court (The), or Modern Gallantry ... As It Was Intended to Have Been Perform'd at One of the Theatres. London, 1732.

Intriguing Courtiers (The), or The Modish Gallants. London, 1732. Appeared also as: The Modish Gallants: A Comedy, in which is introduced An Interlude, Call'd The Promis'd Marriage, or The Dissappointed [sic] Lady. London, 1733. A five-act comedy; only the interlude is in the ballad-opera form.

Jew Decoy'd (The), or The Progress of a Harlot. London, 1733.

Johnson, Charles. The Village Opera. London, 1729 (Drury Lane, 1729).

Jovial Crew (The): A Comic Opera. London, 1731 (Drury Lane, 1731). Attributed to Roome, Concanen, and Sir William Yonge.

Judgment of Paris (The), or The Triumph of Beauty. London, 1731 (Lincoln's Inn Fields, 1731).

*Keepers (The). 1734.

Kelly, John. The Plot. London, 1735 (Drury Lane, 1735).

———Timon in Love, or The Innocent Theft. London, 1733 (Drury Lane, 1733).

Ladies of the Palace (The), or The New Court Legacy. London, 1735. Except for the title-page, identical with The Court Legacy, 1733.

Langford, Abraham. The Lover His Own Rival. London, 1736 (Goodman's Fields, 1736).

Lillo, George. Silvia, or The Country Burial: An Opera. Dublin, 1730 (according to Nicoll); London, 1731 (Lincoln's Inn Fields, 1730).

Lord Blunder's Confession, or Guilt Makes a Coward ... By the Author of Vanelia. London, 1733.

Love and Revenge, or The Vintner Outwitted: An Opera. London, 1729 (Haymarket, 1729).

[Manley, Mrs. Mary de la Rivière.] The Court Legacy ... By the Author of the New Atalantis. London, 1733.

[Maxwell, John.] *The Shepherd's Opera. York, 1739.

———*The Trepan, or Virtue Rewarded. York, 1739.

Mitchell, Joseph. The Highland Fair, or Union of the Clans. London, 1731 (Drury Lane, 1731).

Momus Turn'd Fabulist, or Vulcan's Wedding: An Opera. London, 1729 (Lincoln's Inn Fields, 1729). Attributed to Ebenezer Forrest.

Mottley, John and Thomas Cooke. Penelope. London, 1728 (Haymarket, 1728).

Odell, Thomas. The Patron, or The Statesman's Opera. London, 1729 (Haymarket, 1729).

Odingsells, Gabriel. Bays's Opera. London, 1730 (Drury Lane, 1730).

Operator (The): A Ballad Opera. London, 1740. Titles of the tunes not indicated.

Oxford Act (The): A New Ballad-Opera, As It Was Perform'd by a Company of Students at Oxford. London, 1733.

Peterson, Joseph. The Rarce Show, or The Fox Trap't. York, 1739 (York, 1739).

Phillips, Edward. Britons, Strike Home, or The Sailor's Rehearsal. London, 1739 (Drury Lane, 1739).

——The Chamber-maid. London, 1730 (Drury Lane, 1730).

——The Livery Rake and Country Lass. London, 1733 (Drury Lane, 1733, as The Livery Rake, or The Intriguing Servants).

——The Mock Lawyer. London, n.d. [1733] (Covent Garden, 1733).

——The Stage-Mutineers, or A Play-House to be Lett: A Tragi-Comi-Farcical Ballad Opera . . . By a Gentleman late of Trinity-College, Cambridge. London, 1733 (Covent Garden, 1733).

Potter, Henry. The Decoy: An Opera. London, 1733 (Goodman's Fields, 1733).

Prisoner's Opera (The). Sadler's Wells, 1730. Attributed by Schultz to Edward Ward.

Ragged Uproar (The), or The Oxford Roratory. London, n.d.

Ralph, James. The Fashionable Lady, or Harlequin's Opera: In the Manner of a Rehearsal. London, 1730 (Goodman's Fields, 1730).

Ramsay, Allan. The Gentle Shepherd. Edinburgh, 1725. Revised in 1729 in form of a ballad opera. (First performance in January, 1729, as a school-play in Taylor's Hall, Edinburgh.)

Randall, John. The Disappointment . . . Alter'd from a Farce after the Manner of the Beggar's Opera. London, 1732 (Haymarket, 1732).

Robin Hood: An Opera. London, 1730 (Bartholomew Fair, Lee's and Harper's Great Theatrical Booth, 1730).

Rome Excis'd: A New Tragi-Comi Ballad-Opera. London, 1733.

Royal Marriage (The) . . . By a Gentleman of the University of Oxford. London, 1736.

Ryan, Lacy. The Cobler's Opera. Dublin, 1729 (Lincoln's Inn Fields, 1728).

Sailor's Opera (The), or A Trip to Jamaica. London, 1745.

*Stage-Coach Opera (The). Published in error by Wilkes in Dublin edition of Farquhar's works; see W. J. Lawrence, "The Mystery of 'The Stage Coach,'" Modern Language Review, XXVII, October, 1932, pp. 392–97. (Drury Lane, 1730; Smock Alley, Dublin, 1730).

State Juggler (The), or Sir Politick Ribband: A New Excise Opera. London, 1733.

Sturdy Beggars (The): A New Ballad Opera. London, 1733.

Thomson, Adam. The Disappointed Gallant, or Buckram in Armour. Edinburgh, 1738 (New Theatre, Edinburgh, 1738).

*Trooper's Opera (The). 1736.

Vanelia, or The Amours of the Great: An Opera. London, 1732.

Walker, Thomas. The Quaker's Opera. London, 1728 (Bartholomew Fair, 1728).

Wanton Countess (The), or Ten Thousand Pounds for a Pregnancy. London, 1733.

Wanton Jesuit (The), or Innocence Seduced. London, 1731 (Haymarket, 1732).

Ward, Henry. The Happy Lovers, or The Beau Metamorphosed. London, 1736 (Lincoln's Inn Fields, 1736).

Wedding (The), or The Country House-Wife. London, 1734.

Whim (The), or The Miser's Retreat: A Farce, Alter'd from the French of La Maison Rustique. London, 1734. (Goodman's Fields, 1734?)

Wilder, James. The Gentleman Gardiner: A Ballad Opera . . . Taken from Dancourt. Dublin, 1751 (Covent Garden, 1749).

Woodward, Henry (under stage name of Lun, Jr.). The Beggar's Pantomime, or The Contending Columbines. London, 1736 (Lincoln's Inn Fields, 1736).

Worsdale, James. A Cure for a Scold. London, [1735] (Drury Lane, 1735).

Yarrow, Joseph. Love at First Sight, or The Wit of a Woman. York, 1742.

II: UNPUBLISHED BALLAD OPERAS

THE AUTHORITY for the inclusion of each piece as a ballad opera is listed after the date of performance. Since absolute evidence is, of necessity, lacking, the list may not be entirely accurate.

Ayres, James. The Kiss Accepted and Returned (Haymarket, 1744. Nicoll).

Barren Island (The), or Petticoat Government (Bartholomew Fair, 1734. Nicoll).

Cheats of Scapin (The) (Bartholomew Fair, 1736. Nicoll).

Chimney Sweeper (The) (Goodman's Fields, 1736. Nicoll).

Chimney Sweeper's Opera (The) (Haymarket, 1728. Nicoll).

Clown's Stratagem (The), or A New Way to Get a Wife (Drury Lane, 1730. Nicoll).

Comical Disappointment (The), or The Miser Outwitted (Haymarket, 1736. Nicoll).

Comical Revenge (A), or A Doctor in Spight of His Teeth (Drury Lane, 1732. Nicoll).

Contract (The), or The Biter Bit (Haymarket, 1736. Nicoll).

Cure for Covetousness (A), or The Cheats of Scapin (Bartholomew Fair, 1733. Nicoll).

Davey, Samuel. Whittington and His Cat (Aungier Street, Dublin, 1739. Lawrence).

Egleton, Mrs. The Maggot (Lincoln's Inn Fields, 1732. Nicoll).

Farmer's Son (The), or The Maiden's Second Slip (Haymarket, 1733. Nicoll).

Father Girard the Sorcerer, or The Amours of Harlequin and Miss Cadiere (Goodman's Fields, 1732. Nicoll).

Hudibras, or Trulla's Triumph (Lincoln's Inn Fields, 1730. Nicoll).

Hunter (The), or The Beggar's Wedding (Bartholomew Fair, 1729. Nicoll).

Imaginary Cuckold (The) (Drury Lane, 1733. Nicoll).

Jealous Taylor (The), or The Intriguing Valet (Haymarket, 1731. Nicoll).

Johnny Bow-wow, or The Wicked Gravedigger (Smock Alley, Dublin, 1732. Lawrence).

Johnson, Charles. The Ephesian Matron (Drury Lane, 1732. Nicoll).

King and No King (A), or The Polish Squabble (Goodman's Fields, 1733. Nicoll).

Macheath in the Shades, or Bayes at Parnassus (Covent Garden, 1735. Nicoll).

Medley (The) (Aungier Street, Dublin, 1736. Lawrence).

Merry Throwster (The) (Goodman's Fields, 1731. Nicoll).

Mock Countess (The) (Drury Lane, 1733. Genest).

Mock Mason (The) (Goodman's Fields, 1733. Nicoll).

Modern Pimp (The), or The Doctor Deceived (Bartholomew Fair, 1736. Nicoll).

Phillips, Thomas. The Rival Captains, or The Imposter Unmasked (Haymarket, 1736. Nicoll).

Politics on Both Sides (Lincoln's Inn Fields, 1735. Nicoll).

Sailor's Opera (The) (Drury Lane, 1731. Nicoll).

Sailor's Opera (The), or An Example of Justice for Present and Future Times (Haymarket, 1737. Nicoll).

Sailor's Wedding (The), or The Humours of Wapping (Goodman's Fields, 1731. Nicoll).

Tho' Strange 'Tis True, or Love's Vagaries (Lincoln's Inn Fields, 1732. Nicoll).

Throwster's Opera (The) (Goodman's Fields, 1731. Nicoll).

Wat Tyler, or The State Menders (Drury Lane, 1733. Nicoll).

Worsdale, James. The Queen of Spain, or Farinelli at Madrid (Aungier Street, Dublin, 1740. Lawrence).

III: BALLAD OPERA SURVIVALS, 1750–1835

WHILE this list makes no pretense at completeness, it includes most of the later ballad operas. A few of the pieces are only partially ballad operas.

Atkinson, Joseph. A Match for a Widow, or The Frolics of Fancy. London, 1788. Only a very few old airs.

Barton, Andrew. The Disappointment, or The Force of Credulity. New York, 1767; 2d ed., enlarged, Philadelphia, 1796. Attributed to Thomas Forrest.

Bow-Street Opera (The). London, 1773.

Coach-Drivers (The): A Political Comic-Opera. London, 1766.

Country Coquet (The), or Miss in Her Breeches ... By a Young Lady. London, 1755.

Dibdin, Thomas. The Covenanters: A Scotch Ballad Opera. London, n.d. (English Opera House, 1835).

King, Thomas. Love at First Sight. Dublin, 1763 (Drury Lane, 1763).

Maclaren, Archibald. The Coup de Main, or The American Adventurers. Perth, 1784 (New Theatre in Dundee).

MacNally, Leonard. Critic upon Critic. 2d ed., London, 1792. Genest believes the bookseller merely affixed a new title-page and cast to the old copies of 1788.

Markoe, Peter. The Reconciliation, or The Triumph of Nature. Philadelphia, 1790.

Mendez, Moses. The Double Disappointment. London, 1760 (Drury Lane, 1746).

O'Keeffe, John. The Poor Soldier. New ed. Dublin, 1785 (Covent Garden). Only partly a ballad opera.

Reed, Joseph. Tom Jones: A Comic Opera. London, 1769 (Covent Garden). Has only a few ballad airs.

Shirrefs, Andrew. Jamie and Bess, or The Laird in Disguise. In Poems, Chiefly in the Scottish Dialect, Edinburgh, 1790.

Sickelmore, Richard. Quarter-Day. Lewes, 1798 (The theatre, Dover).

[Worsdale, James.] Gasconado the Great. London, 1759. Only partly a ballad opera.

General Bibliography

ATTENTION is called to Bibliography of Ballad Operas, Sections I and III, where the published ballad operas have been listed in alphabetical order. The bibliography given below offers merely a selected list of the works which have proved most helpful in the present study. I have omitted a vast number of items of secondary importance, including many contemporary plays, operas, and pamphlets.

Albert, Maurice. Les Théâtres de la foire (1660–1789). Paris, 1900.

Amhurst, Nicholas. Terræ-Filius, or The Secret History of the University of Oxford. London, 1726.

Armstrong, A. J. Operatic Performances in England before Handel. Baylor University Bulletin No. 4, Waco, Texas, 1918.

[Aubert, Mrs.] Harlequin-Hydaspes, or The Greshamite. London, 1719.

Baker, David E. The Companion to the Playhouse. 2 vols., London, 1764.

Baskervill, Charles Read. The Elizabethan Jig and Related Song Drama. Chicago, 1929.

Bateson, F. W. The English Comic Drama, 1700–1750. Oxford, 1929.

Beljame, Alexandre. Le Public et les hommes de lettres en Angleterre au dix-huitième siècle, 1660–1774. 2d ed., Paris, 1897.

Bernardin, N. M. La Comédie italienne en France et les théâtres de la foire et du boulevard (1570–1791). Paris, 1902.

Biographia Dramatica, or A Companion to the Playhouse. Compiled by David E. Baker, Isaac Reed, and Stephen Jones. 3 vols., London, 1812.

Brome, Richard. A Jovial Crew, or The Merry Beggars. London, 1684.

Buckingham, George Villiers, 2d Duke of. The Rehearsal, edited by Montague Summers. Stratford-upon-Avon, 1914.

Bullock, Christopher. A Woman's Revenge, or A Match in Newgate. London, 1715. Appended to this are "A Key to the Beggar's Opera. In a Letter to Caleb Danvers, Esq." and several ballads.

Burnet, Alexander. Achilles Dissected: Being a Compleat Key of the Political Characters in That New Ballad Opera, Written by the Late Mr. Gay. London, 1733.

Burney, Charles. A General History of Music. 4 vols., London, 1782–89.

Carey, Henry. The Dramatick Works of Henry Carey. London, 1743.

—————The Poems of Henry Carey, edited by Frederick T. Wood. London, [1930].

Carmody, Francis J. Le Répertoire de l'opéra-comique en vaudevilles de 1708 à 1764. Berkeley, California, 1933.

Chappell, William. Popular Music of the Olden Time. 2 vols., London, [1859].

Charke, Charlotte. A Narrative of the Life of Mrs. Charlotte Charke, Daughter of Colley Cibber. New York, 1930.

Chetwood, W. R. A General History of the Stage. London, 1749.

Cibber, Colley. An Apology for the Life of Colley Cibber. 4th ed., 2 vols., London, 1756.

Collection of the Most Esteemed Farces and Entertainments Performed on the British Stage (A). 6 vols., Edinburgh, 1792.

Cooke, William. Memoirs of Macklin, Comedian. London, 1804.

Coxe, William. Memoirs of the Life and Administration of Sir Robert Walpole, Earl of Orford. 3 vols., London, 1798.

Cross, Wilbur L. The History of Henry Fielding. 3 vols., New Haven, 1918.

Dancing-Master (The), or Directions for Dancing Country Dances, with the Tunes to Each Dance for the Treble-violin. 10th ed., 2 vols. in 1, [London,] 1698.

Day, Cyrus Lawrence. "Pills to Purge Melancholy." *Review of English Studies*, VIII, (No. 30; April, 1932), 177–84.

——The Songs of John Dryden. Cambridge, Mass., 1932.

——The Songs of Thomas D'Urfey. Cambridge, Mass., 1933.

Dent, Edward J. Foundations of English Opera. Cambridge, 1928.

Dictionary of National Biography.

Dryden, John. The Works of John Dryden, edited by Scott and Saintsbury. 18 vols., London, 1882–93.

Duffett, Thomas. The Empress of Morocco. London, 1674.

——The Mock Tempest, or The Enchanted Castle. London, 1675.

Dunhill, Thomas F. Sullivan's Comic Operas: A Critical Appreciation. New York and London, 1928.

D'Urfey, Thomas. New Opera's, with Stories and Poems. London, 1721.

——Wit and Mirth, or Pills to Purge Melancholy; Being a Collection of the Best Merry Ballads and Songs, Old and New. 6 vols., London, 1719.

——Wonders in the Sun, or The Kingdom of the Birds: a Comick Opera, with Great Variety of Songs in All Kinds, Set to Musick by Several of the Most Eminent Masters of the Age. London, 1706.

Fielding, Henry. The Tragedy of Tragedies, edited by James T. Hillhouse. New Haven, 1918.

——The Works of Henry Fielding, Esq., with an Essay on his Life and Genius by Arthur Murphy, edited by James P. Browne. 11 vols., London, 1902–3.

Fitzgerald, Percy. The Life of Mrs. Clive. London, 1888.

Forsythe, Robert Stanley. A Study of the Plays of Thomas D'Urfey. Cleveland, 1916.

Gaiffe, Felix. Le Drame en France au XVIIIe siècle. Paris, 1910.

Gay, John. The Poetical Works of John Gay, edited by G. C. Faber. London, 1926.

——The Poetical Works of John Gay, edited by John Underhill. London and New York, 1893.

Genest, Rev. John. Some Account of the English Stage. 10 vols., Bath, 1832.

Gentleman, Francis. The Dramatic Censor, or Critical Companion. 2 vols., London, 1770.

Gherardi, Evaristo. Le Théâtre italien de Gherardi. 6 vols., Paris, 1700.

Gibson, Andrew. New Light on Allan Ramsay. Edinburgh, 1927.

Godwin, A. H. Gilbert and Sullivan: A Critical Appreciation of the Savoy Operas. London and Toronto; New York, 1916.

Goulding, Sybil. "Eighteenth Century French Taste and 'The Beggar's Opera.'" *Modern Language Review,* XXIV (1929), 276–93.

Grannis, Valleria B. Dramatic Parody in Eighteenth Century France. New York, 1931.

Graves, Thornton S. "Some Facts about Anthony Aston." *Journal of English and Germanic Philology,* XX (1921), 391–96.

Griffith, R. H. "Tony Aston's Fool's Opera." *Journal of English and Germanic Philology,* XXI (1922), 188–89.

Hawkins, Sir John. A General History of the Science and Practice of Music. 5 vols., London, 1776.

Hazlitt, William. "A View of the English Stage." In The Collected Works of William Hazlitt, 12 vols., London, 1903.

Hervey, John. Memoirs of the Reign of George the Second, edited by John Wilson Croker. 2 vols., London, 1855.

——Some Materials Toward Memoirs of the Reign of King George II, edited by Romney Sedgwick. 3 vols., London, 1931.

Hillhouse, James T. The Grub-street Journal. Durham, N. C., 1928.

Hindle, C. J. "The School-boy's Opera." Letter in the *Times Literary Supplement.* June 11, 1931, p. 467.

Historical Manuscripts Commission. Manuscripts of the Earl of Egmont: Diary of Viscount Percival, afterwards First Earl of Egmont. 3 vols., London, 1920.

Hogarth, George. Memoirs of the Musical Drama. 2 vols., London, 1838.

Hughes, Helen Sard. "Fielding's Indebtedness to James Ralph." *Modern Philology,* XX (1922), 19–34.

Iacuzzi, Alfred. The European Vogue of Favart. New York, 1932.

Irving, William Henry. John Gay's London. Cambridge, Mass., 1928.

Johnson, Samuel. Lives of the English Poets. With an Introduction by Arthur Waugh. "The World's Classics," 2 vols., Oxford, 1929.

Kidson, Frank. The Beggar's Opera: Its Predecessors and Successors. Cambridge, 1922.

Kitchin, George. A Survey of Burlesque and Parody in English. Edinburgh, 1931.

Kretzschmar, Hermann. Geschichte der Oper. Leipzig, 1919.

Lawrence, W. J. "Early Irish Ballad Opera and Comic Opera." *The Musical Quarterly,* VIII (July, 1922), 397–412.

——"The Mystery of 'The Stage Coach.'" *Modern Language Review,* XXVII (October, 1932), 392–97.

——"Reviving 'The Gentle Shepherd.'" *The Graphic* (London), September 1, 1932, p. 312.

Lea, K. M. Italian Popular Comedy. 2 vols., Oxford, 1934.

Lesage, A. R., and D'Orneval. Le Théâtre de la foire, ou L'Opéra-comique. 9 vols., Paris, 1737.

Leveridge, Richard. A Collection of Songs with the Musick. 2 vols. in one. London, 1727.

——The Comick Masque of Pyramus and Thisbe. London, 1716.

Levy, Bernard. The Unpublished Plays of Carolet. New York, 1931.

Life of Mr. James Quin, Comedian (The). London, 1766.

Lillo, George. Dramatic Works, with Memoirs of the Author by Thomas Davies. 2 vols., London, 1810.

Lintilhac, Eugène. Histoire générale du théâtre en France. 5 vols., Paris, [1904–11].

Loiseau, J. "John Gay et le *Beggar's Opera.*" *Revue Anglo-Américaine,* XII (1934), 3–19.

Mark, Jeffrey. "Ballad Opera and its Significance in the History of English Stage-Music." *London Mercury,* VIII (1923), 256–78.

Martin, Burns. Allan Ramsay: A Study of his Life and Works. Cambridge, Mass., 1931.

Melville, Lewis. Life and Letters of John Gay (1685–1732), Author of "The Beggar's Opera." London, 1921.

Miles, Dudley Howe. The Influence of Molière on Restoration Comedy. New York, 1910.

Miller, James. Harlequin-Horace, or The Art of Modern Poetry. London, 1731.

Nettleton, G. H. English Drama of the Restoration and Eighteenth Century (1642–1780). New York, 1914.

Newspapers and periodicals (eighteenth century)—from the collections at Harvard and Yale: *The British Journal; The Daily Courant; The Daily Post; Fog's Weekly Journal; The Gentleman's Magazine; The Grub-street Journal.*

Nichols, John. Biographical Anecdotes of William Hogarth. 3d ed., London, 1785.

Nicoll, Allardyce. A History of Early Eighteenth Century Drama, 1700–1750. 2d ed., Cambridge, 1929.

——A History of Late Eighteenth Century Drama, 1750–1800. Cambridge, 1927.

——A History of Restoration Drama, 1660–1700. 2d ed., Cambridge, 1928.

Nouveau théâtre italien (Le), ou Recueil général des comédies représentées par les comédiens italiens ordinaires du roi. 10 vols., Paris, 1753.

Odell, George C. D. Annals of the New York Stage. 9 vols., New York, 1927–37.

——Shakespeare from Betterton to Irving. 2 vols., New York, 1920.

Oxford History of Music. 7 vols., Oxford, 1901–34.

Pearce, Charles E. "Polly Peachum": being the Story of Lavinia Fenton (Duchess of Bolton) and "The Beggar's Opera." London, 1913.

Percival, Milton. Political Ballads Illustrating the Administration of Sir Robert Walpole. Oxford Historical and Literary Studies, Vol. VIII. Oxford, 1916.

Pilkington, Letitia. Memoirs of Mrs. Letitia Pilkington, 1712–1750, Written by Herself. With an introduction by Iris Barry. London, [1928].

Prunières, Henry. Le ballet de cour en France avant Benserade et Lully. Paris, 1913.

Purcell, Henry. Orpheus Britannicus. 2d ed., 2 vols., London, 1706.

Ralph, James. The Taste of the Town, or a Guide to All Publick Diversions. London, 1731.

Ramsay, Allan. The Tea-Table Miscellany, or A Collection of Choice Songs, Scots and English. 12th ed., 4 vols., Edinburgh, 1760.

Richards, A. E. "A Literary Link between Thomas Shadwell and Christian Felix Weisse." *Publications of The Modern Language Association,* XXI (1906), 808–30.

Riemann, Hugo. Dictionnaire de musique, traduit par Georges Humbert. 3d ed., Paris, 1931.

——Opern-handbuch. Leipzig. First supplement, 1881–86; second supplement, 1892.

Rolland, Romain. Les Origines du théâtre lyrique moderne; histoire de l'opéra en Europe avant Lully et Scarlatti. Paris, 1895.

Saint-Evremond [Charles de Marguetel de Saint Denis], Seigneur de. Œuvres mêlées. 3 vols., Paris, 1865.

Schultz, William Eben. Gay's Beggar's Opera: Its Content, History and Influence. New Haven, 1923.

Settle, Elkanah. The World in the Moon. 2d ed., London, 1698.

Smith, Winifred. The Commedia dell' arte. New York, 1912.

Sonneck, O. G. T. Catalogue of Opera Librettos Printed before 1800. 2 vols., Washington, 1914.

——Early Opera in America. New York, 1914.

Spence, Rev. Joseph. Anecdotes, Observations, and Characters, of Books and Men. 2d ed., London, 1858.

Squire, William Barclay. "An Index of Tunes in the Ballad Operas." *Musical Antiquary,* II (1910), 1–17.

Stevens, David Harrison. Some Immediate Effects of *The Beggar's Opera.* "Manley Anniversary Studies in Language and Literature," Chicago, 1923.

Streitfeild, R. A. Handel. 2d ed., London, 1910.

Sutherland, James R. "The Beggar's Opera." *Times Literary Supplement,* April 25, 1935, p. 272.

Swaen, A. E. H. "The Airs and Tunes of John Gay's Beggar's Opera." *Anglia,* XLIII (1919), 152–90.

Thorndike, Ashley. English Comedy. New York, 1929.

Thorp, Willard. Songs from the Restoration Theater. Princeton, 1934.

Trusler, Rev. John. The Works of William Hogarth. 2 vols., London, [18–].

Tufts, George. "Ballad Operas: A List and Some Notes." *The Musical Antiquary,* IV (1913), 61–86.

——A Bibliography of Ballad Opera. Typewritten Ms. Cambridge, Mass., 1911.

Victor, Benjamin. The History of the Theatres of London and Dublin, from the Year 1730 to the Present Time. 3 vols., London, 1761.

Walpole, Horace. The Letters of Horace Walpole, Fourth Earl of Orford, edited by Paget Toynbee. Oxford, 1903.

——Reminiscences, with Notes and Index by Paget Toynbee. Oxford, 1924.

Wells, John Edwin. "Some New Facts concerning Fielding's *Tumble-Down Dick* and *Pasquin.*" *Modern Language Notes,* XXVIII (May, 1913), 137–42.

West, Albert C. L'Influence française dans la poésie burlesque en Angleterre entre 1660 et 1700. Paris, 1931.

Wheatley, Henry B. Hogarth's London. New York, 1909.

Whincop, Thomas. Scanderbeg, or Love and Liberty . . . To Which Are Added, A List of All the Dramatic Authors with Some Account of Their Lives; and of All the Dramatic Pieces Ever Published in the English Language, to the Year 1747. London, 1747.

Williams, I. A. "The Author of The Beggar's Opera." *London Mercury,* III (1920), 166–79.

Wood, Frederick T. " 'The Disappointment.' " *Review of English Studies,* V (1929), 66–69.

Young, J. R. Allan Ramsay. *London Mercury,* XXI (1929), 26–36.

Index